JOHN WILLIS'

SCREEN WORLD

1972

Volume 23

Crown Publishers, Inc.

419 Park Avenue South

New York

Copyright © 1972 by John Willis. Manufactured in the U.S.A.
Library of Congress Catalog Card No. 50-3023
ISBN: 0-517-501287

To

CHARLES SPENCER CHAPLIN

*whose unique genius for comedy and pathos
touched the hearts of the world and brought
laughter to millions; whose many other talents are
largely responsible for the development of the
cinematic arts throughout the world; and whose
warmth when accepting the industry's belated
personal acknowledgment came from the same
source of greatness.*

4

LILLIAN GISH with press
after receiving an Honorary Academy Award
April 14, 1971

CONTENTS

EDITOR: JOHN WILLIS

Assistant Editor: Stanley Reeves

Staff: Frances Crampon, Raymond Frederick, Lucy Williams

1. John Wayne

2. Clint Eastwood ·

3. Paul Newman

4. Steve McQueen

5. George C. Scott

6. Dustin Hoffman

7. Walter Matthau

8. Ali McGraw

9. Sean Connery

10. Lee Marvin

11. Ryan O'Neal

12. Candice Bergen

13. Jack Nicholson

14. Sidney Poitier

15. Robert Redford

16. Barbra Streisand

TOP 25 BOXOFFICE STARS OF 1971

17. James Garner

18. Elliott Gould

19. Ann-Margret

20. Dean Martin

1971 RELEASES

21. Jane Fonda

22. Donald Sutherland

23. Jack Lemmon

24. Dyan Cannon

25. Elvis Presley

Catherine Deneuve

Marcello Mastroianni

Glenda Jackson

THE PROJECTIONIST

(MARON) Produced, Directed, and Written by Harry Hurwitz; Assistant Director, Roy Frumkes; Associate Producer, David Wolfson; Photography, Victor Petrashevic; Music, Igo Kantor, Erma E. Levin; A Maglan Films Production in Technicolor; Rating GP; 85 minutes; January release.

CAST

Projectionist/Flash	Chuck McCann
The Girl	Ina Balin
Renaldi/The Bat	Rodney Dangerfield
Candy Man/Scientist	Jara Kohout
Friendly Usher	Harry Hurwitz
TV Pitchman	Robert Staats
Premiere Announcer	Robert King
Fat Man/Henchman	David Holiday
Minister	Stephen Phillips
Crazy Lady	Clara Rosenthal
Nude on Bearskin	Jacqueline Glenn
Belly Dancer	Morocco
Ushers/Henchmen	Mike Gentry, Lucky Kargo, Sam Stewart, Robert Lee, Alex Stevens

**Right: Ina Balin, Chuck McCann
Below: Rodney Dangerfield**

**Robert Walker, Mimsy Farmer
Above: Robert Walker, Rita Hayworth**

ROAD TO SALINA

(AVCO EMBASSY) Producers, Robert Dorfmann, Yvon Guezel; Director, George Lautner; Screenplay, George Lautner, Pascal Jardin, Jack Miller; Based on novel "Sur La Route de Salina" by Maurice Cury; Photography, Maurice Fellous; Music, Bernard Gerard, Christophe, Ian Anderson; Costumes, Jean Bouquin; Presented by Joseph E. Levine; In DeLuxe Color; Rating R; 96 minutes; February release.

CAST

Billie	Mimsy Farmer
Jonas	Robert Walker
Mara	Rita Hayworth
Warren	Ed Begley
Charlie	Bruce Pecheur
Sheriff	David Sachs
Linda	Sophie Hardy
Rocky	Marc Porel

RAID ON ROMMEL

(UNIVERSAL) Producer, Harry Tatelman; Director, Henry Hathaway; Screenplay, Richard Bluel; Photography, Earl Rath; Music, Hal Mooney; Assistant Director, Jim Fargo; In Technicolor; Rating GP; 99 minutes; February release.

CAST

Foster	Richard Burton
Mackenzie	John Colicos
Major Tarkington	Clinton Greyn
Rommel	Wolfgang Preiss
Vivi	Danielle De Metz
Schroeder	Karl Otto Alberty
Conscientious Objector	Christopher Cary
Garth	John Orchard
Reilly	Brook Williams
Brown	Greg Mullavey
Admiral	Ben Wright
Wembley	Michael Sevareid
Tank Sergeant	Chris Anders

Right: Richard Burton

Mike Kulscar, Wolfgang Preiss, (also above), Clinton Greyn, Richard Burton

Christopher Cary, Danielle DeMetz Above: Brook Williams, John Orchard, Richard Burton

COLD TURKEY

(UNITED ARTISTS) Producer-Director, Norman Lear; Executive Producer, Bud Yorkin; Screenplay, Norman Lear; Story, Norman Lear, William Price Fox, Jr.; Music, Randy Newman; Photography, Charles F. Wheeler; Associate Producer, Edward S. Stephenson; Costumes, Rita Riggs; Assistant Director, Claude Binyon, Jr.; In DeLuxe Color; Rating GP; 106 minutes; February release.

CAST

Rev. Clayton Brooks	Dick Van Dyke
Natalie Brooks	Pippa Scott
Mr. Stopworth	Tom Poston
Hiram C. Grayson	Edward Everett Horton
TV Personalities	Bob and Ray
Merwin Wren	Bob Newhart
Mayor Wrappler	Vincent Gardenia
Dr. Procter	Barnard Hughes
Amos Bush	Graham Jarvis
Mrs. Wrappler	Jean Stapleton
Letitia	Barbara Cason
Odie	Judith Lowry
Cissy	Sudie Bond
Mrs. Watson	Helen Page Camp
Zen Buddhist	Paul Benedict
Mr. Kandiss	Simon Scott
Homer Watson	Raymond Kark
Mrs. Procter	Peggy Rea
Tobacco Executive	Woodrow Parfrey
Bishop Manley	George Mann
Colonel Galloway	Charles Pinney
Art	M. Emmet Walsh
The Hooker	Gloria LeRoy
Dennis	Eric Boles
TV Stage Manager	Jack Grimes
Tobacco Executive	Walter Sande
Hypnotist	Harvey Jason

Right: Vincent Gardenia, Dick Van Dyke

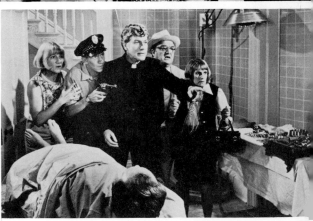

**Dick Van Dyke, Pippa Scott
Above: Woodrow Parfrey, Edward Everett
Horton, Simon Scott**

**Barbara Cason, Raymond Kark, Dick Van Dyke,
Vincent Gardenia, Sudie Bond Above: Bob
Newhart, Judith Lowry, Graham Jarvis**

THE PURSUIT OF HAPPINESS

(COLUMBIA) Producer, David Susskind; Director, Robert Mulligan; Screenplay, Jon Boothe, George L. Sherman; Based on novel by Thomas Rogers; Music, Dave Grusin; Song written and sung by Randy Newman; Associate Producer, Alan Shayne; Photography, Dick Kratina; Art Director, George Jenkins; Assistant Director, Peter Scoppa; Costumes, Ann Roth; In Color; 98 minutes; Rating GP; February release.

CAST

William Popper	Michael Sarrazin
Jane Kauffman	Barbara Hershey
Melvin Lasher	Robert Klein
Ruth Lawrence	Sada Thompson
Detective Cromie	Ralph Waite
John Popper	Arthur Hill
Daniel Lawrence	E. G. Marshall
Mrs. Conroy	Maya Kenin
Mrs. O'Mara	Rue McClanahan
Terence Lawrence	Peter White
Holmes	Joseph Attles
Josephine	Beulah Garrick
Mrs. Popper	Ruth White
Judge Vogel	Barnard Hughes
James Moran	David Doyle
George Wilson	Gilbert Lewis
McArdle	Albert Henderson
Defense Attorney Keller	Tom Rosqui
Judge Palumbo	Jack Somack
First Guard	Edward Kovens
Second Guard	Charles Durning
Policeman	Ed Setrakian
Traffic Cop	Ted Beniades
Pilot	William Devane

Right: Sada Thompson, Michael Sarrazin
Below: Barbara Hershey, Robert Klein, Michael Sarrazin

Marcia Rodd, Elliott Gould
Above: Elizabeth Wilson, Elliott Gould, Vincent Gardenia

LITTLE MURDERS

(20th CENTURY-FOX) Producer, Jack Brodsky; Director, Alan Arkin; Screenplay, Jules Feiffer; Based on his play of same title; Associate Producer, Burtt Harris; Photography, Gordon Willis; Costumes, Albert Wolsky; Music, Fred Kaz, Assistant Director, Peter Scoppa; A Brodsky/Gould Production in DeLuxe Color; Rating R; 110 minutes; February release.

CAST

Alfred Chamberlain	Elliott Gould
Patsy Newquist	Marcia Rodd
Mr. Newquist	Vincent Gardenia
Mrs. Newquist	Elizabeth Wilson
Kenny	Jon Korkes
Mr. Chamberlain	John Randolph
Mrs. Chamberlain	Doris Roberts
Minister	Donald Sutherland
Judge	Lou Jacobi
Detective	Alan Arkin

MRS. POLLIFAX—SPY

(UNITED ARTISTS) Producer, Frederick Brisson; Director, Leslie Martinson; Screenplay, C. A. McKnight; Based on novel "The Unexpected Mrs. Pollifax" by Dorothy Gilman; Associate Producer, Charles Forsythe; Assistant Directors, Fred Gammon, Fred Giles; Music, Lalo Schifrin; Dance Music and "Merdita" theme, Andre Previn; Photography, Joe Biroc; Costumes, Noel Taylor; In DeLuxe Color; Rating G; 110 minutes; March release.

CAST

Mrs. Pollifax	Rosalind Russell
Farrell	Darren McGavin
Berisha	Nehemiah Persoff
Nexdhet	Harold Gould
Perdido	Albert Paulsen
Lulash	John Beck
Carstairs	Dana Elcar
Mason	James Wellman
Bishop	Dennis Cross
Stefan	Nick Katurich
DeGamez	Don Diamond
Larrabee	Robert Donner
Roger	Tom Hallick

Left: Rosalind Russell, Darren McGavin
Below: Rosalind Russell, Harold Gould

BROTHER JOHN

(COLUMBIA) Producer, Joel Glickman; Director, James Goldstone; Screenplay, Ernest Kinoy; Photography, Gerald Perry Finnerman; Music, Quincy Jones; "Children of Summer" sung by Clydie King; Art Director, Al Brenner; Assistant Directors, Tom Schmidt, Charles Washburn; An E & R Production in Color; 94 Minutes; Rating GP; March release.

CAST

John Kane	Sidney Poitier
Doc Thomas	Will Geer
Lloyd Thomas	Bradford Dillman
Louisa MacGill	Beverly Todd
Orly Ball	Ramon Bieri
George	Warren J. Kemmerling
Charley Gray	Lincoln Kilpatrick
Rev. MacGill	P. Jay Sidney
Frank	Richard Ward
Henry Birkardt	Paul Winfield
Miss Nettie	Zara Cully
Cleve	Michael Bell
Jimmy	Howard Rice
Marsha	Darlene Rice
Turnkey	Harry Davis
Sarah	Lynn Hamilton
Calvin	Gene Tyburn
Perry	E. A. Nicholson
Bill Jones	Bill Crane
Lab Deputy	Richard Bay
Henry's friend	John Hancock
Nurse	Lynne Arden
Motel Owner	William Houze
Neighbors	Maye Henderson, Lois Smith

Lincoln Kilpatrick, Beverly Todd, Sidney Poitier
Above: Will Geer, Sidney Poitier

VANISHING POINT

(20th CENTURY-FOX) Producer, Norman Spencer; Director, Richard C. Sarafian; Executive Producer, Michael Pearson; Screenplay, Guillermo Cain; Story, Malcolm Hart; Music, Jimmy Bowen; Photography, John A. Alonzo; Assistant Director, Richard Glassman; A Cupid Production in De Luxe Color; Rating GP; 107 minutes; March release.

CAST

Kowalski	Barry Newman
Super Soul	Cleavon Little
Prospector	Dean Jagger
Vera	Victoria Medlin
Young Cop	Paul Koslo
Older Cop	Bob Donner
Angel	Timothy Scott
Nude Rider	Gilda Texter
First Male Hitch-hiker	Anthony James
Second Male Hitch-hiker	Arthur Malet
Clerk	Karl Swenson
J. Hovah	Severn Darden
J. Hovah's Singers	Delaney and Bonnie & Friends
Jake	Lee Weaver
First Girl	Cherie Foster
Second Girl	Valerie Kairys
Sheriff	Tom Reese
Communications Officer	Owen Bush

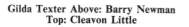

Gilda Texter Above: Barry Newman
Top: Cleavon Little

Dean Jagger, Barry Newman

13

THE ANDROMEDA STRAIN

(UNIVERSAL) Producer-Director, Robert Wise; Screenplay, Nelson Gidding; From novel by J. Michael Crichton; Production Designer, Boris Leven; Photography, Richard H. Kline; Music, Gil Melle; Costumes, Helen Colvig; Assistant Director, Ridgeway Callow; In Panavision and Technicolor; Rating G; 137 minutes; March release.

CAST

Dr. Jeremy Stone	Arthur Hill
Dr. Charles Dutton	David Wayne
Dr. Mark Hall	James Olson
Dr. Ruth Leavitt	Kate Reid
Karen Anson	Paula Kelly
Jackson	George Mitchell
Major Manchek	Ramon Bieri
Dr. Robertson	Kermit Murdock
Grimes	Richard O'Brien
General Sparks	Peter Hobbs
Senator from Vermont	Eric Christmas

Right: James Olson, Arthur Hill

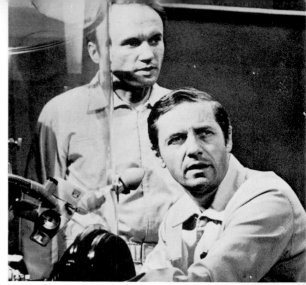

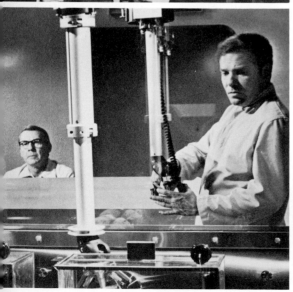

**David Wayne Above:
Arthur Hill, Susan Stone**

**Paula Kelly Above: David Wayne,
Arthur Hill, Kate Reid**

THE BEGUILED

(UNIVERSAL) Producer-Director, Donald Siegel; Associate Producer, Claude Traverse; Photography, Bruce Surtees; Screenplay, John B. Sherry, Grimes Grice; Based on novel by Thomas Cullinan; Production Designer, Ted Haworth; Music, Lalo Schifrin; Costumes, Helen Colvig; Assistant Director, Burt Astor; A Jennings Lang Production; A Malpaso Company Presentation; In Technicolor; Rating R; 109 minutes; March release.

CAST

John McBurney	Clint Eastwood
Martha	Geraldine Page
Edwina	Elizabeth Hartman
Carol	Jo Ann Harris
Doris	Darleen Carr
Hallie	Mae Mercer
Amy	Pamelyn Ferdin
Abigail	Melody Thomas
Lizzie	Peggy Drier
Janie	Pattye Mattick

Right: Geraldine Page, Clint Eastwood, Elizabeth Hartman

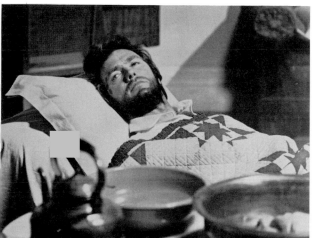

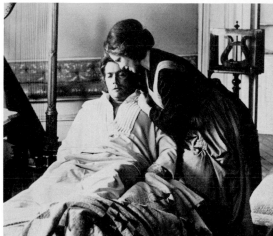

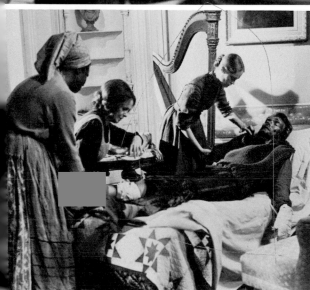

Mae Mercer, Geraldine Page, Elizabeth Hartman, Clint Eastwood (also above)

Clint Eastwood, Elizabeth Hartman Above: Clint Eastwood, Geraldine Page

A NEW LEAF

(PARAMOUNT) Producer, Joe Manduke; Direction and Screenplay, Elaine May; Based on short story "The Green Heart" by Jack Ritchie; Photography, Gayne Rescher; Associate Producer, Florence Nerlinger; Assistant Director, Steven Mussman; Designer, Warren Clymer; Costumes, Anthea Sylbert; In Movielab Color; 102 minutes; Rating G; March release.

CAST

Henry Graham	Walter Matthau
Henrietta Lowell	Elaine May
Andrew McPherson	Jack Weston
Harold	George Rose
Beckett	William Redfield
Uncle Harry	James Coco
Bo	Graham Jarvis
Mrs. Graggert	Doris Roberts
Gloria Cunliffe	Rose Arrick
Sharon Hart	Renee Taylor
John	Mark Gordon
Frank	Jess Osuna
Mel	David Doyle
Mr. Van Rensaeller	Fred Stewart

Left: Renee Taylor, Walter Matthau

Elaine May, Walter Matthau
Above: Walter Matthau, Rose Arrick, Elaine May

Walter Matthau, Elaine May, George Rose
Above: Jack Weston, Elaine May, Walter Matthau

Jack Weston, Elaine May, Walter Matthau
Above: (and top) Elaine May, Walter Matthau

Walter Matthau, Elaine May
Above: Walter Matthau, Doris Roberts

THE MEPHISTO WALTZ

(20th CENTURY-FOX) Producer, Quinn Martin; Director, Paul Wendkos; Screenplay, Ben Maddow; Based on novel by Fred Mustard Stewart; Associate Producer, Arthur Fellows; Photography, William W. Spencer; Music, Jerry Goldsmith; "The Mephisto Waltz" played by Jakob Gimpel; Costumes, Moss Mabry; Assistant Director, David Hall; A QM Production in De Luxe Color; Rating R; 108 minutes; March release.

CAST

Myles Clarkson	Alan Alda
Paula Clarkson	Jacqueline Bisset
Duncan Ely	Curt Jurgens
Roxanne	Barbara Parkins
Bill Delancey	Bradford Dillman
Dr. West	William Windom
Maggie West	Kathleen Widdoes
Abby Clarkson	Pamelyn Ferdin
Agency Head	Curt Lowens
Conductor	Gregory Morton
Agency Head's Girl	Janee Michelle
Woman Writer	Lilyan Chauvin
Zanc Theun	Khigh Dhiegh
Bennet	Alberto Morin
Raymont	Berry Kroeger
Richard	Terence Scammell

Right: Barbara Parkins, Curt Jurgens
Above: Jacqueline Bisset, Alan Alda, Barbara Parkins

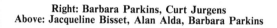
Alan Alda, Jacqueline Bisset

Barbara Parkins

TAKING OFF

(UNIVERSAL) Producer, Alfred W. Crown; Director, Milos Forman; Associate Producer, Michael Hausman; Screenplay, Milos Forman, John Guare, Jean-Claude Carriere, John Klein; Photography, Miroslav Ondricek, Louis San Andres; Assistant Directors, Philip Goldfarb, Edward Folger; In Movielab Color; Rating R; 93 minutes; March release.

CAST

Lynn Tyne	Lynn Carlin
Larry Tyne	Buck Henry
Jeannie Tyne	Linnea Heacock
Margot	Georgia Engel
Tony	Tony Harvey
Ann Lockston	Audra Lindley
Ben Lockston	Paul Benedict
Schiavelli	Vincent Schiavelli
Jamie	David Gittler
Ike and Tina Turner	Themselves
Mrs. Divito	Rae Allen
Corinna Divito	Corinna Cristobal
Norman	Allen Garfield
Schuyler	Barry Del Rae
Committee Man	Frank Berle
Policeman	Phillip Bruns
Nancy Lockston	Gail Busman
Dr. Bronson	Robert Dryden
Committee Woman	Madeline Geffen
Ellen Lubar	Anna Gyory
Dr. Besch	Jack Hausman
Laurie	Carrie Kotkin
SPFC President	Herman Meeker
SPFC Member	Ultra Violet

Audition Singers .... Sari and Jamie Freeman, Nina Hart, Michelle Scheideler, Debbie Robbins, Nancy Bell, Nancy Ferland, Jane Bedrick, Susan Chafitz, Meryl Schneiderman, Janie Rosenberg, Kay Beckett, Bobo Bates, Carly Simon, Mary Mitchell, Catherine Heriza, Shellen Lubin, Jinx Rubin, Caren Klugman

Linnea Heacock
Top Right: Buck Henry, Audra Lindley, Paul Benedict

Lynn Carlin, Audra Lindley Above:
Buck Henry, Paul Benedict

19

SHINBONE ALLEY

(ALLIED ARTISTS) Producer, Preston M. Fleet; Executive Producer-Director, John D. Wilson; Associate Producer-Supervising Director, David Detiege; Screenplay-Lyrics, Joe Darion; Based on "archy and mehitabel" stories by Don Marquis, and musical "shinbone alley" by Joe Darion and Mel Brooks; Music, George Kleinsinger; Photography, Wally Bullock, Gene Borghi, Ted Bemiller; A Fine Arts Film in Color; Rating G; 86 minutes; March release.

CAST
archy .... voice of Eddie Bracken
mehitabel .... voice of Carol Channing
Tyrone T. Tattersall .... voice of John Carradine
Big Bill .... voice of Alan Reed, Sr
also voices of Jackie Ward Singers, Ken Sansom, Hal Smith, Joan Gerber, Sal Delano

Left: Mehitabel

BANANAS

(UNITED ARTISTS) Executive Producer, Charles H. Joffe; Producer, Jack Grossberg; Director, Woody Allen; Associate Producer, Ralph Rosenblum; Screenplay, Woody Allen, Mickey Rose; Music, Marvin Hamlisch; Photography, Andrew M. Costikyan; Production Designer, Ed Wittstein; Assistant Director, Fred T. Gallo; Costumes, Gene Coffin; In DeLuxe Color; Rating GP; 82 minutes; April release.

CAST
Fielding Mellish .... Woody Allen
Nancy .... Louise Lasser
General Vargas .... Carlos Montalban
Yolanda .... Natividad Abascal
Esposito .... Jacob Morales
Luis .... Miguel Suarez
Sanchez .... David Ortiz
Diaz .... Rene Enriquez
Arroyo .... Jack Axelrod
Howard Cosell .... Howard Cosell
Roger Grimsby .... Roger Grimsby
Don Dunphy .... Don Dunphy
Mrs. Mellish .... Charlotte Rae
Dr. Mellish .... Stanley Ackerman
Priest .... Dan Frazer
Dr. Feigen .... Martha Greenhouse
Semple .... Conrad Bain
Perez .... Tigre Perez
Ambassador .... Baron DeBeer
Judge .... Arthur Hughes
Prosecutor .... John Braden
J. Edgar Hoover .... Dorthi Fox
Sharon .... Dagne Crane
and Axel Anderson, Ted Chapman, Ed Barth, Nicholas Saunders, Eulogio Peraza, Norman Evans, Robert O'Connel, Robert Dudley, Marilyn Hengst, Ed Crowley, Beeson Carroll, Allen Garfield, Princess Fatosh, Dick Callinan

Left Center: Woody Allen, Louise Lasser

SWEET SWEETBACK'S BAADASSSSS SONG

(CINEMATION) Produced, Directed, Written, Composed, and Edited by Melvin Van Peebles; Photography, Bob Maxwell; Assistant Director, Clyde Houston; In Color; 97 minutes; Rating X; April release.

CAST
The Black Community: Simon Chuckster, Hubert Scales, John Dullaghan, West Gale, Niva Rochelle, Rhetta Hughes, Nick Ferrari, Ed Rue, Johnny Amos, Lavelle Roby, Ted Hayden, Marlo Peebles, Sonja Dunson, Michael Augustus, Peter Russell, Norman Fields, Bruce Adams, Ron Prince, Steve Cole, Megan Peebles, Joe Tornatore, Mike Angel, The Copeland Family, Jeff Goodman, Curt Matson, Marria Evonee, Jon Jacobs, Bill Kirschner, Vincent Barbi, Chet Norris, Joni Watkins, Jerry Days, John Allen

Melvin Van Peebles

SUMMERTREE

(COLUMBIA) Producer, Kirk Douglas; Director, Anthony Newley; Screenplay, Edward Hume, Stephen Yafa; Based on play of same name by Ron Cowen; Photography, Richard C. Glouner; Assistant Director, David Salven; Song "Having the Time of Our Lives" by David Shire, Richard Maltby; Sung by Hamilton Camp; Associate Producer, Mark Rubin; Music, David Shire; A Bryna Production in Eastman Color; 88 minutes; Rating GP; April release.

CAST

Jerry	Michael Douglas
Herb	Jack Warden
Vanetta	Brenda Vaccaro
Ruth	Barbara Bel Geddes
Marvis	Kirk Callaway
Tony	Bill Vint
Bennie	Jeff Siggens
Don	Rob Reiner
Draft Lawyer	William Smith
Ginsberg	Garry Goodrow
Shelly	Dennis Clark Fimple
Girl in dorm	June Fairchild
Man in conservatory	Richard Stahl

Left: Barbara Bel Geddes, Jack Warden

Michael Douglas, Kirk Calloway
Above: Brenda Vaccaro, Michael Douglas

Michael Douglas, Brenda Vaccaro, and
above with Kirk Calloway

21

SUMMER OF '42

(WARNER BROS.) Producer, Richard A. Roth; Director, Robert Mulligan; Screenplay, Herman Raucher; Photography, Robert Surtees; Production Designer, Albert Brenner; Associate Producer, Don Kranze; Music, Michel Legrand; Assistant Directors, Don Kranze, Mel Efros, Irby Smith; In Technicolor; Rating R; 102 minutes; April release.

CAST

Dorothy	Jennifer O'Neill
Hermie	Gary Grimes
Oscy	Jerry Houser
Benjie	Oliver Conant
Aggie	Katherine Allentuck
Miriam	Christopher Norris
Druggist	Lou Frizzell

Academy Award for Best Original Dramatic Score in 1971

Gary Grimes, Jennifer O'Neill
Above: Gary Grimes, Jerry Houser, Oliver Conant

22

Jerry Houser, Oliver Conant, Gary Grimes
Above: Gary Grimes, Jennifer O'Neill

Christopher Norris, Jerry Houser

23

MAKING IT

(20th CENTURY-FOX) Producer, Albert S. Ruddy; Director, John Erman; Screenplay, Peter Bart; Based on novel "What Can You Do?" by James Leigh; Associate Producer, Gray Frederickson; Photography, Richard C. Glouner; Music, Charles Fox; Lyrics, Norman Gimpel; Assistant Director, Thomas J. Schmidt; An Alfran Production in DeLuxe Color; Rating R; 97 minutes; April release.

CAST

Phil Fuller	Kristoffer Tabori
Betty Fuller	Joyce Van Patten
Yvonne	Marlyn Mason
Wilkie	Bob Balaban
Mallory	Lawrence Pressman
Mrs. Wilson	Louise Latham
Ames	John Fiedler
Debbie	Sherry Miles
Skeeter	Denny Miller
Librarian	Doro Merande
Miss Schneider	Maxine Stuart
Dr. Shurtleff	Tom Troupe
Mr. Fanning	David Doyle
Warren	Dick Van Patten
Mrs. Mallory	Carol Arthur
Ray	Paul Appleby
Bar Girl	Pamela Hensley

Right: Joyce Van Patten, Kristoffer Tabori

Kristoffer Tabori, Gray Frederickson

Kristoffer Tabori, Marlyn Mason

THE BAREFOOT EXECUTIVE

(BUENA VISTA) Producer, Bill Anderson; Director, Robert Butler; Screenplay, Joseph L. McEveety; Story, Lila Garrett, Bernie Kahn, Stewart C. Billett; Photography, Charles F. Wheeler; Music, Robert F. Brunner; Lyrics, Bruce Belland; Assistant Director, Ted Schilz; A Walt Disney Production in Technicolor; Rating G; 96 minutes; April release.

CAST

Steven Post	Kurt Russell
Francis X. Wilbanks	Joe Flynn
E. J. Crampton	Harry Morgan
Mertons	Wally Cox
Jennifer Scott	Heather North
Farnsworth	Alan Hewitt
Clifford	Hayden Rorke
Raffles	Raffles
Roger	John Ritter
Tom	Jack Bender
Dr. Schmidt	Tom Anfinsen
Network Executive	George N. Neise
Announcer	Ed Reimers
Advertising Executive	Morgan Farley
Sponsors	Glen Dixon, Robert Shayne, Tris Coffin
Network Executive	J. B. Douglas
Justice Department	Ed Prentiss
Jackhammer Man	Fabian Dean
Woman Shopper	Iris Adrian
Clatworthy	Jack Smith
Mrs. Crampton	Eve Brent
Mrs. Wilbanks	Sandra Gould
Father O'Leary	James Flavin
Policemen	Pete Renoudet, Judson Pratt, Vince Howard, Hal Baylor
Navigator	Bill Daily
Doorman	Dave Willock
TV Salesman	Anthony Teague
Reporter	Edward Faulkner

Right: Kurt Russell Below: Wally Cox, Joe Flynn, John Ritter Right: Kurt Russell, Heather North

"The World of Hans Christian Andersen"

THE WORLD OF HANS CHRISTIAN ANDERSEN

(UNITED ARTISTS) Executive Producers, Bill Yellin, Herb Gelbspan; Producer, Sean Productions; Directors, Chuck McCann, Al Kilgore; English Version, Al Kilgore, Chuck McCann; Music, Ron Frangiapane; Lyrics, Al Kilgore; In Cinemascope and DeLuxe Color; Rating G; 75 minutes; May release.

CAST

Uncle Oley	Chuck McCann
Hans	Hetty Galen
Elisa/Kitty Kat/Little Boy/ Match Girl	Corinne Orr
Karen	Sidney Filson
Kaspar Kat/Governor Hans/ Father	Jim MacGeorge
Hannibal Mouse/Mayor/ Watchdog	Lionel Wilson
Elisa's Grandmother	Ruth Ballew
Mice	Frances Russell, Jim Yoham, Corinne Orr
Ducks/Theatre Manager	Earl Hammond

ESCAPE FROM THE PLANET OF THE APES

(20th CENTURY-FOX) Producer, APJAC Productions; Director, Don Taylor; Screenplay, Paul Dehn; Based on characters created by Pierre Boulle; Associate Producer, Frank Capra, Jr.; Photography, Joseph Biroc; Music, Jerry Goldsmith; Assistant Director, Pepi Lenzi; An Arthur P. Jacobs Production in Panavision and DeLuxe Color; Rating G; 98 minutes; May release.

CAST

Cornelius	Roddy McDowall
Zira	Kim Hunter
Dr. Lewis Dixon	Bradford Dillman
Dr. Stephanie Branton	Natalie Trundy
Dr. Otto Hasslein	Eric Braeden
The President	William Windom
Milo	Sal Mineo
E-1	Albert Salmi
E-2	Jason Evers
Chairman	John Randolph
General Winthrop	Harry Lauter
Aide	M. Emmet Walsh
Lawyer	Roy E. Glenn, Sr.
Cardinal	Peter Forster
Army Officer	Norman Burton
Naval Officer	William Woodson
Orderly	Tom Lowell
Marine Captain	Gene Whittington
Curator	Donald Elson
TV Newscaster	Bill Bonds
Referee	Army Archerd
General Faulkner	James Bacon
Armando	Ricardo Montalban

Kim Hunter, Roddy McDowall, also above with Eric Braeden, Bradford Dillman

Bradford Dillman, Natalie Trundy, Kim Hunter
Above: Kim Hunter, Ricardo Montalban Top Left: Sal Mineo, Kim Hunter, Roddy McDowall

Kim Hunter, Roddy McDowall
Top: Bradford Dillman, Kim Hunter

Bradford Dillman,
Natalie Trundy

RED SKY AT MORNING

(**UNIVERSAL**) Producer, Hal B. Wallis; Associate Producer, Paul Nathan; Director, James Goldstone; Screenplay, Marguerite Roberts; Based on novel by Richard Bradford; Photography, Vilmos Zsigmond; Music, Billy Goldenberg; Costumes, Edith Head; Assistant Director, Donald Roberts; In Technicolor; Rating GP; 112 minutes; May release.

CAST

Josh Arnold	Richard Thomas
Marcia Davidson	Catherine Burns
Steenie Moreno	Desi Arnaz, Jr.
Frank Arnold	Richard Crenna
Ann Arnold	Claire Bloom
Jimbob Buel	John Colicos
Romeo Bonino	Harry Guardino
John Cloyd	Strother Martin
Amadeo Montoya	Nehemiah Persoff
Chango Lopez	Pepe Serna
Lindo Velarde	Mario Aniov
Viola Lopez	Victoria Racimo
Chamaco	Gregory Sierra
Venery Ann Cloyd	Lynne Marta
Velva Mae Cloyd	Christina Hart
Shirley	Elizabeth Knowles
Gwendolyn	Linda Burton
Excilda Montoya	Alma Beltran
Paolo Bertucci	Jerome Guardino
Corky	Joy Bang
Native	Claudio Miranda
Ratoncito	Joaquin Garay
Miss Rudd	Karen Klett

Right: Mario Aniov, Richard Thomas Below: (L) Desi Arnaz, Jr., Catherine Burns (R) Joy Bang, Richard Thomas

The Great White Shark

BLUE WATER, WHITE DEATH

(**NATIONAL GENERAL**) Producer, Peter Gimbel; Directors, Peter Gimbel, James Lipscomb; Screenplay, Peter Gimbel; Associate Producer, Stanton Waterman; Photography, Peter Gimbel, Stanton Waterman, Ron Taylor, James Lipscomb; Narrator, Wally King; A Blue Water Film Corporation Production in Techniscope and Technicolor; Songs sung by Tom Chapin; Rating G; 99 minutes; May release.

CAST

Peter Gimbel
Ron Taylor
Rodney Jonklaas
Stanton Waterman
Valerie Taylor
Peter A. Lake

SUPPORT YOUR LOCAL GUNFIGHTER

(UNITED ARTISTS) Executive Producer, Burt Kennedy; Producer, Bill Finnegan; Director, Burt Kennedy; Screenplay, James Edward Grant; Photography, Harry Stradling; Assistant Director, Al Jennings; Costumes, Lambert Marks, Pat Norris; In DeLuxe Color; Rating G; 92 minutes; May release.

CAST

Latigo Smith	James Garner
Patience Barton	Suzanne Pleshette
Jug May	Jack Elam
Jenny	Joan Blondell
Taylor Barton	Harry Morgan
Goldie	Marie Windsor
Ez	Henry Jones
Colonel Ames	John Dehner
Swifty Morgan	Chuck Conners
Doc Schultz	Dub Taylor
Mrs. Perkins	Kathleen Freeman
Abigail	Ellen Corby
Bud Barton	Dick Curtis
Fat	Herb Vigran
Croupier	John Wheeler
Bartender	Mike Wagner
Colorado	Ben Cooper
McLaglen	Willis Bouchey
Storekeeper	Grady Sutton
Morris	Walter Burke
Butcher	Gene Evans
Thug	Terry Wilson
Headwaiter	Roy Glenn
Maid	Virginia Capers
Ortiz	Pedro G. Gonzalez

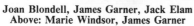

Joan Blondell, James Garner, Jack Elam
Above: Marie Windsor, James Garner

James Garner, Suzanne Pleshette
Top: Harry Morgan, James Garner

29

BIG JAKE

(NATIONAL GENERAL) Producer, Michael Wayne; Director, George Sherman; Story and Screenplay, Harry Julian Fink, R. M. Fink; Photography, William Clothier; Music, Elmer Bernstein; Assistant Director, Newton Arnold; A Batjac Production in Panavision and Technicolor; Rating G; 110 minutes; May release.

CAST

Jacob McCandles	John Wayne
John Fain	Richard Boone
Martha McCandles	Maureen O'Hara
James McCandles	Patrick Wayne
Michael McCandles	Chris Mitchum
Jeff McCandles	Bobby Vinton
Sam Sharpnose	Bruce Cabot
O'Brien	Glenn Corbett
Pop Dawson	Harry Carey, Jr.
Buck Dugan	John Doucette
Head of Lynching Party	Jim Davis
Bert Ryan	John Agar
John Goodfellow	Gregg Palmer
Will Fain	Robert Warner
Trooper	Jim Burke
Kid Duffy	Dean Smith
Little Jake McCandles	John Ethan Wayne
Delilah	Virginia Capers
Moses Brown	William Walker
Stubby	Jerry Gatlin
Saloon Brawler	Tom Hennesy
Saloon Bully	Don Epperson
Walt Devries	Everett Creach
Billy Devries	Jeff Wingfield
Hank	Hank Worden

Bruce Cabot, Chris Mitchum, John Wayne, Patrick Wayne
Top Left: Richard Boone

Standing: John Wayne, John Ethan Wayne, Maureen O'Hara
Seated: Patrick Wayne, Bobby Vinton, Chris Mitchum

BILLY JACK

(WARNER BROS.) Producer, Mary Rose Solti; Director, T. C. Frank; Screenplay, Frank and Teresa Christina; Photography, F. Koenekamp, John Stephens; Associate Producers, Ed Haldeman, Earl D. Elliot; Music, Mundell Lowe; Assistant Directors, Mike Dmytryk, Joseph E. Richards; A National Student Film Corporation Production in Technicolor; Rating GP; 112 minutes; May release.

CAST

Billy Jack	Tom Laughlin
Jean Roberts	Delores Taylor
Sheriff Cole	Clark Howat
Posner	Bert Freed
Barbara	Julie Webb
Deputy	Ken Tobey
Doctor	Victor Izay
Kit	Debbie Schock
Martin	Stan Rice
Carol	Teresa Kelly
Maria	Katy Moffatt
Cindy	Susan Foster
Councilman	Paul Bruce
Sarah	Lynn Baker
Sunshine	Susan Sosa
Bernard	David Roya
Angela	Gwen Smith
Dinosaur	John McClure
Miss Eyelashes	Cissie Colpitts

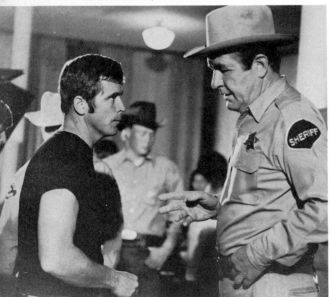

Tom Laughlin, Clark Howat
Top: Delores Taylor, Tom Laughlin

Ken Tobey (L) Above: Clark
Howat Top: David Roya, Ken Tobey

Delores Taylor Above: Bert Freed (L)
Top: Tom Laughlin

33

PLAZA SUITE

(PARAMOUNT) Producer, Howard W. Koch; Director, Arthur Hiller; Screenplay, Neil Simon; Adapted from the play of the same name by Mr. Simon; Photography, Jack Marta; Music, Maurice Jarre; Assistant Director, Howard Roessel; Costumes, Jack Bear; In Technicolor; 115 minutes; Rating GP; May release.

CAST

Sam Nash	Walter Matthau
Karen Nash	Maureen Stapleton
Jesse Kiplinger	Walter Matthau
Muriel Tate	Barbara Harris
Roy Hubley	Walter Matthau
Norma Hubley	Lee Grant
Mimsey Hubley	Jennie Sullivan
Borden Eisler	Tom Carey
Waiter	Jose Ocasio
Bellhop	Dan Ferrone
Miss McCormack	Louise Sorel

Right: Maureen Stapleton

Barbara Harris, Walter Matthau Above: Maureen Stapleton, Louise Sorel, Walter Matthau

Walter Matthau, Barbara Harris Above: Walter Matthau, Maureen Stapleton

34

Walter Matthau, Lee Grant Top:
Walter Matthau, Jennie Sullivan

Walter Matthau, Lee Grant, Jennie
Sullivan, Tom Carey

35

THE ANDERSON TAPES

(COLUMBIA) Producer, Robert M. Weitman; Director, Sidney Lumet; Screenplay, Frank R. Pierson; Based on novel by Lawrence Sanders; Music, Quincy Jones; Associate Producer, George Justin; Photography, Arthur J. Ornitz; Designer, Benjamin J. Kasazkow; Costumes, Gene Coffin; Assistant Director, Alan Hopkins; In Color; 98 minutes; Rating GP; June release.

CAST

Anderson	Sean Connery
Ingrid	Dyan Cannon
Haskins	Martin Balsam
Delaney	Ralph Meeker
Angelo	Alan King
The Kid	Christopher Walken
Parelli	Val Avery
Spencer	Dick Williams
Everson	Garrett Morris
Pop	Stan Gottlieb
Jimmy	Paul Benjamin
Psychologist	Anthony Holland
Werner	Richard B. Schull
Dr. Rubicoff	Conrad Bain
Miss Kaler	Margaret Hamilton
Mrs. Hathaway	Judith Lowry
Bingham	Max Showalter
Mrs. Bingham	Janet Ward
Jerry Bingham	Scott Jacoby
Longene	Norman Rose
Mrs. Longene	Meg Miles
O'Leary	John Call
D'Medico	Ralph Stanley
Vanessi	John Braden
Nurse	Paula Trueman
First Agent	Michael Miller
Johnson	Michael Prince
Papa Angelo	Frank Macetta
Eric	Jack Doroshow
Eric's friend	Michael Clary
Receptionist	Hildy Brooks
Doctor	Robert Dagny
TV Watcher	Bradford English
Judge	Reid Cruckshanks
Sync Man	Tom Signorelli
Detective A	Carmine Caridi
Sgt. Claire	Michael Fairman
Detective B	George Patelis
Detective C	William Da Prato
Private Detective	Sam Coppola

Martin Balsam, Sean Connery

Christopher Walken, Stan Gottlieb, Sean Connery

Sean Connery, Val Avery
Top: Dyan Cannon, Sean Connery

Ralph Meeker, Garrett Morris

DRIVE, HE SAID

(COLUMBIA) Executive Producer, Bert Schneider; Producers, Jack Nicholson, Steve Blauner; Director, Jack Nicholson; Screenplay, Jeremy Larner, Jack Nicholson; From novel by Jeremy Larner; Co-producer, Harry Gittes; Associate Producer, Fred Roos; Photography, Bill Butler; Assistant Director, Sheldon Schrager; Music, David Shire; A BBS Production in Color; 90 minutes; Rating R; June release

CAST

Hector	William Tepper
Olive	Karen Black
Gabriel	Michael Margotta
Coach Bullion	Bruce Dern
Richard	Robert Towne
Conrad	Henry Jaglom
Easly	Mike Warren
Sylvie	June Fairchild
Director of Athletics	Don Hanmer
Dance Instructor	Lynn Bernay
Announcers	Joey Walsh, Harry Gittes
Jollop	Charles Robinson
Finnegan	Bill Sweek
Pro Owner	David Stiers
Pro Lawyer	B. J. Merholz
Secretary	I. J. Jefferson
President Wallop	Kenneth Bayle
Rosemary	Cathy Bradford
Pfc. Johnson	Eric Johnson
Phoneman	Bill Kenney
Policeman	Lenny Lockabaugh
M. P.	Clyde Crawford
Psychiatrist	Mark Malinsuskee
Doctors	Douglas McKenzie, Robert Page, Oliver O'Ferrall
Manager	Douglas Ryan
Manager's girl friend	Cindy Williams
Buckholder	Gunnar Malm
Trainer	Bill Duffy

Right: William Tepper, Karen Black

Karen Black

Mike Warren, William Tepper

WILLY WONKA AND THE CHOCOLATE FACTORY

(PARAMOUNT) Producers, Stan Margulies, David L. Wolper; Director, Mel Stuart; Screenplay, Roald Dahl; Based on his book "Charlie and the Chocolate Factory"; Photography, Arthur Ibbetson; Lyrics, Leslie Bricusse; Music, Anthony Newley; Choreography, Howard Jeffrey; Assistant Directors, Jack Roe, Wolfgang Glattes; In Technicolor; 110 minutes; Rating G; June release.

CAST

Willy Wonka	Gene Wilder
Grandpa Joe	Jack Albertson
Charlie	Peter Ostrum
Augustus Gloop	Michael Bollner
Mrs. Gloop	Ursula Reit
Violet Beauregarde	Denise Nickerson
Mr. Beauregarde	Leonard Stone
Veruca Salt	Julie Dawn Cole
Mr. Salt	Roy Kinnear
Mike Teevee	Paris Themmen
Mrs. Teevee	Dodo Denney
Mrs. Bucket	Diana Sowle
Mr. Bill	Aubrey Wood
Mr. Turkentine	David Battley
Mr. Slugwork	Gunter Meissiner
Tinker	Peter Capell
Jopeck	Werner J. Heyking
Grandpa George	Ernest Ziegler
Grandma Georgina	Dora Altmann
Grandma Josephine	Franziska Liebing

Top: Oompa Loompas at work (R) Peter Ostrum, Gene Wilder, Jack Albertson

Peter Ostrum, Jack Albertson, Gene Wilder, Ursula Reit
Above: Jack Albertson, Peter Ostrum

THE HELLSTROM CHRONICLE

(CINEMA 5) Producer-Director, Walon Green; Music, Lalo Schifrin; Photography, Ken Middleham, Helmut Barth, Walon Green; Written by David Seltzer; Associate Producer, Sascha Schneider; Music, Jack Tillar; A David L. Wolper Production in color; 90 minutes; Rating G; June release.

CAST
Dr. Nils Hellstrom .... Lawrence Pressman

Lawrence Pressman
Academy Award for Best Feature Documentary in 1971

McCABE AND MRS. MILLER

(WARNER BROS.) Producers, David Foster, Mitchell Brower; Director, Robert Altman; Screenplay, Robert Altman, Brian McKay; Based on Novel "McCabe" by Edmund Naughton; Photography, Vilmos Zsigmond; Designer, Leon Ericksen; Associate Producer, Robert Eggenweiler; Assistant Director, Tommy Thompson; Songs, Leonard Cohen; In Panavision and Technicolor; Rating R; 120 minutes; June release.

CAST

John McCabe	Warren Beatty
Constance Miller	Julie Christie
Sheehan	Rene Auberjonois
Butler	Hugh Millais
Lawyer	William Devane
Ida Coyle	Shelley Duvall
Sears	Michael Murphy
Smalley	John Schuck
Mr. Elliott	Corey Fischer

Julie Christie, Warren Beatty
Top: Julie Christie

KLUTE

(WARNER BROS.) Producer-Director, Alan J. Pakula; Co-Producer, David Lange; Screenplay, Andy and Dave Lewis; Photography, Gordon Willis; Executive Associate Producer, C. Kenneth Deland; Music, Michael Small; Costumes, Ann Roth; Assistant Director, William Gerrity; In Panavision and Technicolor; 114 minutes; Rating R; June release.

CAST

Bree Daniels	Jane Fonda
John Klute	Donald Sutherland
Peter Cable	Charles Cioffi
Frank Ligourin	Roy R. Scheider
Arlyn Page	Dorothy Tristan
Trina	Rita Gam
Psychiatrist	Vivian Nathan
Trask	Nathan George
Mr. Goldfarb	Morris Strassberg
Berger	Barry Snider
Actor's Agent	Anthony Holland
Sugarman	Richard Shull
Holly Gruneman	Betty Murray
Man in Hotel	Fred Burrell
Goldfarb's Secretary	Jean Stapleton
Tom Gruneman	Robert Milli

**Donald Sutherland, Dorothy Tristan, Barry Snider
Top: Donald Sutherland, Jane Fonda (also right)**

*Jane Fonda received Academy Award
for Best Actress in 1971*

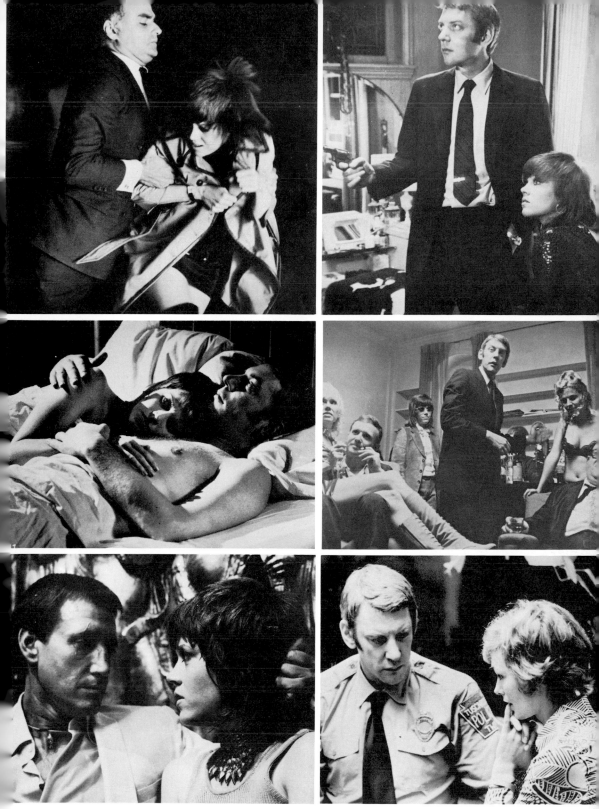

Roy Scheider, Jane Fonda Above: Jane
Fonda, Donald Sutherland Top: Charles
Cioffi, Jane Fonda

Donald Sutherland, Betty Murray Above: Jane
Fonda, Donald Sutherland (also top)

LE MANS

(NATIONAL GENERAL) Executive Producer, Robert E. Relyea; Producer, Jack N. Reddish; Director, Lee H. Katzin; Screenplay, Harry Kleiner; Music, Michel Legrand; Photography, Robert B. Hauser, Rene Guissart, Jr.; Associate Producer, Alan Levine; Designer, Phil Abramson; Costumes, Ray Summers; Assistant Directors, Gus Agosti, Les Sheldon; A Solar Production in DeLuxe Color; 106 minutes; Rating G; June release.

CAST

Michael Delaney	Steve McQueen
Erich Stahler	Siegfried Rauch
Lisa Belgetti	Elga Andersen
David Townsend	Ronald Leigh-Hunt
Johann Ritter	Fred Haltiner
Claude Aurac	Luc Merenda
Larry Wilson	Christopher Waite
Anna Ritter	Louise Edlind
Lugo Abratte	Angelo Infanti
Paul Jacques Dion	Jean-Claude Bercq
Vito Scalise	Michele Scalera
Loretto Fuselli	Gino Cassani
Tommy Hopkins	Alfred Bell
Paolo Scandenza	Carlo Cecchi
Bruno Frohm	Richard Rudiger
Chris Barnett	Hal Hamilton
Jonathan Burton	Jonathan Williams
Peter Wiese	Peter Parten
Tony Elkins	Conrad Pringle
Josef Hauser	Erich Glavitza
Max Kummel	Peter Huber

Steve McQueen, also top left

THEY MIGHT BE GIANTS

(UNIVERSAL) Producers, Paul Newman, John Foreman; Director, Anthony Harvey; Associate Producer, Frank Caffey; Photography, Victor Kemper; Screenplay, James Goldman; Based on his play; Assistant Director, Louis A. Stroller; Designer, John Lloyd; Costumes, Anne Roth, Fern Buchner; A Jennings Lang Production in DeLuxe Color; 88 minutes; Rating G; June release.

CAST

Dr. Watson	Joanne Woodward
Justin Playfair	George C. Scott
Wilbur Peabody	Jack Gilford
Blevins Playfair	Lester Rawlins
Daisy	Rue McClanahan
Dr. Strauss	Ron Weyand
Grace	Kitty Winn
Her Boyfriend	Peter Fredericks
Maud	Sudie Bond
Miss Finch	Jenny Egan
Peggy	Theresa Merritt
Messenger	Al Lewis
Mr. Small	Oliver Clark
Telephone Operators	Jane Hoffman, Dorothy Greener
Sanitation Men	M. Emmet Walsh, Louis Zorich
Telephone Guard	Michael McGuire
Policeman	Eugene Roche
Mr. Brown	James Tolkan
His Driver	Jacques Sandulescu
Mr. Bagg	Worthington Miner
Mrs. Bagg	Frances Fuller
Teenage Boy	Matthew Cowles
Teenage Girl	Candy Azzara
Police Lieutenant	John McCurry
Chief	Tony Capodilupo
Usher	F. Murray Abraham
Winthrop	Staats Cotsworth
Chestnut Vendor	Paul Benedict
Store Manager	Ralph Clanton
Cab Driver	Ted Beniades

Joanne Woodward, George C. Scott
(also top)

WILD ROVERS

(MGM) Producers, Blake Edwards, Ken Wales; Direction and Screenplay, Blake Edwards; Music, Jerry Goldsmith; Photography, Philip Lathrop; Assistant Director, Alan Callow; Costumes, Jack Bear; In Color; 109 minutes; Rating GP; June release.

CAST

Ross Bodine	William Holden
Frank Post	Ryan O'Neal
Walter Buckman	Karl Malden
Sada Billings	Lynn Carlin
John Buckman	Tom Skerritt
Paul Buckman	Joe Don Baker
Nell Buckman	Leora Dana
Joe Billings	James Olson
Ben	Moses Gunn
Sheriff	Victor French
Maybell	Rachel Roberts
Hansen	Sam Gilman
Savage	Charles Gray
Hereford	William Bryant
Cap Swilling	Jack Garner
Bodine's Girl	Caitlin Wyles
Sada's Mother	Mary Jackson
Ruff	William Lucking
Gambler	Ed Bakey
Benson Sheriff	Ted Gehring
Palace Bartender	Alan Carney
Cassidy	Ed Long
Leaky	Lee DeBroux
Mack	Hal Lynch
Sheepmen	Red Morgan, Bennie Dobbins
Bathhouse Attendant	Bob Beck
Attendant's Son	Geoffrey Edwards
Piano Player	Studs Tanney
Cantina Bartender	Bruno VeSoto
Deputy	Dick Crockett

Right: William Holden, Ryan O'Neal

Debbie Reynolds, Shelley Winters

WHAT'S THE MATTER WITH HELEN?

(UNITED ARTISTS) Executive Producer, Edward S. Feldman; Producer, George Edwards; Director, Curtis Harrington; Screenplay, Henry Farrell; Associate Producer, James C. Pratt; Photography, Lucien Ballard; Music, David Raksin; Costumes, Morton Haack; Choreographer, Tony Charmoli; Assistant Director, Claude Binyon, Jr.; A Filmways-Raymax Production; In DeLuxe Color; Presented by Martin Ransohoff; 101 minutes; Rating GP; June release.

CAST

Adelle Bruckner	Debbie Reynolds
Helen Hill	Shelley Winters
Lincoln Palmer	Dennis Weaver
Sister Alma	Agnes Moorehead
Hamilton Starr	Micheal MacLiammoir
Winona Palmer	Samee Lee Jones
Rosalie Greenbaum	Robbi Morgan
Mrs. Greenbaum	Helene Winston
Mrs. Rigg	Molly Dodd
Mrs. Schultz	Peggy Rea
Mrs. Barker	Yvette Vickers
Mrs. Plumb	Paulle Clark
Kiddy M.C.	Pamelyn Ferdin
Sue Anne Schultz	Devvie Van Den Houten
Charlene Barker	Tammy Lee
Donna Plumb	Teresa De Rose
Gigolo	Swen Swenson
Tramp	Timothy Carey
Malcolm Hays	Harry Stanton
Cab Driver	James Dobson
Detective West	Logan Ramsey
Ellie Banner	Peggy Lloyd Patten
Matt Hill	Gary Combs
Midget Lady	Sallie Delfino
Spinster	Annette Davis
Widow	Helene Heigh
Old Man	Peter Brocco
Old Lady	Minta Durfee Arbuckle
Young Girl	Peggy Walton
Fanatical Man	Douglas Deane

WHO IS HARRY KELLERMAN AND WHY IS HE SAYING THOSE TERRIBLE THINGS ABOUT ME?

(NATIONAL GENERAL) Producer-Director, Ulu Grosbard; Producer-Writer, Herb Gardner; Associate Producer, Fred C. Caruso; Photography, Victor J. Kemper; Assistant Directors, Pete Scoppa, Larry Albucher; Designer, Harry Horner; Costumes, Anna Hill Johnstone; Songs, Shel Silverstein; A Cinema Center Presentation; A Harry Kellerman Production; In DeLuxe Color; 108 minutes; Rating GP; June release.

CAST

Georgie	Dustin Hoffman
Allison	Barbara Harris
Dr. Moses	Jack Warden
Leon	David Burns
Irwin	Dom DeLuise
Margot	Betty Walker
Gloria	Rose Gregorio
Sid	Gabriel Dell
Susan	Amy Levitt
Marty	Joe Sicari
Halloran	Ed Zimmermann
Chomsky	Josip Elic
Newsdealer	Rudy Bond
Flower Vendor	Walter Hyman
Sally	Candy Azzara
Samantha	Robyn Millan
Lemuel	James Hall
Ruthie	Regina Baff

Right: Dustin Hoffman

Barbara Harris, Dustin Hoffman

CARNAL KNOWLEDGE

(AVCO EMBASSY) Producer-Director, Mike Nichols; Screenplay, Jules Feiffer; Executive Producer, Joseph E. Levine; Associate Producer, Clive Reed; Photography, Giuseppe Rotunno; Designer, Richard Sylbert; Costumes, Anthea Sylbert; Assistant Director, Tim Zinnemann; In Panavision and Technicolor; 96 minutes; Rating R; June release.

CAST

Jonathan	Jack Nicholson
Susan	Candice Bergen
Sandy	Arthur Garfunkel
Bobbie	Ann-Margret
Louise	Rita Moreno
Cindy	Cynthia O'Neal
Jennifer	Carol Kane

Left: Jack Nicholson, Arthur Garfunkel

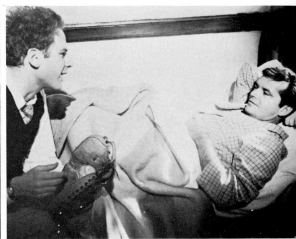

Jack Nicholson, Ann-Margret
Above: Candice Bergen, Jack Nicholson

Arthur Garfunkel, Candice Bergen
Above: Arthur Garfunkel, Jack Nicholson

Jack Nicholson, Rita Moreno Above: Ann-Margret,
Jack Nicholson Top: Cynthia O'Neal, Arthur Garfunkel

Arthur Garfunkel, Ann-Margret Above:
Jack Nicholson, Arthur Garfunkel,
Carol Kane Top: Arthur Garfunkel,
Jack Nicholson

WILLARD

(CINERAMA) Producer, Mort Briskin; Director, Daniel Mann; Screenplay, Gilbert A. Ralston; Based on novel "Ratman's Notebooks" by Stephen Gilbert; Photography, Robert B. Hauser; Music, Alex North; Art Director, Howard Hollander; Assistant Director, Robert Goodstein; A BCO Production in DeLuxe Color; 95 minutes; Rating GP; June release.

CAST

Willard Stiles	Bruce Davison
Henrietta Stiles	Elsa Lanchester
Al Martin	Ernest Borgnine
Joan	Sondra Locke
Brandt	Michael Dante
Charlotte Stassen	Jody Gilbert
Alice	Joan Shawlee
Barskin	William Hansen
Jonathan Farley	J. Pat O'Malley
Carlson	John Myhers
Mrs. Becker	Helen Spring
Ida Stassen	Pauline Drake
Carrie Smith	Almira Sessions

and Alan Baxter, Sherry Presnell, Lola Kendrick, Robert Golden, Minta Durfee Arbuckle, Arthur Tovey, Shirley Lawrence, Louise De Carlo.

Right: Bruce Davison, Elsa Lanchester
Below: Sondra Locke, Bruce Davison Left:
Bruce Davison, Ernest Borgnine

Trish Van Devere, Tony Musante, George C. Scott

THE LAST RUN

(MGM) Producer, Carter De Haven; Director, Richard Fleischer; Screenplay, Alan Sharp; Photography, Sven Nykvist; Art Directors, Roy Walker, Jose Maria Tapiador; Music, Jerry Goldsmith; Assistant Directors, Antonio Tarruella, Stefano Capriati; In MetroColor; 99 minutes; Rating GP; July release.

CAST

Harry Garmes	George C. Scott
Paul Ricard	Tony Musante
Claudie Scherrer	Trish Van Devere
Monique	Colleen Dewhurst

and Aldo Sanbrell, Antonio Tarruella, Robert Coleby, Robert J. Zurica, Rocky Taylor

BUNNY O'HARE

(AMERICAN INTERNATIONAL) Producers, Gerd Oswald, Norman T. Herman; Executive Producers, Samuel Z. Arkoff, James H. Nicholson; Screenplay, Stanley Z. Cherry, Coslough Johnson; From story by Mr. Cherry; Photography, Loyal Griggs, John Stephens; Music, Billy Strange; Assistant Director, Rusty Meek; In Technicolor; 91 minutes; Rating GP; July release.

CAST

Bunny O'Hare	Bette Davis
Bill Green	Ernest Borgnine
Detective Greeley	Jack Cassidy
R. J. Hart	Joan Delaney
Banker	Jay Robinson
Lulu	Reva Rose
Ad	John Astin
Commissioner Dingle	Robert Foulk
Frank	Brayden Linden
Lola	Karen Mae Johnson
Rhett	Francis R. Cody
Elvira	Darra Lyn Tobin
Speed	Hank Wickham
State Trooper	David Cargo

**Right: Ernest Borgnine, Bette Davis
Below: Joan Delaney, Jack Cassidy**

BLESS THE BEASTS & CHILDREN

(COLUMBIA) Producer-Director, Stanley Kramer; Screenplay, Mac Benoff; Based on novel by Glendon Swarthout; Music, Barry De Vorzon, Perry Botkin, Jr.; Title song performed by The Carpenters; Photography, Michel Hugo; Assistant Director, Sheldon Schrager; Associate Producer, George Glass; 109 minutes; Rating GP; In Color; July release.

CAST

Teft	Bill Mumy
Cotton	Barry Robins
Shecker	Miles Chapin
Goodenow	Darel Glaser
Lally 1	Bob Kramer
Lally 2	Marc Vahanian
Sid Shecker	Jesse White
Wheaties	Ken Swofford
Camp Director	Dave Ketchum
Cotton's Mother	Elaine Devry
Hustler	Wayne Sutherlin
Hustler	Bruce Glover
Mr. Goodenow	William Bramley
Mrs. Goodenow	Vanessa Brown
Captain Cotton	Charles H. Gray
Mr. Teft	Vincent Van Lynn
Mom	June C. Ellis
Doctor	Frank Farmer
Young Shooter	Jess Smart

Bill Mumy, Marc Vahanian, Barry Robins, Bob Kramer, Miles Chapin, Darel Glaser, and also above

THE PANIC IN NEEDLE PARK

(20th CENTURY-FOX) Producer, Dominick Dunne; Director, Jerry Schatzberg; Screenplay, Joan Didion, John Gregory Dunne; From book by James Mills; Associate Producer, Roger M. Rothstein; Photography, Adam Holender; Costumes, Jo Ynocencio; Assistant Directors, Robert Greenhut, James F. Inch; A Dunne-Didion-Dunne Production; In DeLuxe Color; 110 minutes; Rating R; July release.

CAST

Bobby	Al Pacino
Helen	Kitty Winn
Hotchner	Alan Vint
Hank	Richard Bright
Chico	Kiel Martin
Sonny	Michael McClanathan
Sammy	Warren Finnerty
Marcie	Marcia Jean Kurtz
Marco	Raul Julia
Irene	Angie Ortega
Mickey	Larry Marshall
Whitey	Paul Mace
Penny	Nancy MacKay
Robins	Gil Rogers
DiBono	Joe Santos
Samuels	Paul Sorvino
Freddy	Arnold Williams
Santo	Vic Ramano
Prep Schoolboy	Bryant Fraser
Pawnshop Lady	Dora Weissman
Doctor	Sully Boyar
Ward Nurse	Florence Tarlow
Admitting Nurse	Ruth Alda
Hotel Clerk	Anthony Palmer

52   Kitty Winn, Alan Vint Above: (C) Al Pacino, Kitty Winn, also top

Al Pacino, Kitty Winn, Above: Marcia Jean Kurtz, Kitty Winn

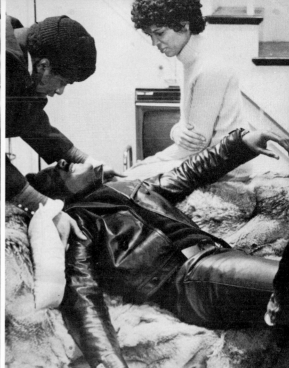

SHAFT

(MGM) Producer, Joel Freedman; Director, Gordon Parks; Screenplay, Ernest Tidyman, John D. F. Black; Based on novel by Ernest Tidyman; Associate Producer, David Golden; Music, Isaac Hayes; Photography, Urs Furrer; Assistant Director, Ted Zachary; Costumes, Joe Aulisi; 100 minutes; Rating R; July release.

CAST

John Shaft	Richard Roundtree
Bumpy	Moses Gunn
Vic Androzzi	Charles Cioffi
Ben Buford	Christopher St. John
Ellie Moore	Gwenn Mitchell
Tom Hannon	Lawrence Pressman
Charlie	Victor Arnold
Marcy	Sherri Brewer
Rollie	Rex Robbins
Dina Greene	Camille Yarbrough
Linda	Margaret Warncke
Byron Leibowitz	Joseph Leon
Cul	Arnold Johnson
Patsy	Dominic Barto
Carmen	George Strus
Lee	Edmund Hashim
Willy	Drew Bundi Brown
Leroy	Tommy Lane
Sims	Al Kirk
Dr. Sam	Shimen Ruskin
Bunky	Antonio Fargas
Old Lady	Gertrude Jeannette
Blind Vendor	Lee Steele
Mal	Damu King
Remmy	Donny Burks

and Tony King (Davies), Benjamin R. Rixson (Newfield), Ricardo Brown (Tully), Alan Weeks (Gus), Glenn Johnson (Char), Dennis Tate (Dotts), James Hainesworth, Adam Wade (Brothers), Clee Burtonya (Sonny), Ed Bernard (Peerce), Ed Barth (Tony), Joe Pronto (Dom), Robin Nolan (Waitress), Ron Tannas (Billy), Betty Bresler (Mrs. Androzzi), Gonzalo Madurga (Counterman), Paul Nevens (Elevator Man), Jon Richards (Starter)

"Theme from Shaft" received Academy Award for Best Song in 1971.

Top: Christopher St. John, Richard Roundtree, Moses Gunn (R) Richard Roundtree, Gwenn Mitchell

Vic Arnold, Richard Roundtree Above: Richard Roundtree, Joseph Leon, Charles Cioffi

53

DUSTY AND SWEETS McGEE

(WARNER BROS.) Producer, Michael S. Laughlin; Direction and Screenplay, Floyd Mutrux; Photography, William A. Fraker; Music, Rick Nelson; Associate Producer, Michael J. Parsons; In Technicolor; 94 minutes; Rating R; July release.

CAST

Pam and Larry, Clifton Tip Fredell, Kit Ryder Beverly, Mitch, Armen, and Bobby Graham are real people, and not actors

Right: Sweets, Dusty, Tip
Below: Larry and Pam

George Kennedy, Anne Baxter Above:
Strother Martin, James Stewart, Kurt Russell

FOOLS' PARADE

(COLUMBIA) Producer-Director, Andrew V. McLaglen; Screenplay, James Lee Barrett; From novel by Davis Grubb; Photography, Harry Stradling, Jr.; Music, Henry Vars; Associate Producer, Harry Bernsen; Assistant Director, Howard W. Koch, Jr.; Costumes, Guy C. Verhille; Produced by Stanmore Productions and Penbar Productions in Eastman Color; 98 minutes; Rating GP; July release.

CAST

Mattie Appleyard	James Stewart
"Doc" Council	George Kennedy
Cleo	Anne Baxter
Lee Cottrill	Strother Martin
Johnny Jesus	Kurt Russell
Roy K. Sizemore	William Windom
Steve Mystic	Mike Kellin
Chanty	Kathy Cannon
Junior Kilfong	Morgan Paull
Willis Hubbard	Robert Donner
Homer Grindstaff	David Huddleston
Enoch Purdy	Dort Clark
Sonny Boy	James Lee Barrett
Clara	Kitty Jefferson Doepken
Station Master	Dwight McConnell
Police Chief	Richard Carl
Prosecuting Attorney	Arthur Cain
Fireman	Paul Merriman
Engineer	Walter Dove
Trusty	Peter Miller
Train Dispatcher	George Metro
Bank Teller	Suzann Stoehr
Bank Clerk	John Edwards

SCANDALOUS JOHN

(BUENA VISTA) Producer, Bill Walsh; Director, Robert Butler; Screenplay, Bill Walsh, Don DaGradi; Based on book by Richard Gardner; Music, Rod McKuen; Photography, Frank Phillips; Associate Producer, Tom Leetch; Designer, Robert Clatworthy; Costumes, Chuck Keehne, Emily Sundby; Assistant Director, Ted Schilz; In Panavision and Technicolor; A Walt Disney Production; 113 minutes; Rating G; July release.

CAST

John McCanless	Brian Keith
Paco Martinez	Alfonso Arau
Amanda	Michele Carey
Jimmy Whitaker	Rick Lenz
Hector Pippin	Harry Morgan
Whitaker Senior	Simon Oakland
Mavis	Iris Adrian
Sheriff Hart	Bill Williams
Card Dealer	Christopher Dark
Farm Woman	Fran Ryan
Sludge	Bruce Glover
Old Indian	Richard Hale
Grotch	James Lydon
Wendell	John Ritter
Bartender	Larry D. Mann
Switchman	Jack Raine
Governor Murray	Booth Colman
Hilary	Edward Faulkner
Abernathy	Bill Zuckert
Wales	John Zaremba
Paco's Cousin	Robert Padilla
Clerk	Alex Tinne
Dr. Kropak	Ben Baker
Pipes	Paul Koslo
Men's Store Clerk	William O'Connell
Bald Head	Sam Edwards
Girl	Leonore Stevens

Right: Brian Keith, Alfonso Arau

Iris Adrian, Brian Keith

Rick Lenz, Michele Carey

THE LIGHT AT THE EDGE OF THE WORLD

(NATIONAL GENERAL) Producer, Kirk Douglas; Director, Kevin Billington; Screenplay, Tom Rowe; Based on novel by Jules Verne; Photography, Henri Decae; Music, Piero Piccioni; Presented by Alexandre Salkind; In Panavision and Eastman Color; 101 minutes; Rating GP; July release.

CAST

Will Denton	Kirk Douglas
Jonathan Kongre	Yul Brynner
Arabella	Samantha Eggar
Virgilio	Jean Claude Drouot
Captain Moriz	Fernando Rey
Montefiore	Renato Salvatori
Felipe	Massimo Ranieri
Tarcante	Aldo Sambrell
Emilio	Tito Garcia

Left: Samantha Eggar, Yul Brynner
Below: Samantha Eggar, Kirk Douglas

THE RETURN OF COUNT YORGA

(AMERICAN INTERNATIONAL) Producer, Michael Macready; Director, Bob Kelljan; Screenplay, Bob Kelljan, Yvonne Wilder; Based on characters created by Bob Kelljan; Music, Bill Marx; Color by Movielab; 97 minutes; Rating GP; August release.

CAST

Count Yorga	Robert Quarry
Cynthia Nelson	Mariette Hartley
Dr. David Baldwin	Roger Perry
Jennifer	Yvonne Wilder
Rev. Thomas	Tom Toner
Lt. Madden	Rudy DeLuca
Tommy	Philip Frame
Prof. Rightstat	George Macready
Bill Nelson	Walter Brooke
Brudah	Edward Walsh
Sgt. O'Connor	Craig Nelson
Jason	David Lampson
Ellen	Karen Houston
Mrs. Nelson	Helen Baron
Mitzi	Jesse Wells
Joe	Mike Pataki
Witch	Corrine Conley
Michael Farmer	Allen Joseph
Claret Farmer	Peg Shirley
Laurie Greggs	Liz Rogers
Jonathan Greggs	Paul Hansen

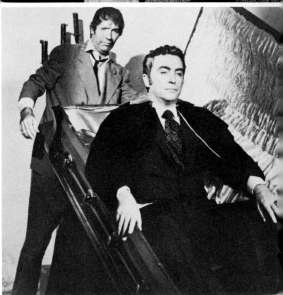

Edward Walsh, Robert Quarry Above:
Robert Quarry, Mariette Hartley, Roger Perry

CHROME AND HOT LEATHER

(AMERICAN INTERNATIONAL) Producer, Wes Bishop; Direction and Photography, Lee Frost; Screenplay, Michael Allen Haynes, David Neibel, Don Tait; Story, Michael Allen Haynes, David Neibel; Music, Porter Jordan; Color by Movielab; 91 minutes; Rating GP; August release.

CAST

T. J.	William Smith
Mitch	Tony Young
Casey	Michael Haynes
Al	Peter Brown
Jim	Marvin Gaye
Hank	Michael Stearns
Susan	Kathy Baumann
Sheriff	Wes Bishop
Ned	Herb Jeffries
Sweet Willy	Bob Pickett
Lt. Reardon	George Carey
Capt. Barnes	Marland Proctor
Kathy	Cherie Moor
Helen	Ann Marie
Sgt. Mack	Robert Ridgely
NCO Bartender	Lee Parrish
Gabe	Larry Bishop

Marvin Gaye, Tony Young
Top: William Smith, Kathy Baumann

Top: Michael Haynes, Kathy Baumann
Below: Ann Marie

JOHNNY GOT HIS GUN

(CINEMATION) Producer, Bruce Campbell; Direction and Screenplay by Dalton Trumbo from his novel; Photography, Jules Brenner; Music, Jerry Fielding; Presented by Jerry Gross; In Color; 111 minutes; Rating GP; August release.

CAST

Joe Bonham	Timothy Bottoms
Kareen	Kathy Fields
Joe's Mother	Marsha Hunt
Joe's Father	Jason Robards
Christ	Donald Sutherland
Fourth Nurse	Diane Varsi
Lucky	Sandy Brown Wyeth
Jody Simmons	Donald Barry
Ancient Prelate	Peter Brocco
Hospital Official	Kendell Clarke
Corporal Timlon	Eric Christmas
Col/Gen. Tillery	Eduard Franz
Little Guy	Craig Bovia
Bakery Girl	Judy Howard Chaikin
Orator	Robert Cole
British Colonel	Maurice Dallimore
Third Doctor	Robert Easton
Russ	Larry Fleischman
Redhead	Tony Geary
Priest	Edmund Gilbert
Second Doctor	Ben Hammer
First Reader	Milton Barnes
Captain	Wayne Heffley
Elizabeth at 6	Lynn Hanratty

and Ernestine Johnston (Farm woman), Joseph Kaufman (Rudy), Mike Lee (Bill), Kerry MacLane (Joe at 10), Charles McGraw (Mike), William Mims (Gentleman), Byron Morrow (Brigadier General), Alice Nunn, Marge Redmond, Jodean Russo (Nurses), David Soul (Swede), Etienne Veazie (Black Boy), Peter Virgo, Jr. (Attendant), Gigi Vorgan (Catherine at 13), Jeff Walker (Fifth Guy), Bruce Watson (Technician), Cynthia Wilson (Catherine at 7)

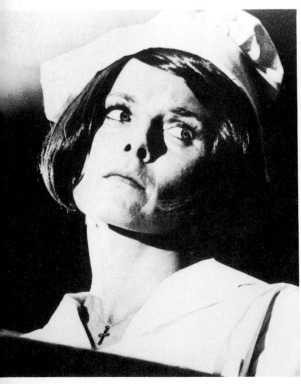

Diane Varsi Top Right: Timothy Bottoms, Kathy Fields

Donald Sutherland Above: Timothy Bottoms, Jason Robards

58

A GUNFIGHT

(PARAMOUNT) Producers, A. Ronald Lubin, Harold Jack Bloom; Director, Lamont Johnson; Screenplay, Harold Jack Bloom; Photography, David Walsh; Designer, Tambi Larsen; Assistant Directors, William Green, William Sheehan; Music, Laurence Rosenthal; Title song by Johnny Cash; A Harvest-Thoroughbred-Joel Production in Color; 90 minutes; Rating GP; August release.

CAST

Will Tenneray	Kirk Douglas
Abe Cross	Johnny Cash
Nora Tenneray	Jane Alexander
Francisco Alvarez	Raf Vallone
Jenny Simms	Karen Black
Bud Tenneray	Eric Douglas
Kyle	Phillip Mead
Toby	John Wallwork
Marv Green	Dana Elcar
Cater	Bob Wilke
Dekker	George Le Bow
Newt Hale	James Cavasos
Cowboy	Keith Carradine

LAWMAN

(UNITED ARTISTS) Producer-Director, Michael Winner; Screenplay, Gerald Wilson; Music, Jerry Fielding; Photography, Bob Paynter; Designer, Stan Jolley; Assistant Director, Michael Dryhurst; A Scimitar Production in Technicolor; 98 minutes; Rating GP; August release.

CAST

Jered Maddox	Burt Lancaster
Cotton Rayn	Robert Ryan
Vincent Bronson	Lee J. Cobb
Laura Selby	Sheree North
Lucas	Joseph Wiseman
Vernon Adams	Robert Duvall
Harvey Stenbaugh	Albert Salmi
Hurd Price	J. D. Cannon
Mayor Sam Bolden	John McGiver
Crowe Wheelwright	Richard Jordan
Jason Bronson	John Beck
Jack Dekker	Ralph Waite
Choctaw Lee	William Watson
Minister	Charles Tyner
Totts	John Hillerman
Hersham	Robert Emhardt
Dusaine	Richard Bull
Moss	Hugh McDermott
Cobden	Lou Frizell
Luther Harris	Walter Brooke
Marc Corman	Bill Brimley

ROMANCE OF A HORSETHIEF

(ALLIED ARTISTS) Producer, Gene Gutowski; Director, Abraham Polonsky; Screenplay, David Opatoshu; Music, Mort Shuman; Costumes, Ruth Myers; Photography, Piero Portalupi; Presented by Emanuel L. Wolf; In Technicolor; 101 minutes; Rating GP; August release.

CAST

Stoloff	Yul Brynner
Kifke	Eli Wallach
Naomi	Jane Birkin
Zanvill	Oliver Tobias
Estusha	Lainie Kazan
Shloime	David Opatoshu
Sigmund	Serge Gainsbourg
Mendel	Henri Sera
Countess Grabowsky	Linda Veras
Lt. Vishinsky	Branko Plesa
Gruber	Vladimir Bacic
Sura	Alenka Rancic
Strugatch	Branko Spoljar
Cheitche	Dina Rutic
Manka	Marilu Tolo
Schoolteacher	Maria Mizar
Grisha	Mile Sosa
Tailor	Aljosa Vuckovic
Piano Player	Mort Shuman
Girls	Vida Jerman, Vera Stanojevic, Mira Blaskovic, Nada Cibic

Karen Black, Johnny Cash Above:
Kirk Douglas, Raf Vallone, Johnny Cash
Top: Jane Alexander, Kirk Douglas

David Opatoshu, Jane Birkin, Lainie
Kazan, Eli Wallach

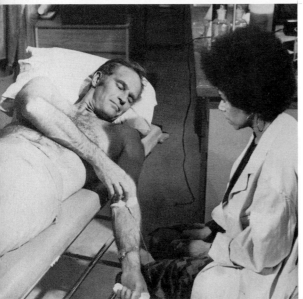

THE OMEGA MAN

(WARNER BROS.) Producer, Walter Seltzer; Director, Boris Sagal; Screenplay, John William, Joyce H. Corrington; from novel by Richard Matheson; Photography, Russell Metty; Music, Ron Grainer; Art Director, Arthur Loel, Walter M. Simonds; Assistant Director, Donald Roberts; In Technicolor; 98 minutes; Rating GP; August release.

CAST

Neville	Charlton Heston
Matthias	Anthony Zerbe
Lisa	Rosalind Cash
Dutch	Paul Kosto
Zachary	Lincoln Kilpatrick
Richie	Eric Laneuville

Left: Charlton Heston, Rosalind Cash
Top: Charlton Heston

LET'S SCARE JESSICA TO DEATH

(PARAMOUNT) Producer, Charles B. Moss, Jr.; Co-Producer, William Badalto; Director, John Hancock; Screenplay, Norman Jonas, Ralph Rose; Photography, Bob Baldwin; Music, Orville Stoeber; Electronic Music, Walter Sear; In Color; 89 minutes; August release.

CAST

Jessica	Zohra Lampert
Duncan	Barton Heyman
Woody	Kevin O'Connor
Girl	Gretchen Corbett
Dorker	Alan Manson
Emily	Mariclare Costello

Barton Heyman, Zohra Lampert, Kevin O'Connor, Gretchen Corbett

THE LOVE MACHINE

(COLUMBIA) Executive Producer, Irving Mansfield; Producer, M. J. Frankovich; Director, Jack Haley, Jr.; Screenplay, Samuel Taylor; From novel by Jacqueline Susann; Photography, Charles B. Lang; Music, Artie Butler; Designer, Lyle R. Wheeler; Assistant Director, Philip L. Parslow; In Eastman Color; 108 minutes; Rating R; August release.

CAST

Robin Stone	John Phillip Law
Judith Austin	Dyan Cannon
Gregory Austin	Robert Ryan
Danton Miller	Jackie Cooper
Jerry Nelson	David Hemmings
Christie Lane	Shecky Greene
Amanda	Jodi Wexler
Cliff	William Roerick
Ethel Evans	Maureen Arthur
Alfie	Clinton Greyn
Maggie Stewart	Sharon Farrell
Tina	Alexandra Hay
Prostitute	Eva Bruce
Bob Summers	Greg Mullavey
Mary	Edith Atwater
Lane's Pals	Gene Baylos, Ben Lessy

Jodi Wexler, Shecky Greene Above: Robert Ryan, Dyan Cannon Top Right: John Phillip Law

Jackie Cooper, David Hemmings Above: John Phillip Law, Jodi Wexler

CRY UNCLE

(CAMBIST) Producer, David Disick; Director, John G. Avildsen; Screenplay, David Odell; From novel by Michael Brett; Photography, John G. Avildsen; Production Manager, Lloyd Kaufman; Associate Producer, Frank Vitale; In Color; Rating X; 87 minutes; August release.

CAST

Jacob Masters	Allen Garfield
Cora Merrill	Madeline le Roux
Keith	Devin Goldenberg
Jason Dominick	David Kirk
Sprigg	Sean Walsh
Connie	Nancy Salmon
Lena	Maureen Byrnes
Olga	Deborah Morgan
Rene	Pamela Gruen
Lt. Fowler	Mel Stuart
Crazy Girl	Marcia Jean Kurtz
Caulk	Bruce Pesheur
Coughing Policeman	Paul Sorvino
Other Policeman	Ray Baron

Allen Garfield, Madeleine le Roux

DOC

(UNITED ARTISTS) Producer-Director, Frank Perry; Screenplay, Pete Hamill; Photography, Gerald Hirschfeld; Designer, Gene Callahan; Music, Jimmy Webb; Assistant Director, Tony Tarruella; In DeLuxe Color; 95 minutes; Rating R; August release.

CAST

John "Doc" Holliday	Stacy Keach
Kate Elder	Faye Dunaway
Wyatt Earp	Harris Yulin
Ike Clanton	Mike Whitney
The Kid	Denver John Collins
Mr. Clum	Dan Greenburg

Stacy Keach, Harris Yulin, Denver John Collins
Above: Harris Yulin (L), Stacy Keach (R)

Faye Dunaway

THE HIRED HAND

(UNIVERSAL) Producer, William Hayward; Director, Peter Fonda; Executive Producer, Stanley A. Weiss; Screenplay, Alan Sharp; Photography, Vilmos Zsigmond; Music, Bruce Langhorne; Assistant Director, Howard Koch; A Pando Production in Technicolor; 93 minutes; Rating GP; August release.

CAST

Collings	Peter Fonda
Harris	Warren Oates
Hannah	Verna Bloom
Dan	Robert Pratt
McVey	Severn Darden
Luke	Ted Markland
Mace	Owen Orr
Will	Gray Johnson
Mexican Woman	Rita Rogers
Bartender	Al Hopson
Mrs. Sorenson	Ann Doran
Janey	Megan Denver
Plummer	Michael McClure

Severn Darden, Rita Rogers, Peter Fonda Top: Peter Fonda, Warren Oates, Megan Denver, Verna Bloom

KOTCH

(CINERAMA) Producer, Richard Carter; Director, Jack Lemmon; Screenplay, John Paxton; From novel by Katharine Topkins; Photography, Richard H. Kline; Music, Marvin Hamlisch; Art Director, Jack Poplin; Assistant Director, Harry Hogan III; An ABC Picture in Metrocolor; 113 minutes; Rating GP; September release.

CAST

Joseph P. Kotcher .... Walter Matthau
Erica Herzenstiel .... Deborah Winters
Wilma Kotcher .... Felicia Farr
Gerald Kotcher .... Charles Aidman
Vera Kotcher .... Ellen Geer
and James Brohead, Jane Connell, Jessica Rains, Paul Picerni, Darrel Larson, Larry Linville, Arlen Stuart

Left: Walter Matthau

Walter Matthau Above: Walter Matthau, Felicia Farr, Charles Aidman

Walter Matthau, and above with Deborah Winters

SKIN GAME

(WARNER BROS.) Producer, Harry Keller; Executive Producer, Meta Rosenberg; Director, Paul Bogart; Screenplay, Pierre Marton (Peter Stone); From story by Richard Alan Simmons; Photography, Fred Koenekamp, Music, David Shire, Art Director, Herman Blumenthal; Assistant Director, Cliff Coleman; In Technicolor; 102 minutes; Rating GP; September release.

CAST

Quincy	James Garner
Jason	Louis Gossett
Ginger	Susan Clark
Naomi	Brenda Sykes
Plunkett	Edward Asner
Calloway	Andrew Duggan

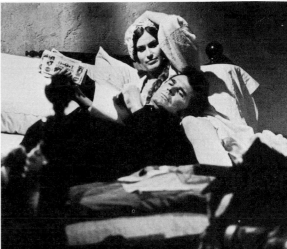

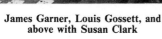
James Garner, Louis Gossett, and above with Susan Clark

James Garner, Louis Gossett (C) Above: James Garner, Susan Clark Top: James Garner, Louis Gossett

DESPERATE CHARACTERS

(ITC) Produced, Directed, and Written by Frank D. Gilroy; Based on novel by Paula Fox; Photography, Urs Furrer; Music, Lee Konitz, Jim Hall, Ron Carter; An ITC-TDJ Presentation in EastmanColor; 88 minutes; September release.

CAST

Sophie	Shirley MacLaine
Otto	Kenneth Mars
Charlie	Gerald O'Loughlin
Claire	Sada Thompson
Leon	Jack Somack
Mike	Chris Gampel
Flo	Mary Ellen Hokanson
Man on subway	Wallace Rooney
Ruth	Rose Gregorio
Young Man	Robert Bauer
Young Girl	Carol Kane
Francis Early	Michael Higgins
Racounteur	Michael McAloney
Saleslady	Elena Karam
Caller	Nick Smith
Hospital Attendant	Robert Delbert
Woman Doctor	Shauneille Ryder
Nurse	Gonzalee Ford
Mr. Haynes	Patrick McVey
Tom	L. J. Davis

Sada Thompson, Shirley MacLaine
Above: Shirley MacLaine, Wallace Rooney

Kenneth Mars, Shirley MacLaine, also top, and above with Robert Delbert

$1,000,000 DUCK

(BUENA VISTA) Producer, Bill Anderson; Director, Vincent McEveety; Screenplay, Roswell Rogers; Based on story by Ted Key; Photography, William Snyder; Costumes, Chuck Keehne, Emily Sundby; Assistant Director, Christopher Hibler; Music, Buddy Baker; In Technicolor; A Walt Disney Production; 92 minutes; Rating G; September release.

CAST

Prof. Albert Dooley	Dean Jones
Katie Dooley	Sandy Duncan
Finley Hooper	Joe Flynn
Fred Hines	Tony Roberts
Rutledge	James Gregory
Jimmy Dooley	Lee Harcourt Montgomery
Dr. Gottlieb	Jack Kruschen
Eunice Hooper	Virginia Vincent
Arvin Wadlow	Jack Bender
Orlo Wadlow	Billy Bowles
Frisby	Sammy Jackson
Mr. Purdham	Arthur Hunnicutt
Bank Manager	Frank Wilcox
Bank Teller	Bryan O'Byrne
Mr. Forbes	Ted Jordan
Mr. Smith	Neil Russell
Mr. Beckert	Pete Renoudet
Assayer	Frank Cady
Parking Attendant	George O'Hanlon
Purchasing Agent	Jonathan Daly
Courthouse Guard	Hal Smith
Morgan	Edward Andrews

Tony Roberts, Dean Jones, Sandy Duncan
Above: Dean Jones Top: Lee Montgomery, Dean Jones, Sandy Duncan

Top and Below: Sandy Duncan, Dean Jones

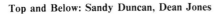

67

BORN TO WIN

(UNITED ARTISTS) Producer, Philip Langner; Director, Ivan Passer; Screenplay, David Scott Milton; Photography, Jack Priestly, Richard Kratina; Music, William S. Fisher; Art Director, Murray Stern; Costumes, Albert Wolsky; In Color; 90 minutes; October release.

CAST

Jay Jay	George Segal
Pam	Karen Black
Veronica	Paula Prentiss
Billy Dynamite	Jay Fletcher
The Greek	Hector Elizondo
Marlene	Marcia Jean Kurtz
Stanley	Irving Selbst
Danny	Robert De Niro
Cashier	Sylvia Syms

George Segal (C), Marcia Jean Kurtz
top: Karen Black, George Segal

68

THE ORGANIZATION

(UNITED ARTISTS) Producer, Walter Mirisch; Director, Don Medford; Screenplay, James R. Webb; Based on character created by John Ball; Photography, Joseph Biroc; Art Director, George B. Chan; Music, Gil Melle; Assistant Director, Jack Reddish; In DeLuxe Color; 107 minutes; Rating GP; October release.

CAST

Virgil Tibbs	Sidney Poitier
Valerie Tibbs	Barbara McNair
Jack Pecora	Gerald S. O'Loughlin
Mrs. Morgan	Sheree North
Bob Alford	Fred Beir
Benjy	Allen Garfield
Lt. Jessop	Bernie Hamilton
William Martin	Graham Jarvis
Juan Mendoza	Raul Julia
Joe Peralez	Ron O'Neal
Stacy Baker	James A. Watson, Jr.
Night Watchman	Charles H. Gray
Larry French	Jarion Monroe
Sgt. Chassman	Dan Travanty
Dave Thomas	Billy "Green" Bush
Rudy	Maxwell Gail, Jr.
Chet	Ross Hagen
Tony	Paul Jenkins
Zach Mills	John Lasell
Annie Sekido	Lani Miyazaki
Capt. Stacy	Garry Walberg
Charlie Blossom	Demond Wilson
Andy Tibbs	George Spell
Ginny Tibbs	Wanda Spell

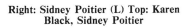

Right: Sidney Poitier (L) Top: Karen Black, Sidney Poitier

Gerald S. O'Loughlin, Sidney Poitier

THE LAST PICTURE SHOW

(COLUMBIA) Executive Producer, Bert Schneider; Producer, Stephen J. Friedman; Director, Peter Bogdanovich; Screenplay, Larry McMurtry, Peter Bogdanovich; Based on novel by Larry McMurtry; Designer, Polly Platt; Photography, Robert Surtees; Associate Producer, Harold Schneider; Assistant Director, Robert Rubin; A BBS Production; 118 minutes; October release.

CAST

Sonny Crawford	Timothy Bottoms
Duane Jackson	Jeff Bridges
Jacy Farrow	Cybill Shepherd
Sam the Lion	Ben Johnson
Ruth Popper	Cloris Leachman
Lois Farrow	Ellen Burstyn
Genevieve	Eileen Brennan
Abilene	Clu Gulager
Billy	Sam Bottoms
Charlene Duggs	Sharon Taggart
Lester Marlow	Randy Quaid
Sheriff	Joe Heathcock
Coach Popper	Bill Thurman
Joe Bob Blanton	Barc Doyle
Miss Mosey	Jessie Lee Fulton
Bobby Sheen	Gary Brockette
Jimmie Sue	Helena Humann
Leroy	Loyd Catlett
Gene Farrow	Robert Glenn
Teacher	John Hillerman
Mrs. Clarg	Janice O'Malley
Oklahoma Patrolman	Floyd Mahaney
Annie-Annie Martin	Kimberly Hyde
Chester	Noble Willingham
Winnie Snips	Marjory Jay
Mrs. Jackson	Joye Hash
Jackie Lee French	Pamela Kelier
Monroe	Gordon Hurst
Johnny	Mike Hosford
Nurse	Faye Jordan
Andy Fanner	Charlie Seybert
Mr. Crawford	Grover Lewis
Marlene	Rebecca Ulrick
Agnes	Merrill Shepherd
Bud	Buddy Wood
Ken	Kenny Wood
Cowboy in cafe	Leon Brown
Truck Driver	Bobby McGriff
Oil Pumper	Jack Mueller
Brother Blanton	Robert Arnold
Tommy Logan	Frank Marshall
Mechanic	Otis Elmore
Roughneck Driver	Charles Salmon
Cowboy	George Gaulden
Gas Station Man	Will Morris Hannis

and the Leon Miller Band

Academy Awards went to Cloris Leachman for Best Supporting Actress, and to Ben Johnson for Best Supporting Actor in 1971

70

**Cybill Shepherd, Ellen Burstyn
Above: Timothy Bottoms, Cloris Leachman**

**Timothy Bottoms, Jeff Bridges
Top Left: Timothy Bottoms, Ben Johnson**

Timothy Bottoms, Cloris Leachman Above:
Timothy Bottoms, Eileen Brennan Top:
Timothy Bottoms, Cybill Shepherd

Cloris Leachman, Timothy Bottoms Above:
Jeff Bridges, Timothy Bottoms Top:
Ben Johnson

THE FRENCH CONNECTION

(20th CENTURY-FOX) Philip D'Antoni/Schine-Moore Production; Director, William Friedkin; Screenplay, Ernest Tidyman; Based on novel by Robin Moore; Photography, Owen Roizman; Executive Producer, G. David Schine; Music, Don Ellis; Assistant Directors, William C. Gerrity, Terry Donnelly; In Technicolor; 104 minutes; Rating R; October release.

CAST

Jimmy Doyle	Gene Hackman
Alain Charnier	Fernando Rey
Buddy Russo	Roy Scheider
Sal Boca	Tony LoBianco
Pierre Nicoli	Marcel Bozzuffi
Devereaux	Frederic De Pasquale
Mulderig	Bill Hickman
Marie Charnier	Ann Rebbot
Weinstock	Harold Gary
Angie Boca	Arlene Farber
Simonson	Eddie Egan
La Valle	Andre Ernotte
Klein	Sonny Grosso
Chemist	Pat McDermott
Drug Pusher	Alan Weeks
The Three Degrees	The Three Degrees

**Top: Gene Hackman, and below
with Arlene Farber**

*Academy Awards for Best Film, Best Director,
Best Screenplay, Best Editing, and Best Actor in 1971*

**Marcel Bozzuffi, Fernando Rey Above:
Gene Hackman, Roy Scheider, Alan Weeks
Top: Gene Hackman, Roy Scheider**

Gene Hackman, Roy Scheider, Bill Hickman
Above: Gene Hackman Top: Sonny Grosso,
Eddie Egan

Gene Hackman, Marcel Bozzuffi Above:
Marcel Bozzuffi Top: Tony LoBianco

73

SHOOT OUT

(UNIVERSAL) Producer, Hal B. Wallis; Associate Producer, Paul Nathan; Director, Henry Hathaway; Screenplay, Marguerite Roberts; Based on novel "The Lone Cowboy" by Will James; Photography, Earl Rath; Music, David Grusin; Assistant Directors, Kenny Williams, Milton Feldman; In Technicolor; 95 minutes; Rating GP; October release.

CAST

Clay Lomax	Gregory Peck
Juliana	Pat Quinn
Bobby Jay	Robert F. Lyons
Alma	Susan Tyrrell
Trooper	Jeff Corey
Sam Foley	James Gregory
Emma	Rita Gam
Decky	Dawn Lyn
Pepe	Pepe Serna
Skeeter	John Chandler
Brakeman	Paul Fix
Homer Page	Arthur Hunnicutt
Dutch	Nicolas Beauvy

Top Left: Gregory Peck, Susan Tyrrell, Robert F. Lyons, John Chandler, Pepe Serna

GOING HOME

(MGM) Producer-Director, Herbert B. Leonard; Screenplay, Lawrence B. Marcus; Photography, Fred Jackman; Music, Bill Walker; Art Director, Peter Wooley; Songs, Red Lane, Larry Henley, Bill Walker; Assistant Director, Howard W. Koch, Jr.; In Metrocolor; 97 minutes; Rating GP; November release.

CAST

Harry K. Graham	Robert Mitchum
Jenny	Brenda Vaccaro
Jimmy Graham	Jan-Michael Vincent
Jimmy at 6	Jason Bernard
Ann Graham	Sally Kirkland
Bonelli	Josh Mostel

(Photos not supplied)

SOMETIMES A GREAT NOTION

(UNIVERSAL) Producer, John C. Foreman; Director, Paul Newman; Associate Producer, Frank Caffey; Screenplay, John Gay; From novel of same name by Ken Kesey; Photography, Richard Moore; Art Director, Philip Jefferies; Costumes, Edith Head; Music, Henry Mancini; "All His Children" sung by Charley Pride; Assistant Director, Mickey McCardle; A Universal/Newman-Foreman Production in Panavision and Technicolor; 113 minutes; Rating GP; November release.

CAST

Hank	Paul Newman
Henry	Henry Fonda
Viv	Lee Remick
Leeland	Michael Sarrazin
Joe Ben	Richard Jaeckel
Jan	Linda Lawson
Andy	Cliff Potts
John	Sam Gilman
Willard Eggleston	Lee de Broux
Biggy Newton	Jim Burk
Elwood	Roy Jenson
Floyd Evenwrite	Joe Maross
Draeger	Roy Poole
Les Gibbons	Charles Tyner

Richard Jaeckel, Henry Fonda, Paul Newman
Above: Paul Newman, Lee Remick

BEDKNOBS AND BROOMSTICKS

(BUENA VISTA) Producer, Bill Walsh; Director, Robert Stevenson; Screenplay, Bill Walsh, Don DaGradi; Based on book by Mary Norton; Photography, Frank Phillips; Music and Lyrics, Richard M. and Robert B. Sherman; Animation Director, Ward Kimball; A Walt Disney Production in Technicolor; 117 minutes; Rating G; November release.

CAST

Eglantine Price	Angela Lansbury
Emelius Browne	David Tomlinson
Mr. Jelk	Roddy McDowall
Bookman	Sam Jaffe
Col. Heller	John Ericson
Swinburne	Bruce Forsyth
General Teagler	Reginald Owen
Mrs. Hobday	Tessie O'Shea
Capt. Greer	Arthur E. Gould-Porter
Street Sweeper	Ben Wrigley
German Sergeants	Rick Traeger, Manfred Lating
Vendor	John Orchard
Paul	Roy Smart
Carrie	Cindy O'Callaghan
Charlie	Ian Weighall
Voice of codfish	Robert Holt
Voice of secretary bird and lion	Lennie Weinrib

Academy Award for Best Special Visual Effects in 1971

Right: Angela Lansbury Top: Roy Snart, Cindy O'Callaghan, Ian Weighill, David Tomlinson, Angela Lansbury

Ian Weighill, Roy Snart,
Angela Lansbury, Cindy O'Callaghan

Barbara Morrison, David Tomlinson, Angela Lansbury

PLAY MISTY FOR ME

(UNIVERSAL) Producer, Robert Daley; Director, Clint Eastwood; Associate Producer, Bob Larson; Screenplay, Jo Heims, Dean Riesner; Story, Jo Heims; Photography, Bruce Surtees; Art Director, Alexander Golitzen; Costumes, Helen Colvig; Music, Dee Barton; "Misty" composed and performed by Errol Garner; "The First Time I Ever Saw Your Face" sung by Roberta Flack; Assistant Director, Bob Larson; A Malpaso Production in Technicolor; 102 minutes; Rating R; November release.

CAST

Dave	Clint Eastwood
Evelyn	Jessica Walter
Tobie	Donna Mills
Sgt. McCallum	John Larch
Frank	Jack Ging
Madge	Irene Hervey
Al Monte	James McEachin
Birdie	Clarice Taylor
Murphy	Donald Siegel
Jay Jay	Juke Everts
Man	George Fargo
Locksmith	Mervin W. Frates
Deputy Sheriff	Tim Frawley
Policeman	Otis Kadani
Anjelica	Brit Lind
Second Man	Paul E. Lippman
Cab Driver	Jack Kosslyn
Madalyn	Ginna Patterson
Man in window	Malcolm Moran

Right: Clint Eastwood, Jessica Walter

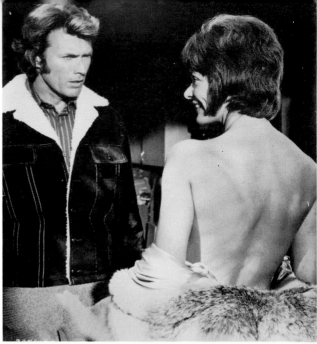

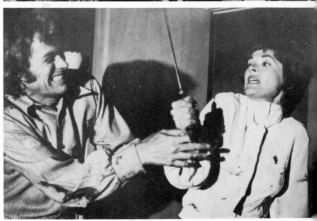

Donald Siegel, Jessica Walter, Clint Eastwood
Above: Walter Spear, Jessica Walter

Clint Eastwood, Jessica Walter
Above: Clint Eastwood, Donna Mills

Jack Klugman, Kevin Riou

WHO SAYS I CAN'T RIDE A RAINBOW!

(TRANSVUE) Producer, Jerry Hammer; Director, Edward Mann; Associate Producer, Mortimer Levitt; Screenplay, Edward Mann, Daniel Hauer; Music, Bobby Scott; Lyrics, Danny Meehan, Richard Ahlert, Joe Scott; Title Song sung by Bobby Vinton; In DeLuxe Color; 85 minutes; Rating G; November release.

CAST

Barney	Jack Klugman
Mary Lee	Norma French
Angel	Reuben Figueroa
David	David Mann
Kevin	Kevin Riou
The Marshal	Val Avery
Afro	Morgan Freeman

and Special Guest Stars Skitch Henderson, Heather MacRae, Otis Stephens

Top: Norma French, Jack Klugmán

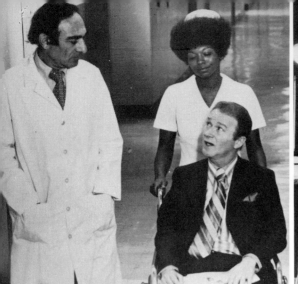

WHO KILLED MARY WHAT'S'ERNAME?

(CANNON) Executive Producer, Christopher C. Dewey; Producer, George Manasse; Director, Ernie Pintoff; Associate Producer, Jeff Lieberman; Screenplay, John O'Toole; Photography, Greg Sandor; In DeLuxe Color; 90 minutes; Rating GP; November release.

CAST

Mickey	Red Buttons
Della	Alice Playten
Christine	Sylvia Miles
Alex	Sam Waterston
Malthus	Dick Williams
Val	Conrad Bain
Dr. Barkunian	Norman Rose
Boulting	David Doyle
Angela	Ellen Gurin
Officer Solomon	Gilbert Lewis
Bartender	Ron Carey
Whitey	Earl Hindman
Joe	Antony Page
Snug Nurse	Sally Birkhead
First Hooker	Stella Longo
Second Hooker	Ellen Faison
Hospital Nurse	Deè Timberlake
Leo	Donald Marye

**Top: Norman Rose, Dee Timberlake, Red Buttons
Below: Mary Boylan (L), Dick Williams (C), Florence Tarlow (second from right)**

**Sam Waterston, Alice Playten, Conrad Bain, Red Buttons
Above: Sylvia Miles, Red Buttons Top: Alice Playten, Red Buttons**

SOMETHING BIG

(NATIONAL GENERAL) Producer-Director, Andrew V. McLaglen; Story and Screenplay, James Lee Barrett; Associate Producer, Harry Bernsen; Title Song, Music, Burt Bacharach; Lyrics, Hal David; Sung by Mark Lindsay; Photography, Harry Stradling, Jr.; Music, Marvin Hamlisch; Art Director, Alfred Sweeney; Assistant Director, Howard W. Koch, Jr.; Costumes, Ray Summers, Richard Bruno; A Cinema Center Films Presentation in Technicolor; 108 minutes; Rating GP; November release.

CAST

Joe Baker	Dean Martin
Colonel Morgan	Brian Keith
Mary Anna Morgan	Honor Blackman
Dover MacBride	Carol White
Jesse Bookbinder	Ben Johnson
Johnny Cobb	Albert Salmi
Tommy MacBride	Don Knight
Polly Standall	Joyce Van Patten
Junior Frisbee	Denver Pyle
Sgt. Fitzsimmons	Merlin Olsen
Angel Moon	Robert Donner
Joe Pickens	Harry Carey, Jr.
Carrie Standall	Judi Meredith
Capt. Tyler	Ed Faulkner
Chief Yellow Sun	Paul Fix
Luis Munos	Armand Alzamora
Malachi Morton	David Huddleston
Teamster #3	Bob Steele
Stagecoach Lady	Shirleena Manchur
Emilio Estevez	Jose Angel Espinosa
Juan Garcia	Juan Garcia
Sam	Robert Gravage
Cpl. James	Chuck Hicks
Barkeeper	John Kelly
Indian Spy	Enrique Lucero
Woman in village	Lupe Amador
Tuffy	Scruffy

Right: Dean Martin, Don Knight Top: Dean Martin, Honor Blackman

Brian Keith, Merlin Olsen

Carol White

FIDDLER ON THE ROOF

(UNITED ARTISTS) Producer-Director, Norman Jewison; Associate Producer, Patrick Palmer; Screenplay, Joseph Stein; Based on musical of same name and Sholem Aleichem stories; Music, Jerry Bock; Lyrics, Sheldon Harnick; Violin Soloist, Isaac Stern; Photography, Oswald Morris; Designer, Robert Boyle; Art Director, Michael Stringer; Assistant Director, Terry Nelson; Choreography after Jerome Robbins by Tom Abbott assisted by Sammy Bayes; Costumes, Elizabeth Haffenden, Joan Bridge; In Panavision and Color; 181 minutes plus intermission; November release.

CAST

Tevye	Chaim Topol
Golde	Norma Crane
Motel	Leonard Frey
Yente	Molly Picon
Lazar Wolf	Paul Mann
Tzeitel	Rosalind Harris
Hodel	Michele Marsh
Chava	Neva Small
Perchik	Michael Glaser
Fyedka	Raymond Lovelock
Shprintze	Elaine Edwards
Bielke	Candy Bonstein
Mordcha	Shimen Ruskin
Rabbi	Zvee Scooler
Constable	Louis Zorich
Avram	Alfie Scopp
Nachum	Howard Goorney
Mendel	Barry Dennen
Russian Official	Vernon Dobtcheff
Fruma Sarah	Ruth Madoc
Grandma Tzeitel	Patience Collier
Fiddler	Tutte Lemkow
Shandel	Stella Courtney
Yankel	Jacob Kalich
Beri	Brian Coburn
Hone	George Little
Farcel	Stanley Fleet
Moishe	Arnold Diamond
Rifka	Marika Rivera
Ezekial	Mark Malicz
Sheftel	Aharan Ipale
Sexton	Roger Lloyd Pack
Priest	Vladimir Medar

Academy Awards for Best Cinematography, Best Sound, and Best Scoring in 1971

Left: Chaim Topol, Norma Crane

Elaine Edwards, Neva Small, Rosalind Harris, Michele Marsh, Candice Bonstein

Leonard Frey, Rosalind Harris

Norma Crane, Molly Picon
Top: Michele Marsh, Michael Glaser

Chaim Topol Top: Neva
Small, Raymond Loreno

HAPPY BIRTHDAY, WANDA JUNE

(COLUMBIA) Producer, Lester Goldsmith; Director, Mark Robson; Screenplay, Kurt Vonnegut, Jr., from his play of the same name; Photography, Fred Koenekamp; Designer, Boris Leven; Assistant Directors, Harry Caplan, Murray Schwartz; Costumes, Michael Woulfe; Produced by The Filmakers Group/Sourdough Ltd./Red Lion Productions in Color; 105 minutes; Rating R; December release.

CAST

Harold Ryan	Rod Steiger
Penelope Ryan	Susannah York
Dr. Norbert Woodley	George Grizzard
Herb Shuttle	Don Murray
Looseleaf Harper	William Hickey
Paul Ryan	Steven Paul
Wanda June	Pamelyn Ferdin
Mildred Ryan	Pamela Saunders
Major Von Kinigswald	Louis Turenne
Mrs. Kestenbaum	C. C. Whitney
Mr. Kestenbaum	Lester M. Goldsmith

Pamelyn Ferdin, Pamela Saunders, Louis Turenne
Top: George Grizzard, Susannah York, Steven Paul, Rod Steiger

DOLLARS

(COLUMBIA) Producer, M. J. Frankovich; Direction and Screenplay, Richard Brooks; Photography, Petrus Schloemp; Music, Quincy Jones; "Money Is" and "Do It" sung by Little Richard; Assistant Director, Tom Shaw; "When You're Smiling" sung by Roberta Flack; In Technicolor; 119 minutes; Rating R; December release.

CAST

Joe Collins	Warren Beatty
Dawn Divine	Goldie Hawn
Mr. Kessel	Gert Frobe
Attorney	Robert Webber
Sarge	Scott Brady
Candy Man	Arthur Brauss
Major	Robert Stiles
Granich	Wolfgang Kieling
Bodyguard	Robert Herron
Helga	Christiane Maybach
Karl	Hans Hutter
Berta	Monica Stender
Bruno	Horst Hesslein
Fur Coat	Wolfgang Kuhlman
Knife Man	Klaus Tschichan
Customs	Tove Platon, Kirsten Lahman
Stripper	Francoise Blanc
Associated Press	Darrell Armstrong
Stars and Stripes	Walter Trott

Goldie Hawn, Gert Frobe Above:
Goldie Hawn, Warren Beatty

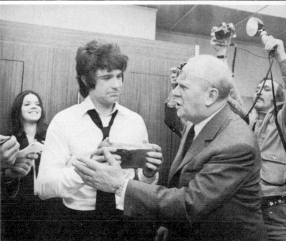

Warren Beatty, Gert Frobe
Top: Goldie Hawn, Warren Beatty

MINNIE AND MOSKOWITZ

(**UNIVERSAL**) Producer, Al Ruban; Direction and Screenplay, John Cassavetes; Associate Producer, Paul Donnelly; Photography, Arthur J. Ornitz; Costumes, Helen Colvig; Music, Bo Harwood; Assistant Directors, Kevin Donnelly, Lou Stroller; In Technicolor; 114 minutes; Rating GP; December release.

CAST

Minnie	Gena Rowlands
Moskowitz	Seymour Cassel
Zelmo Swift	Val Avery
Morgan Morgan	Tim Carey
Sheba Moskowitz	Katherine Cassavetes
Girl	Elizabeth Deering
Florence	Elsie Ames
Georgia Moore	Lady Rowlands
Irish	Holly Near
Wife	Judith Roberts
Dick Henderson	Jack Danskin
Mrs. Grass	Eleanor Zee
Ned	Sean Joyce
Minister	David Rowlands

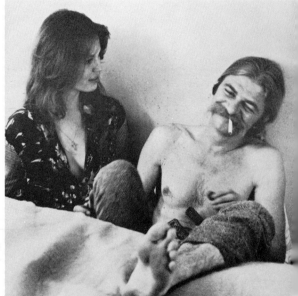

Seymour Cassel (C) Above: Gena Rowlands, Seymour Cassel Top: Seymour Cassel

Seymour Cassel, Gena Rowlands Above: Elizabeth Deering, Seymour Cassel

MADE FOR EACH OTHER

(20th CENTURY-FOX) Producer, Roy Townshend; Director, Robert B. Bean; Screenplay, Renee Taylor, James Bologna; Photography, William Storz; Music, Trade Martin; In Color; 107 minutes; Rating GP; December release.

CAST

Pandora	Renee Taylor
Giggy	Joseph Bologna
Giggy's father	Paul Sorvino
Giggy's mother	Olympia Dukakis
Pandora's mother	Helen Verbit
Helen's father	Louis Zorich
Dr. Furro	Norman Shelly

Renee Taylor, Olympia Dukakis, Paul Sorvino
Top: Joseph Bologna, Renee Taylor

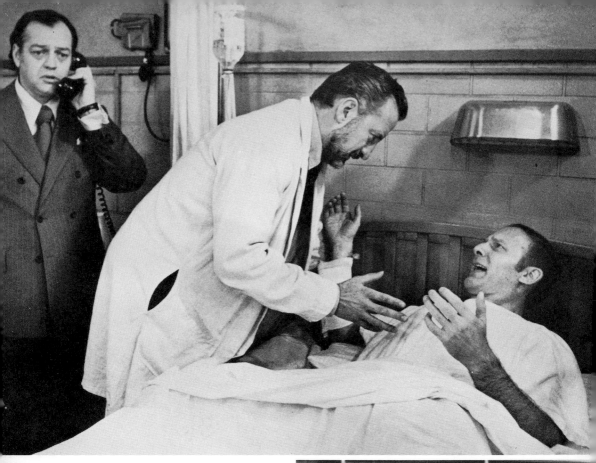

THE HOSPITAL

(UNITED ARTISTS) Producer, Howard Gottfried; Director, Arthur Hillwe; Screenplay, Paddy Chayefsky; Photography, Victor J. Kemper; Music, Morris Surdin; Art Director, Gene Rudolf; Assistant Director, Pete Scoppa; In DeLuxe Color; 103 minutes; Rating GP; December release.

CAST
Dr. Herbert Bock	George C. Scott
Barbara Drummond	Diana Rigg
Drummond	Barnard Hughes
Head Nurse	Nancy Marchand
Hospital Executives	Stephen Elliott, Donald Harron
Hospital Victim	Roberts Blossom
Drummond's Victims	Lenny Baker, Robert Anthony, Angie Ortega
Dr. Welbeck	Richard Dysart
Psychiatrist	David Hooks
Young Doctor	Robert Walden
Indian	Arthur Junuluska
Dr. Spezic	Rehn Scofield

Academy Award for Best Story and Screenplay in 1971

Stephen Elliott (C) Top:
George C. Scott (C)

STAR SPANGLED GIRL

(PARAMOUNT) Producer, Howard W. Koch; Director, Jerry Paris; Screenplay, Arnold Margolin, Jim Parker; From play by Neil Simon; Photography, Sam Leavitt; Music, Charles Fox; Lyrics, Norman Gimbel; Designer, Lawrence G. Paull; Assistant Director, Marty Moss; In Movielab Color; 92 minutes; December release.

CAST

Amy Cooper	Sandy Duncan
Andy Hobart	Tony Roberts
Norman Cornell	Todd Susman
Landlady	Elizabeth Allen
Mr. Karlson	Artie Lewis
Laundryman	Allen Jung
YWCA Receptionist	Helen Kleeb
Cowboy on bus	Harry Northup
Man in car	Peter Hobbs
Karlson's boys	Gordon Bosserman, Jim Connors

Sandy Duncan, Tony Roberts
Top: Tony Roberts, Sandy Duncan, Todd Susman

SUCH GOOD FRIENDS

(PARAMOUNT) Producer-Director, Otto Preminger; Screenplay, Esther Dale (Elaine May); From novel by Lois Gould; Adapted by David Shaber; Photography, Gayne Rescher; Music, Thomas Z. Shepard; Lyrics, Robert Brittan; Designer, Rouben Ter-Arutunian; Assistant Director, Charles Okun; In Movielab Color; 100 minutes; Rating R; December release.

CAST

Julie Messinger	Dyan Cannon
Dr. Timmy Spector	James Coco
Miranda Graham	Jennifer O'Neill
Cal Whiting	Ken Howard
Mrs. Wallman	Nina Foch
Richard Messinger	Laurence Luckinbill
Marcy Berns	Louise Lasser
Bernard Kalman	Burgess Meredith
Uncle Eddie	Sam Levene
Barney Halsted	William Redfield

Right: Dyan Cannon, Nina Foch, Jennifer O'Neill, Ken Howard

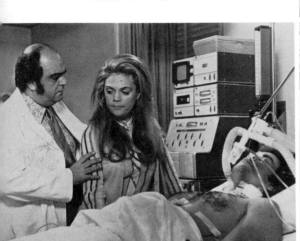

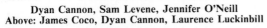

Dyan Cannon, Sam Levene, Jennifer O'Neill
Above: James Coco, Dyan Cannon, Laurence Luckinbill

Dyan Cannon, Laurence Luckinbill,
Above: Dyan Cannon, James Coco

88

SOMEONE BEHIND THE DOOR

(GSF) Producer, Raymond Danon; Director, Nicolas Gessner; Screenplay, Jacques Robert, Mac Dehm, Nicolas Gessner, Lorenzo-Ventavoli; Based on novel by Jacques Robert; Music, Georges Garvarentz; Photography, Pierre Lhomme; Assistant Directors, Michel Lang, Guy Sauteret; In Eastmancolor; 97 minutes; Rating GP; December release.

CAST

The Stranger	Charles Bronson
Laurence	Anthony Perkins
Frances	Jill Ireland
Paul	Henri Garcin
Andrew	Adriano Magestretti
Lucy	Agathe Natanson
Young girl on the beach	Viviane Everly
Intern	Andre Penvern

**Right: Jill Ireland, Charles Bronson
Below: Anthony Perkins, Charles Bronson**

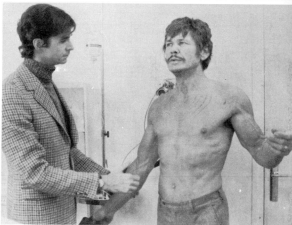

Lilli Palmer, Jason Robards Above:
Jason Robards, Jose Calvo, Christine Kaufmann

MURDERS IN THE RUE MORGUE

(AMERICAN INTERNATIONAL) Executive Producers, James H. Nicholson, Samuel Z. Arkoff; Producer, Louis M. Heyward; Director, Gordon Hessler; Screenplay, Christopher Wicking, Henry Slesar; Based on novel by Edgar Allan Poe; Photography, Manuel Berenguer; Music, Waldo de los Rios; Designer, Jose Luis Galicia; Assistant Director, Juan Carlos Lopez Rodero; In Movielab Color; 87 minutes; Rating GP; December release.

CAST

Cesar Charron	Jason Robards
Marot	Herbert Lom
Madeleine	Christine Kaufmann
Vidocq	Adolfo Celi
Madeleine's mother	Lilli Palmer
Genevre	Maria Perschy
Pierre	Michael Dunn
Hunchback	Jose Calvo
Aubert	Peter Arne
Theatre Manager	Werner Umburg
Actor	Luis Rivera
Lucie	Virginia Stach
Jacques	Dean Selmeir
Orsini	Marshall Jones
Gabrielle	Rosalind Elliot
Orsini's assistant	Ruth Platt

**Country Joe and The Fish
in "Zachariah"**

**Steve Forrest, Vera Miles, Clint Howard
in "The Wild Country"**

ZACHARIAH (Cinerama) Producer-Director, George Englund; Screenplay, Joe Massot, The Firesign Theatre (Philip Austin, Peter Bergman, David Ossman, Philip Proctor); Photography, Jorge Stahl; Music, Jimmie Haskell; Songs, Joe McDonald, Barry Melton, Joe Walsh, Jim Fox, Dale Peters, Doug Kershaw, Michael Kamen, Martin Fulterman, Byard Ray, Obray Ramsey, Arthur Gorson, John Rubenstein; Designer, Asheton Gordon; Assistant Director, Terry Morse, Jr.; In Metrocolor; 91 minutes; Rating GP; January release. CAST: John Rubinstein (Zachariah), Pat Quinn (Belle), Don Johnson (Matthew), Country Joe and The Fish (Crackers), Elvin Jones (Job), Doug Kershaw (Fiddler), William Challee (Old Man), Robert Ball (Stage manager), Dick Van Patten (Dude), Lawrence Kubik (Man in bar), and The James Gang, New York Rock Ensemble, White Lightnin'.

TALES (New Line) Producer, Bill Snyder; Screenplay, Cassandra Gerstein; Photography, Andrea Loomis; 70 minutes; January release. No other credits.

HOW TO FRAME A FIGG (Universal) Producer, Edward J. Montagne; Director, Alan Rafkin; Screenplay, George Tibbles; Story, Edward J. Montagne, Don Knotts; Photography, William Margulies; Music, Vic Mizzy; Costumes, Helen Colvig; Assistant Director, Mel A. Bishop; In Technicolor; 103 minutes; Rating G; February release. CAST: Don Knotts (Figg), Joe Flynn (Kermit), Edward Andrews (Mayor), Elaine Joyce (Ema), Yvonne Craig (Glorianna), Frank Welker (Prentiss), Parker Fennelly (Old Charley), Bill Zuckert (Commissioner), Pitt Herbert (Doctor), Robert P. Lieb (Hayes), Bob Hastings (Chris), Bruce Kirby (Dale), Stuart Nisbet (Gentry), James Millhollin (Funeral Director), Fay DeWitt (Grace), Savannah Bentley (Ethel), Athena Lorde (Agnes), Bill Quinn (Carmoni), John Archer (Gerard), Eddie Quillan (Old Man), Benny Rubin (Max), Billy Sands (Bowling Manager), Clay Tanner (Officer).

PINOCCHIO (Eve) Producer, Chris Warfield; Director, Corey Allen; Screenplay, Chris Warfield, Corey Allen; Music, John Barber; Photography, Ray Dennis Steckler; Art Director, Earl Marshall; Assistant Director, Gene Marum; In Technicolor; 79 minutes; Rating X; January release. CAST: Alex Roman (Pinocchio), Karen Smith (Mabelle), Eduardo Ranez (Jojo), Dyanne Thorne (Fairy Godmother), Monica Gayle (Geppeta), and Neola Graef, Debbie Osborne, Vincene Wallace, Lavinia Dawson, Elizabeth Bell, Gwen Van Dam.

THE WILD COUNTRY (Buena Vista) Producer, Ron Miller; Director, Robert Totten; Screenplay, Calvin Clements, Jr., Paul Savage; Based on "Little Britches" by Ralph Moody; Photography, Frank Phillips; Music, Robert F. Brunner; Assistant Director, Paul Nichols; A Walt Disney Production in Technicolor; Rating G; 100 minutes; February release. CAST: Steve Forrest (Jim), Jack Elam (Thompson), Ronny Howard (Virgil), Frank deKova (Two Dog), Morgan Woodward (Ab), Vera Miles (Kate), Clint Howard (Andrew), Dub Taylor (Phil), Woodrow Chambliss (Dakota), Karl Swenson (Jensen), Mills Watson (Feathers).

DOCTORS' WIVES (Columbia) Producer, M. J. Frankovich; Director, George Schaefer; Screenplay, Daniel Taradash; From novel of same name by Frank G. Slaughter; Photography, Charles B. Lang; Music, Elmer Bernstein; In Color; 100 minutes; Rating R; February release. CAST: Dyan Cannon (Lorrie), Richard Crenna (Pete), Gene Hackman (Dave), Carroll O'Connor (Joe), Rachel Roberts (Della), Janice Rule (Amy), Diana Sands (Helen), Cara Williams (Maggie), Richard Anderson (D.A.), Ralph Bellamy (Jake), John Colicos (Mort), George Gaynes (Paul), Marian McCargo (Elaine).

THE LEXINGTON EXPERIENCE (Corda) Executive Producer, John Brent; Producer-Director, Lawrence Schiller; Screenplay, L. M. Kit Carson; Photography, Charles Levey, Ed Lynch, Lawrence Schiller; In Eastman-Color; 85 minutes; February release. Rock documentary about drug abuses featuring the Pacific Gas & Electric rock group.

**Pat Quinn, John Rubinstein
in "Zachariah"**

**Elaine Joyce, Don Knotts
in "How to Frame a Figg"**

"Bright College Years"

Jill O'Hara, Jordan Christopher
in "Pigeons"

BRIGHT COLLEGE YEARS (AVCO Embassy) Produced, Directed and Photographed by Peter Rosen in Color; 52 minutes; Rating G; February release. No other credits.

PIGEONS (Plaza) Original title "Sidelong Glances of a Pigeon Kicker"; Executive Producer, William P. Wilson; Producer, Richard Lewis; Director, John Dexter; Screenplay, Ron Whyte; Based on novel "Sidelong Glances . . ." by David Boyer; Photography, Urs Furrer; Music, Pat Williams, Lee Holdridge, Edd Kalehoff, Chris Dedrick, Warren Marley; Assistant Director, Stanley Panesoff; Songs sung by Warren Marley; Art Direction, Manny Gerard; Costumes, Domingo Rodriguez; Associate Producers, Tom Sternberg, James Signorelli; A Saturn Picture-Lois Holland Callaway Presentation in Movielab Color; 87 minutes; Rating R; February release. CAST: Jordan Christopher (Jonathan), Jill O'Hara (Jennifer), Robert Walden (Winslow), Kate Reid (Jonathan's mother), William Redfield (William's father), Lois Nettleton (Mildred), Boni Enten (Naomi), Elaine Stritch (Tough lady), Melba Moore (Model), Peter Link (Oliver), Kristoffer Tabori (Oliver's boyfriend), Don Warfield (Stutterer), Jean Shevlin (Mrs. Abelman), Ethel Smith (Blowsy Lady), Matt Warner (Mr. Abelman), Mary Orr (Saleslady), Nancy Andrews (Passenger with crying child), Tony Capodilupo (Van man), Christian Ericson (Gordon), Maria Cellario (Girl in laundromat), Pat Ast (Fat girl), Sara Wilson (Lesbian), Helen Ludlam (Old lady on train), Paul Norman (Orderly), Richard Clarke (Englishman), Janet Maria Burtis (Cranky lady), Bert Bertram (Doorman), Ellis Richardson and Buddy Butler (Negro passersby), Adam Reed (Redhaired boy), Sean Campbell (Boy on crutches), Margaret Brewster (Pigeon lady), Arthur Anderson (Floorwalker), Steve Dawson (Desk Sgt.), Bonnie Paul (Crying girl), Bill Herndon (Cop), Anne Shropshire (Mother in Dept. Store), Esther Bussler (Shopper in cab), Salo Douday (Sad bum), Frank Hamilton (Man in hospital), Wyman Pendleton (Doctor), David Doyle (Seigbert), Edward Dunne (Fag), Sean Bersell (Boy in cab).

ROOMMATES (Pantages) Producers, Harvey Bernstein, Leo Baran; Direction and Screenplay, Jack Baran; Photography, Bruce Sparks; Music, Earth Opera; A Gulliver Production in Color; 97 minutes; Rating R; February release. CAST: Dan Mason (Henry), Harvey Marks (Solly), Barbara Press (Sandy), Theon Banos (Rhoda), Allen Garfield (Martin), Rick Wessler (Bookmaster), Stanley Brock (Madison).

OKAY BILL (Four Star Excelsior) Producer, David Disick; Direction, Screenplay, Photography, John Avildsen; Music, Charles G. Morrow; A Cake Company Presentation in Pathe Color; 91 minutes; Rating R; February release. CAST: Bob Brady (Bill), Nancy Salmon (Nancy), Gordon Felio (Zachary), Roz Kelly (Roz).

MONA (Sherpix) Producer-Director, Bill Osco; A Graffitti Production in Color; 75 minutes; Rating X; February release. CAST: Fifi Watson (Mona), Judy Angel (Mother).

BLOOD AND LACE (American International) Producers, Ed Carlin, Gil Lasky; Associate Producer, Chase Mishkin; Director, Philip Gilbert; Screenplay, Gil Lasky; Photography, Paul Hipp; Art Director, Lee Fischer; Music, John Rons; A Contemporary Filmakers/Carlin C. Production in Movielab Color; 87 minutes; Rating GP; March release. CAST: Gloria Grahame (Mrs. Deere), Melody Patterson (Ellie), Milton Selzer (Mullins), Len Lesser (Tom), Vic Tayback (Calvin), Terri Messina (Bunch), Ronald Taft (Walter), Dennis Christopher (Pete), Peter Armstrong (Ernest), Maggie Corey (Jennifer), Mary Strawberry (Nurse), Louise Sherrill (Edna).

RED, WHITE AND BLUE (Entertainment Ventures) Produced, Directed, Written, Photographed, and Edited by Ferd and Beverly Sebastian; Music, New Hope, Quixote Productions; Narration, Robert Fitzpatrick; 90 minutes; Rating X; March release. A documentary on censorship and obscenity in America.

Marian McCargo, Dyan Cannon, Cara Williams,
Janice Rule, Rachel Roberts in "Doctors' Wives"

Melody Patterson, Gloria Grahame
in "Blood and Lace"

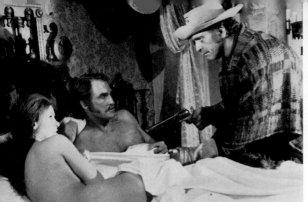

**Susan Clark, Jon Cypher, Burt Lancaster
in "Valdez Is Coming"**

**Louise Sorel, Peter Kastner
in "B.S. I Love You"**

VALDEZ IS COMING (United Artists) Executive Producer, Roland Kibbee; Producer, Ira Steiner; Director, Edwin Sherin; Screenplay, Roland Kibbee, David Rayfiel; Based on novel by Elmore Leonard; Music, Charles Gross; Associate Producer, Sam Manners; Photography, Gabor Pogany; Assistant Directors, Tony Ray, Jose Maria Ochoa, Luis Gomez; Costumes, Louis Brown; A Norlan-Ira Steiner Production in DeLuxe Color; 90 minutes; Rating GP; March release. CAST: Burt Lancaster (Bob Valdez), Susan Clark (Gay), Jon Cypher (Tanner), Barton Heyman (El Segundo), Richard Jordan (R. L.), Frank Silvera (Diego), Hector Elizondo (Mexican Rider), Phil Brown (Malson), Ralph Brown (Beaudry), Juanita Penaloza (Apache Woman), Lex Monson (Rincon), Robert Haynes (Polly), Maria Montez (Anita), Marta Tuck (Rosa), Jose Garcia (Carlos), James Lemp (Bony Man), Sylvia Poggioli (Segundo's Girl), Werner Hasselman (Sheriff), Concha Hombria (Inez), Per Barclay (Bartender), Vic Albert (Rancher), Allan Russell (Rancher), Michael Hinn (Merchant), Rudy Ugland (Tracker), Joaquin Parra (Tracker), Losada (Tracker), and Santiago Santos, Losardo Iglesias, Juan Fernandez, Tony Eppers, Mario Barros, Raul Castro, Nick Cravat, Santiago Garcia, Jeff Kibbee, Linc Kibbee, Ian MacLean, Tom McFadden, Jose Morales, Mario Sanz, Lee Thaxton, Robin Thaxton, Julian Vidrie, Manolin Vidrie.

JOE COCKER/MAD DOGS AND ENGLISHMEN (MGM) Executive Producer, Jerry Moss; Associate Producer, Sidney Levin; Producers, Pierre Adidge, Harry Marks, Robert Abel; Director, Pierre Adidge; Photography, David Myers; An A & M Production in association with Creative Film Associates in Color; 114 minutes; March release. CAST: Joe Cocker, Leon Russell, Chris Stainton, Carl Radle, Jim Price, Bobby Keys, Jim Gordon, Jim Keltner, Don Preston, Sandy Konikoff, Chuck Blackwell, Rita Coolidge, Claudia Lennear, Donna Washburn, Donna Weiss, Pamela Polland, Nicole Barclay, Matthew Moore, Dan Moore, Bobby Jones.

B. S. I LOVE YOU (20th Century-Fox) Producer, Arthur M. Broidy; Direction and Screenplay, Steven Hillard Stern; Music, Jimmy Dale, Mark Shekter; Lyrics, Mark Shekter; Photography, David Dans; Associate Producer, Hurley A. Graffius; Assistant Director, Claude Binyon, Jr.; A Motion Pictures International Production in DeLuxe Color; 99 minutes; Rating R; March release. CAST: Peter Kastner (Paul), JoAnna Cameron (Marilyn/Michele), Louise Sorel (Ruth), Gary Burghoff (Ted), Richard B. Shull (Harris), Joanna Barnes (Jane), John Gerstad (Paul's Father), Mary Lou Mellace (Car Rental Girl), Jeanne Sorel (Paul's Mother), Joe Kottler (Cab Driver), Tom Ruisinger (Travel Agent), Frank Orsatti (Manuel), Barry Woloski (Hippie).

THE SPORTING CLUB (AVCO Embassy) Executive Producer, Joseph E. Levine; Producer, Lee M. Rich; Director, Larry Peerce; Screenplay, Lorenzo Semple, Jr.; Based on novel by Thomas McGuane; Photography, John Courtland; Music, Michael Small; Associate Producer, Joshua Darr; Assistant Director, Stephen Barnett; Costumes, Ronald Talsky; A Lorimar Production in Color; 105 minutes; Rating R; March release. CAST: Robert Fields (Vernor), Nicolas Coster (James), Maggie Blye (Janey), Jack Warden (Earl), Richard Dysart (Spengler), William Roerick (Fortesque), Logan Ramsey (Scott), Leon B. Stevens (Olds), John Seymour (Newcombe), Helen Craig (Mrs. Olds), Diane Rousseau (Barbara), Lois Markle (Sheilah), James Noble (Canon), Ralph Purdum (Murray), Ralph Waite (Olson), Jo Ann Harris (Lu), Linda Blair (Barby).

HARLOT (Graffitti) Producer, Bill Osco; Directors, Howard Ziehm, Mike Light; Screenplay, Lester Romano; Photography, Howard Ziehm; In Color; 70 minutes; Rating X; March release. CAST: Fran Spector (Mary), Patty Alexon (Melody), John McGaughtery (1st Rider), Bill Pruner (2nd Rider), Leroy Jones (James), Judy Angel (Miss Gladstone), Zeb (Biker).

Joe Cocker/Mad Dogs and Englishmen

**Jack Warden, James Noble, John Seymour, Helen
Craig, Lois Markle in "The Sporting Club"**

**Nicolas Coster, Maggie Blye, Robert Fields
in "The Sporting Club"**

**Calvin Culver, Cheri Caffaro
in "Ginger"**

THREE HUNDRED YEAR WEEKEND (Cinerama) Direction and Screenplay, Victor Stoloff; Additional Dialogue, William Devane, Jerome Alden; Photography, Joseph Brun; Music, Gilber Fuller; Art Director, Trevor Williams; Assistant Director, Tony Thatcher; An ABC Picture in Metrocolor; 84 minutes; Rating GP; March release. CAST: Michael Tolan (Marshall), Sharon Laughlin (Nancy), Roy Cooper (Hal), Gabriel Dell (Wynter), M'el Dowd (Carole), Bernard Ward (Rockne), Dorothy Lyman (Jean), William Devane (Tom), James Congdon (Dr. Roland), Carole Demas (Joy).

THE WORLD IS JUST A 'B' MOVIE (Robinson) Produced, Directed, Written, Photographed, and Edited by R. D. Robinson; Music, Bob Lind; In EastmanColor; 90 minutes; March release. CAST: James Christopher (Jonathan), Robert Lincoln Robb (Harry), Riki Ferguson (Gandalf), Georgina Clegg (Alice), Willie Harris (Speaker), Walter Jones (Mitch), and Jerry Charburn, Pigeon Darbo, Uschi Digaid, Eleanor Dixson, Monica Gayle, Mike Hall, Hans Ludermilk, Nadra McClain, Carl MacIntire, Colin MacKenzie, Patti Newby, Joe Saunders, Alan Stecker, Don Vandergriff, Linda York.

THE FLANDERS AND ALCOTT REPORT ON SEX RESPONSE (Films International) Director, Eric Jeffrey Haims; Story, Dr. Ann Foster; Photography, Jim Hastings, David Worth; Music, Randy Scott; A Xerxes Picture in EastmanColor; 83 minutes; Rating X; March release. CAST: John Dunnigan (Dr. Leon Flanders), Sheri Enid (Dr. Phyllis Alcott).

GINGER (Joseph Brenner) Producers, Ralph T. Desiderio, Anthony J. Desiderio; Direction and Screenplay, Don Schain; Photography, R. Kent Evans; Music, Robert G. Orpin; A Derio Picture in Color; 102 minutes; Rating X; March release. CAST: Cheri Caffaro (Ginger), Cindy Barnett (Jean), Herb Kerr (Jimmy), William Grannell (Jason), Michele Norris (Vicki), Lise Mauer (Elizabeth), Herndon Ely (Allison), Duane Tucker (Rex), Calvin Culver (Rodney), David Ross (D. J.), Chuck Ames (Brad), Art Burns (William), Tom Potter (Stanley).

FIVE BLOODY GRAVES (Independent International) Producer-Director, Al Adamson; Story and Screenplay, Robert Dix; Photography, William Zsigmond; Associate Producers, John Cardos, Robert Dix; In Techniscope and Technicolor; A Dix International Presentation; 88 minutes; Rating GP; March release. CAST: Robert Dix (Ben), Scott Brady (Jim), Jim Davis (Clay), John Carradine (Boone), Paula Raymond (Kansas), John Cardos (Joe/Satago), Tara Ashton (Althea), Kent Osbourne (Dave), Vicki Volante (Nora), Denver Dixon (Rawhide), Ray Young (Horace), Julie Edwards (Lavinia), Fred Meyers (Driver), Maria Polo (Little Fawn), Gene Raymond (Voice of Death).

HORROR OF THE BLOOD MONSTERS (Independent International) Executive Producers, Charles McMullen, Zoe Phillips; Producer-Director, Al Adamson; Screenplay, Sue McNair; Photography, William Zsigmond, William G. Troiano; Music, Mike Velarde; Associate Producer, Ewing Brown; A TAL Production; In Movielab Color; 85 minutes; Rating GP; March release. CAST: John Carradine (Dr. Rynning), Robert Dix (Col. Manning), Vicki Volante (Valerie), Joey Benson (Willy), Jennifer Bishop (Lian), Bruce Powers (Bryce), Fred Meyers (Bob), Britt Semand (Linda).

RUBY (Bartlett) Produced, Directed, Photographed, and Edited by Dick Bartlett; Screenplay, Ray Loring, Dick Bartlett; Music, Ray Loring; In Color; 90 minutes; March release. CAST: Ruth Hurd (Ruby), Phillip Webber (Clifford), Joanie Andrews (Mother), George Bartlett (Father), Danny Kosow (Singer), Susan Peters (Girl).

WANDA (Bardene International) Producer, Foundation for Filmmakers of New York; Directed and Written by Barbara Loden; Photography, Nicholas T. Proferes; In Color; 101 minutes; March release. CAST: Barbara Loden (Wanda), Michael Higgins (Dennis), Charles Dosinan (Dennis' father), Frank Jourdano (Soldier), Valerie Manches (Girl in roadhouse).

**Peter Kastner, Joanna Barnes
In "B. S. I Love You"**

**Michael Higgins, Barbara Loden
in "Wanda"**

**Joan Baez
in "Celebration at Big Sur"**

**Rock Hudson
in "Pretty Maids All in a Row"**

DEVIATIONS ON GRATIFICATIONS (Sherpix) Director, Jack Genero; Screenplay, Richard Ray; Photography, Jack Mathew; A Reel Art Production in Color; 82 minutes; Rating X; March release. Documentary on sex.

BRANDY IN THE WILDERNESS (New Line) Producers, and Writers, Stanton Kaye, Michaux French; Director, Stanton Kaye; Photography, Stanton Kaye; In Black and White; 87 minutes; March release. CAST: Michaux French (Brandy), Stanton Kaye (Simon).

CELEBRATION AT BIG SUR (20th Century-Fox) Producer, Carl Gottlieb; Associate Producer, Allison Caine; Photography, Baird Bryant, Bill Kaplan, Gary Weis, Peter Smokler, Joan Churchill; Music, Kit Kalionzes; A Ted Mann Production; In DeLuxe Color; Rating GP; 82 minutes; April release. CAST: Joan Baez, Carol Ann Cisneros, David Crosby, Chris Ethridge, Mimi Farina, Joni Mitchell, Dorothy Morrison, Graham Nash, Julie Payne, Greg Reeves, John Sebastian, Steve Stills, Dallas Taylor, Neil Young, The Combs Sisters, Struggle Mountain Resistance Band, Christopher Ross, Don Sturdy, Lillian Roxon, Ron Martin, Ben Weaver, Peter Melchior, Dr. Francis X. Rigny, Kyle Lawton, Milan Melvin, Barry Adams, John Adams, Bob Cambridge, Patrick Cassidy, Fred Case, William S. Gay, Cynthia Harris, Jack Poet, Star, Yabo Yablonsky.

BRANCHES (New Line) Produced by Cornell University Cinema; Director, Ed Emshwiller; 103 minutes; April release. CAST: Bill Weidner (Bill), Connie Brady (Girl), Al Capogrossi (Her other boy friend), Richard Perlmutter (His side kick), Erica Saxe (Girl after Bill), Christian Larson (Storyteller).

SKEZAG (Soho Cinema) Produced and Directed by Joel L. Freedman, Philip F. Messina; A Cinnamon Production in Color; 76 minutes; April release. CAST: Wayne Shirley, Louis "Sonny" Berrios, Angel Sanchez.

PRETTY MAIDS ALL IN A ROW (MGM) Producer, Gene Roddenberry; Director, Roger Vadim; Screenplay, Gene Roddenberry; Based on novel by Francis Pollini; Music, Lalo Schifrin; Photography, Charles Rosher; Art Directors, George W. Davis, Preston Ames; Assistant Directors, David Silver, Robert Dijoux; Costumes, William Ware Theiss; In Color; Rating R; 92 minutes; April release. CAST: Rock Hudson (Tiger), Angie Dickinson (Miss Smith), Telly Savalas (Surcher), John David Carson (Ponce), Roddy McDowall (Proffer), Kennan Wynn (Pooldaski), James Doohan (Follo), William Campbell (Grady), Susan Tolsky (Miss Craymire), Barbara Leigh (Jean), Gretchen Burrell (Marjorie), Amy Eccles (Hilda), JoAnna Cameron (Yvonne), Margaret Markov (Polly), June Fairchild (Sonny), Joy Bang (Rita), Brenda Sykes (Pamela), Diane Sherry (Sheryl), Phillip Brown (Jim), Mark Malmborg (Dink), Kyle Johnson (Dave), Warren Seabury (Harold), Stephanie Mizrahi (Tiger's Daughter), Orville Sherman (Pastor), and Gary Tigerman, Tim Ray, Alberto Isaac, Dawn Roddenberry, Larry Marmorstein, Judy Michie, Adriana Bentley, Joyce Williams, Chris (Allen) Woodley, Fredricka Myers, Linda Morand, Topo Swope, Jomarie Ward, Otis Greene, Guy Remsen, Joe Quinn, Estrellita Rania. Photos not supplied.

SIMON, KING OF THE WITCHES (Fanfare) Producer, David Hammond; Director, Bruce Kessler; Screenplay, Robert Phippeny; Photography, David Butler; Music, Stu Phillips; Assistant Director, Arthur Levinson; In EastmanColor; 91 minutes; Rating R; April release. CAST: Andrew Prine (Simon), Brenda Scott (Linda), George Paulsin (Turk), Norman Burton (Rackum), Gerald York (Hercules), and Ultra Violet, Michael C. Ford, Lee J. Lambert, William Martel, Angus Duncan, Richard Shepard, Richard Ford Grayling, Allyson Ames, Harry Rose, Mike Kopcha, John Yates, Jerry Brooks, Ray Galvin, Buck Holland, David Vaile, Helen Jay, Art Hern, John Hart, Sharon Berryhill.

POWDER BURNS (De Renzy) Produced, Directed, Written, and Photographed by Alex de Renzy; In Color; 74 minutes; Rating X; April release. No cast listing.

Wayne Shirley, Angel Sanchez, Joel L. Freedman, Philip F. Messina in "Skeezag"

Graham Nash, Joni Mitchell, John Sebastian, Steve Stills, Joan Baez in "Celebration at Big Sur"

Lyndal, Tom, Eileen, Robin
in "Saturday Morning"

Carolyn Moreland
in "Derby"

SATURDAY MORNING (Columbia) Producer-Director, Kent Mackenzie; Executive Producer, Gary Goldsmith; Photography, Erik Daarstad, John Morrill, Ken Plotin, Paul Deason; Titles, Don Record; A Dimension Film in Color; 82 minutes; Rating GP. No other credits.

THE HARD RIDE (American International) Executive Producer, Burt Topper; Producer, Charles Hanawalt; Direction and Screenplay, Burt Topper; Associate Producer, Byron Roberts; Photography, Robert Sparks; Music, Harley Hatcher; Songs sung by Paul Wibier, Bill Medley, Junction, The Arrows, Bob Moline, Thelma Camacho; A Burwalt Production in Movielab Color; 93 minutes; Rating GP; April release. CAST: Robert Fuller (Phil), Sherry Bain (Sheryl), Tony Russel (Big Red), William Bonner (Grady), Marshall Reed (Father Tom), Mikel Angel (Ralls), Biff Elliot (Mike), Al Cole (Mooch), Phyllis Selznick (Rita), R. L. Armstrong (Jason), Robert Swan (Ted), Larry Eisley (Rice), Frank Charolla (Meyers), Herman Rudin (Little Horse), Alfonso Williams (Lenny).

DERBY (Cinerama) Producer, William Richert; Direction and Photography, Robert Kaylor; A Jerry Seltzer-Michael Hamilburg Presentation in Color; 96 minutes; Rating R; April release. CAST: Roller Derby Stars Charlie O'Connell, Eddie Krebs, Mike Snell, Christina Snell, Butch Snell.

TOUCH ME (Fortune) Producer, Larry Price; Director, Sam Weston; Story and Screenplay, Michael Abel, Stanley Zero; Photography, Dale Smallin; Assistant Director, Marvin Almeas; In EastmanColor; 80 minutes; Rating X; April release. No cast listing.

RIGHT ON! (Concept East) Producers, Woodie King, Jr., Herbert Danska; Director, Herbert Danska; Written by The Original Last Poets; Photography, Amin Chaudri, Joe Zysman, Herbert Danska; 80 minutes; April release. CAST: The Original Last Poets, Gylan Kain, David Nelson, Felipe Lucano.

THE AMERICAN DREAMER (EYR) Producer, Lawrence Schiller; Executive Producer, Jason G. Brent; Directors, Lawrence Schiller, L. M. Kit Carson; Screenplay, Dennis Hopper, L. M. Kit Carson, Lawrence Schiller; Photography, Chuck Levey; Music, Nick Venet; Assistant Director, Jack Bernstein; A Corda-Kaback Production in EastmanColor; 93 minutes; April release. Purported autobiography of actor-director Dennis Hopper in documentary form, starring Dennis Hopper.

THE TENDER WARRIOR (Safari) Producer, William Thompson; Director, Stewart Raffill; Screenplay, Stewart Raffill, David Dalie; Photography, Gerardo H. Wenziner; Music, Kenneth Wannberg; In Techniscope and Technicolor; 77 minutes; Rating G; April release. CAST: Dan Haggerty (Cal), Charles Lee (Sammy), Liston Elkins (Pa).

JOHNNY MINOTAUR (Impact) Conceived, Directed, and Photographed by Charles Henri Ford; A Minotaur Production in EastmanColor; 80 minutes; Rating X; April release. CAST: Nikos Koulizakis (Nikos), Yiannis Koutsis (Johnny), Chuzzer Miles (Karolos), Shelley Scott (Shelley), and Allen Bole, Billy Bones, Derek, Stavros Georgiakakis, Babis Gnardellis, Charles Haldeman, Dick Johnson, John Kirk, Terry Kouridakis, Stefano, Sotiris Nomikos, Costas Papanikos, Florence Phillips, Jorgos Rantis, Andrea Tagliahue, Lynn Tillman, Yiannia Tsakalozos, The Boys of Chanea.

ONLY YOU KNOW, AND I KNOW (Shoeshine) Producers, Robert Simon, Alan Ruskin; Direction and Screenplay, Alan Ruskin; Photography, Bill Markle; In Radiant Color; 92 minutes; Rating X; April release. CAST: Patrice Barnett (Piano Teacher), Josephine Mitchell (Stripper), Peaches Harden (Sportswoman), Carol Sanders (Girl with car), Philadelphia Frank (Mechanic), Dolce Mann (Actress), Hardy Harrison (Hardy), Michael Merlin (Pornographer).

Tony Russel, Sherry Bain, Robert Fuller
in "The Hard Ride"

Mike Snell, Christina Snell, Butch Snell
in "Derby"

**George Peppard, France Nuyen
in "One More Train to Rob"**

**Scott Wilson, Kim Darby
in "The Grissom Gang"**

ONE MORE TRAIN TO ROB (Universal) Producer, Robert Arthur; Director, Andrew V. McLaglen; Screenplay, Don Tait, Dick Nelson; Story, William Roberts; Photography, Alric Edens; Music, David Shire; Lyrics, Richard Maltby, Jr.; Sung by Tim Morgan; Costumes, Grady Hunt; Assistant Director, Phil Bowles; In Technicolor; Rating GP; 108 minutes; May release. CAST George Peppard (Harker Fleet), Diana Muldaur (Kat John Vernon (Timothy X. Nolan), France Nuyen Toy), Steve Sandor (Jim), Soon-Taik Oh (Yung), C Yang (Wong), John Doucette (Monte), Robert Do (Adams), George Chandler (Conductor), Marie Win (Louella), Joan Shawlee (Big Nellie), Harry Carey (Red), Timothy Scott (Slim), Hal Needham (Bert), Jim Burk (Skinner), Ben Cooper (Deputy), Guy Lee (Sen), Ray Dimas (Herbert), Pamela McMyler (Cora May), Merlin Olsen (Eli), Phil Olsen (Luke).

THE HOLY OUTLAW (New Yorker) Producers, Lee Lockwood, Don Lenzer; Associate Producers, Sharon Shoper, Marc N. Weiss; Photography, Robert Fitch, Lee Lockwood; 59 minutes; May release. CAST: Father Daniel Berrigan, his family, and associates in a documentary.

CYCLES SOUTH (DAL Arts) Produced, Directed, and Edited by Don Marshall; Screenplay, Patrick McNamara; Photography, Dick Johnson; Music, Don Marshall, Thomas J. Valentino, J. J. Monroe; In EastmanColor; 89 minutes; Rating GP; May release. CAST: Don Marshall, Vaughn Everly, Bobby Garcia.

HAMPTON (MGA) Documentary in black and white made about and partly with the late Black Panther leader Fred Hampton; 88 minutes; May release. No other credits.

A FABLE (MFR) Producer, Victor Ramos, Jr.; Director, Al Freeman, Jr.; Screenplay, LeRoi Jones from his play "Slave"; Photography, Bruce Sparks; In Color by Kodak; 80 minutes; May release. CAST: Al Freeman, Jr. (Leader), Hildy Brooks (Wife), James Patterson (Husband).

MAKING THE BLUE FILM (National Adult Film Alliance) Producer, Jeraldo Stuarti; Director, J. Nehemara; In Color; 100 minutes; May release. No other credits.

PINK NARCISSUS (Sherpix) Produced, Written and Photographed by Anonymous; Music, Martin Jay Sadoff, Gary Goch; In Color; 70 minutes; May release. CAST: Bobby Kendall (Boy).

THE GRISSOM GANG (Cinerama) Producer-Director, Robert Aldrich; Screenplay, Leon Griffiths; From novel by James Hadley Chase; Photography, Joseph Biroc; Music, Gerald Fried; Art Director, James Vance; Costumes, Norma Koch; Associate Producer, Walter Blake; Assistant Directors, Malcolm Harding, William Morrison; An ABC Pictures and Associates & Aldrich Production in Metrocolor; 127 minutes; May release. CAST: Kim Darby (Barbara), Scott Wilson (Slim), Tony Musante (Eddie), Irene Dailey (Ma), Robert Lansing (Dave), Connie Stevens (Anna), Joey Faye (Doc), Don Keefer (Wopper), Ralph Waite (Mace), Wesley Addy (John), Dotts Johnson (Johnny), Mort Marshall (Heinie), Michael Baseleon (Connor), Alvin Hammer (Sam), Dave Willock (Rocky), Hal Baylor (Chief McLaine), Matt Clark (Bailey).

DIRTYMOUTH (Superior) Produced, Directed, and Written by Herbert S. Altman; Photography, Bert Spielvogel; Music, Manny Bardi, Lenny Hambro; 95 minutes; May release. CAST: Bernie Travis (Lenny Bruce), Courtney Sherman (Iris), Lyn Irwin (Lou), Harry Spillman (Fred), Miss Sam Teardrop (Marlene).

DARK DREAMS (213 Releasing Organization) Executive Producer, Damion Dark; Producer, Canidia Ference; Director, Roger Guermontes; Screenplay, Canidia Ference; Photography, Werner Hlinka; Music, Charles Morrow; An Initiation Production in Color; 75 minutes; Rating X; June release. CAST: Tina Russell, Tim Long, June DuLu, Patrice DeVeur, Arlana Blue, Alan Martin, Yoryck Yegno, Darby Lloyd Raines, Kitty Kat.

**Irene Dailey, Don Keefer, Ralph Waite, Tony Musante,
Joey Faye in "The Grissom Gang"**

**Zooey Hall, Danny Freedman, Michael Greer,
Wendell Burton in "Fortune and Men's Eyes"**

**Mitch Ryan, Topo Swope
in "My Old Man's Place"**

**Butch Van Arstdalen
in "Pacific Vibrations"**

MY OLD MAN'S PLACE (Cinerama) Formerly "Glory Boy"; Producer, Philip A. Waxman; Director, Edwin Sherin; Screenplay, Stanford Whitmore; Based on Novel by John Sanford; Music, Charles Gross; Lyrics, Norma Green, Associate Producers, Jack Solomon, Irving Tanner; Photography, Richard C. Glouner; Assistant Directors, Michael Glick, Joseph Ellis; A Philip Waxman/Jerome Minskoff Production in Color; Rating R; 93 minutes; June release. CAST: Arthur Kennedy (Walter), Mitchell Ryan (Sgt. Flood), William Devane (Jimmy), Michael Moriarty (Trubee), Topo Swope (Helen), Lloyd Gough (Dr. Paul), Ford Rainey (Sheriff), Peter Donat (Car Salesman), Sandra Vacey (Darlene), Paula Kauffman (Bubbles), Eve Marchand (Streetwalker), Gary Lemel sings "Glory Boy."

FORTUNE AND MEN'S EYES (MGM) Producers, Lester Persky, Lewis M. Allen; Director, Harvey Hart; Screenplay, John Herbert from his play of same name; Music, Galt MacDermot; Co-Producer, Donald Ginsberg; Photography, Georges Dufaux; Designer, Earl G. Preston; Assistant Director, Arthur Voronka; Choreography, Jill Courtney; Costumes, Marcel Carpenter; In MetroColor; 102 minutes; Rating R; June release. CAST: Wendell Burton (Smitty), Michael Greer (Queenie), Zooey Hall (Rocky), Danny Freedman (Mona), Larry Perkins (Screwdriver), James Barron (Holyface), Lazaro Perez (Catso), Jon Granik (Sgt), Tom Harvey (Warden), Hugh Webster (Rabbit), Kirk McColl (Guard), Vance Davis (Sailor), Robert Goodier (Doctor), Cathy Wiele (Cathy), Georges Allard (Fiddler), Modesto (One-Eye), Michel Gilbert (Young Prisoner), Robert Saab (Drummer), A. Zeytounian (Pianist).

FIDEL (New Yorker) Produced, Directed, and Written by Saul Landau; Photography, Irving Sharaf; Music by Cuban groups; In EastmanColor; 96 minutes; A Documentary of a revolutionary filmed in Cuba in 1968.

PACIFIC VIBRATIONS (American International) Producer-Director, John Severson; Associate Editor, Fred Talmage; Additional Photography, Spyder Wills, Robert Grant, Curt Mastalka, Brad Barrett; Color by MovieLab; 92 minutes; Rating G; A Documentary on surfing; June release. CAST: Jock Sutherland, Rolf Aurness, Corky Carroll, Tom Stone, Mike Tabeling, Rick Griffin, Spyder Wills, Chuck Dent, Mike Purpus, Bill Hamilton, David Huuhiwa, Merv Larson, Jeff Hakman, Angie Feno, Brad McCaul, Mickey Dora, Steve Bigler.

THE BATTLE OF LOVE'S RETURN (Standard) Producers, Lloyd Kaufman, Frank Vitale; Executive Producer, Garrard Glenn; Direction and Screenplay, Lloyd Kaufman; Photographer and Associate Director, Frank Vitale; Music, Lloyd Kaufman, Andre Golino; In Color and Black and White; 82 minutes; Rating G; June release. CAST: Lloyd Kaufman (Abacrombie), Lynn Lowry (Dream Girl), Andy Kay (Loafer), Stanley Kaufman (Crumb), Ida Goodcuff (Elderly woman), Jim Crispi (Bridge foreman), Bernard Brown (Det. Glass), Roderick Ghyka (Dr. Finger), Bonnie Sacks (Sgt.), Robert S. Walker (Preacher).

THE WINDSPLITTER (POP) Producer, David L. Ford; Directed and Written by Julius D. Feigelson; Music, Jackie Mills, Al Capps; In Color; 95 minutes; Rating GP; June release. CAST: Jim McMullan (Bobby Joe), I. Van Charles (Louis), Joyce Taylor (Jenny), Paul Lambert (Buford), Richard Everett (R. T.), Jim Sedlow (Mr. Smith), Chris Wilson (Mrs. Smith), Anne Layne (Annie), and John Martin, Carter Smith, Ray O'Leary, Ruth Roberts, Greg Ford, Lee Ryan, Mahlon Foreman, Tobe Hooper, John Barten.

Arthur Kennedy, William Devane, Mitch Ryan, Topo Swope, Michael Moriarty in "My Old Man's Place"

**Lloyd Kaufman
in "The Battle of Love's Return"**

**James Taylor, Dennis Wilson
in "Two-Lane Blacktop"**

**Yvonne DeCarlo
in "The Seven Minutes"**

RUN THE WILD RIVER (Currey) Produced, Directed, Written, and Photographed by Jack Currey; Music, Cine-Sound; In Color; 95 minutes; June release. No other credits. An adventure documentary of a rapids-shooting trip down Mexico's Grijalva River.

SUB ROSA RISING (Sherpix) Directed, Photographed, and Edited by Jerry Abrams; Narration, John Wasserman; Narrated by Allan Jones; Music, Loose Gravel, David Litwin, International Explosion, Barrett Bassick; Assistant Director, Marilyn Ashmun; Interviewers, Jack Teach, Mary Smith; A Jahl Production in EastmanColor; 98 minutes; Rating X; June release. No other listings. A purported documentary on sex life in San Francisco.

AMERICAN SEXUAL REVOLUTION (Pussycat) Producer, Stephen A. Burroughs; Director, John William Abbott; Photography, Olaf Svenson; Music, Carlos Rodriguez; Narration, Colin Beardsley; A Sunset-Western Production in EastmanColor; 80 minutes; Rating X; June release. Interviews with street public on the sexual revolution.

TWO-LANE BLACKTOP (Universal) Producer, Michael S. Laughlin; Director, Monte Hellman; Screenplay, Rudolph Wurlitzer, Will Corry; Story, Will Corry; Associate Producer, Gary Kurtz; Photography, Jack Deerson; Costumes, Richard Bruno; Assistant Director, Ken Swor; In Technicolor; 101 minutes; Rating R; July release. CAST: James Taylor (driver), Warren Oates (G.T.O.), Laurie Bird (girl), Dennis Wilson (mechanic), David Drake (station attendant), Richard Ruth (station mechanic), Rudolph Wurlitzer (hot rod driver), Jaclyn Hellman (driver's girl), Bill Keller (Texas hitchhiker), H. D. Stanton (Oklahoma Hitchhiker), Don Samuels, Charles Moore (policemen), Tom Green (Boswell attendant), W. H. Harrison (parts store owner), Alan Vint (man in roadhouse), Illa Ginnaven (waitress), George Mitchell (driver at accident), Katherine Squire (old woman), Melissa Hellman (child), Jay Wheatley, Jim Mitchum (men at race track), Kreag Caffey (motorcyclist), Tom Witenbarger (pick up driver), Glen Rogers (Soldier).

THE SEVEN MINUTES (20th Century-Fox) Producer-Director, Russ Meyer; Screenplay, Richard Warren Lewis; Based on novel by Irving Wallace; Associate Producers, Red Hershon, Eve Meyer; Photography; Music, Stu Phillips; Assistant Director, David Hall; Costumes, Bill Thomas; In DeLuxe Color; 116 minutes; Rating R; July release. CAST: Wayne Maunder (Mike), Marianne McAndrew (Maggie), Philip Carey (Elmo), Jay C. Flippen (Luther), Edy Williams (Faye), Lyle Bettger (Frank), Jackie Gayle (Norman), Ron Randell (Merle), Charles Drake (Kellogg), John Carradine (O'Flanagan), Harold J. Stone (Judge), Tom Selleck (Phil), James Iglehart (Clay), John Sarno (Jerry), Stanley Adams (Irwin), Billy Durkin (George), Yvonne D'Angers (Sheri), Robert Moloney (Ben), Olan Soule (Harvey), Jan Shutan (Anna Lou), Alex D'Arcy (Christian), David Brian (Cardinal), Berry Kroeger (Paul), Ralph Story (Commentator), Charles Napier (Iverson), Kay Peters (Olivia), Richard Angarola (Father Sarfatti), Baby Doll Shawn Devereaux (Luther's Girlfriend), Regis Cordic (Louis), John Lawrence (Howard), and Yvonne De Carlo (Constance).

THE INCREDIBLE TWO-HEADED TRANSPLANT (American International) Executive Producer, Nicholas Wowchuck; Producer, John Lawrence; Co-Producer, Wolodymyr Kowal; Associate Producers, Arthur N. Gilbert, Alvin L. Fast; Director, Anthony M. Lanza; Screenplay, James Gordon White, John Lawrence; Music, John Barber; Photography, Jack Steely, Glen Gano, Paul Hipp; In DeLuxe Color; 88 minutes; July release. CAST: Bruce Dern (Roger), Pat Priest (Linda), Casey Kasem (Ken), Albert Cole (Cass), John Bloom (Danny), Berry Kroeger (Max), Larry Vincent (Andrew), Jack Lester (Sheriff), Jerry Patterson (Deputy), Darlene Duralia (Miss Pierce), Robert Miller (Station Attendant), Leslie Cole (Young Danny), Ray Thorn, Donald Brody, Mary Ellen Clawsen (Motorcyclists), Janice Gelman, Mike Espe, Andrew Schneider, Eva Sorensen (Teenagers), Bill Collins, Jack English (Patrolmen), Laura Lanza, Carolyn Gilbert (Nurses).

**Laurie Bird
in "Two-Lane Blacktop"**

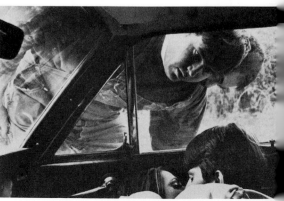

"The Incredible Two-Headed Transplant"

**Mert Lawwill, Malcolm Smith, Steve McQueen
in "On Any Sunday"**

**John Phillip Law
in "Von Richthofen and Brown"**

ON ANY SUNDAY (Cinema 5) Produced, Directed, Written, Narrated by Bruce Brown; Music, Dominic Frontiere, Lyrics, Sally Stevens; Photographers, Bob Bagley, Don Shoemaker, Bruce Brown, Allan Seymour, Gordon Brettelle, Bob Collins, Dan Wright, Richard Carrillo, Nelson Tyler, Mark Zavad, James Odom, Mark Brelsford; In Technicolor; 91 minutes; Rating G; July release. CAST: Malcolm Smith, Mert Lawwill, Steve McQueen. A documentary on motorcycling.

SHAFT (MGM) Producer, Joel Freeman; Director, Gordon Parks; Screenplay, Ernest Tidyman, John D. F. Black; Based on novel by Ernest Tidyman; Associate Producer, David Golden; Music, Isaac Hayes; Photography, Urs Furrer; Assistant Director, Ted Zachary; Costumes, Joe Aulisi; 100 minutes; Rating R; July release. CAST: Richard Roundtree (Shaft), Moses Gunn (Bumpy), Charles Cioffi (Vic), Christopher St. John (Ben), Gwenn Mitchell (Ellie), Lawrence Pressman (Tom), Victor Arnold (Charlie), Sherri Brewer (Marcy), Rex Robbins (Rollie), Camille Yarbrough (Dina), Margaret Warncke (Linda), Joseph Leon (Byron), Arnold Johnson (Cul), Dominic Barto (Patsy), George Strus (Carmen), Edmund Hashim (Lee), Drew Bundini Brown (Willy), Tommy Lane (Leroy), Al Kirk (Sims), Shimen Ruskin (Dr. Sam), Antonio Fargas (Bunky), Gertrude Jeannette (Old Lady), Lee Steele (Blind Vendor), Damu King (Mal), Donny Burks (Remmy), Tony King (Davies), Benjamin R. Rixson (Bey), Ricardo Brown (Tully), Alan Weeks (Gus), Glenn Johnson (Char), Dennis Tate (Dotts), Adam Wade, James Hainesworth (Brothers), Clee Burtonya (Sonny), Ed Bernard (Peerce), Ed Barth (Tony), Joe Pronto (Dom), Robin Nolan (Waitress), Ron Tannas (Billy), Betty Bresler (Mrs. Androzzi), Jon Richards (Starter), Paul Nevens (Elevator Man), Gonzalo Madurga (Counterman).

VON RICHTHOFEN AND BROWN (United Artists) Producer, Gene Corman; Director, Roger Corman; Screenplay, John and Joyce Corrington; Music, Hugo Friedhofer; Photography, Michael Reed; Assistant Director, Jake Wright; In DeLuxe Color; 97 minutes; Rating GP; July release. CAST: John Philip Law (von Richthofen), Barry Primus (Goering), Peter Masterson (Boelcke), Robert LaTourneaux (Udet), George Armitage (Wolff), Steve McHattie (Voss), Brian Foley (Lothar von Richthofen), David Osterhout (Holzapfel), Clint Kimbrough (Von Hoeppner), Gordon Phillips (Cargonico), Peadar Lamb (German Staff Major), Seamus Forde (Kaiser), Karen Huston (Ilse), Ferdy Mayne (Father Richthofen), Maureen Cusack (Mother Richthofen), Fred Johnson (Jeweller), Hurd Hatfield (Fokker), Vernon Hayden (Trackl), Michael Fahey (Richthofen at 3), Robert Walsh (Richthofen at 13), Don Stroud (Brown), Corin Redgrave (Hawker), Tom Adams (Owen), David Weston (Murphy), Brian Sturdivant (May), Des Nealon (Intelligence Officer), John Flanagan (Thompson), Lorraine Rainier (Girl in woods).

EVEL KNIEVEL (Fanfare) Producers, Joe Solomon, George Hamilton; Director, Marvin Chomsky; Screenplay, Alan Caillou, John Milius; Photography, David Walsh; Art Director, Norman Houle; Music, Pat Williams; Assistant Directors, Thomas J. Schmidt, Arthur Levinson; In Metrocolor; 90 minutes; Rating GP; July release. CAST: George Hamilton (Evel), Sue Lyon (Linda), Bert Freed (Doc), Rod Cameron (Charlie), Dub Taylor (Turquoise), and Pius Ron Masak, Hal Baylor, Judy Baldwin, Kathy Baumann, Ben Bentley, Betty Bronson, Alana Collins, Jan Davis, Lee De Broux, Roger Edington, Frank Ellis, John Garwood, Richard Ford Grayling, Mary Grover, Bob Harris, Sylvia Hayes, John Haymer, Ted Henningsen.

BLACK CHARIOT (Goodwin) Produced, Directed, and Written by Robert L. Goodwin; In Color; 90 minutes; July release. No other credits. CAST: Bernie Casey, Barbara O. Jones.

**Edy Williams, Wayne Maunder
in "The Seven Minutes"**

**George Hamilton
in "Evel Knievel"**

**Jack Palance, Omar Sharif
in "The Horsemen"**

**Joe Namath, Victoria George
in "The Last Rebel"**

THE HORSEMEN (Columbia) Producer, Edward Lewis; Director, John Frankenheimer; Screenplay, Dalton Trumbo; From novel by Joseph Kessel; Assistant Director, Jose Lopez Rodero; Photography, Claude Renoir; Designer, Pierre Thevenet; Costumes, Jacqueline Moreau; In SuperPanavision and Color; 105 minutes; Rating GP; July release. CAST: Omar Sharif (Uraz), Leigh Taylor-Young (Zereh), Jack Palance (Tursen), David De (Mukhi), Peter Jeffrey (Hayatal), Mohammed Shamsi (Osmen Bey), George Murcell (Mizrar), Eric Pohlmann (Merchant), Despo (Uljan), Vernon Dobtcheff (Zam), Ishaq Bux (Amjad Khan), Saeed Jaffrey (Chief), John Ruddock (Scribe), Mark Colleano (Rahim), Sy Temple (Quadir), Aziz Resh (Bacha), Vida St. Romaine (Gypsy), Leon Lissek (Proprietor), Milton Reid (Aqqul).

CREATURES THE WORLD FORGOT (Columbia) Produced and Written by Michael Carreras; Director, Don Chaffey; Assistant Directors, Ferdinand Fairfax, Simon Peterson; Photography, Vincent Cox; Designer, John Stoll; Music, Mario Nascimbene; A Hammer Production in Technicolor; 94 minutes; Rating GP; July release. CAST: Julie Ege (Girl), Tony Bonner (Fair Boy), Robert John (Dark Boy), Brian O'Shaughnessy (Father), Sue Wilson (Mother), Rosalie Crutchley (Old Crone), Marcia Fox (Dumb Girl), Gerard Bonthuys (Young Fair Boy), Hans Kiesouw (Young Dark Boy), Josje Kiesouw (Young Dumb Girl), Beverly Blake, Doon Baide (Young Lovers), Don Leonard (Old Leader), Frank Hayden (Murderer), Rosita Moulan (Dancer), Fred Swart (Marauder Leader), Ken Hare (Fair Tribe Leader).

CRY DR. CHICAGO (Leahy) Producers, Margaret Leahy, Robert Halper; Directed, Written, and Photographed by George Manupelli; Music, George Burt; In EastmanColor; 98 minutes; July release. CAST: Alvin Lucier (Dr. Chicago), Mary Ashley (Sheila Marie), Steve Paxton (Steve), Claude Kipnis (Clo Clo), Viera Collaro (Viera/Lily), and Joseph Wehrer, William Finneran, Alan Schreiber, Michael Frost, Betty Wong, Shirley Wong, Lincoln Scott, Pat Oleszko, Roberts Bloom, Ruth Reichl, Liz Hall, Kathy Schuetz, Carol Kladder, Nick Bertoni, Jack Starkweather.

THE BUS IS COMING (Thompson International) Producer, Horace Jackson; Director, Wendell James Franklin; Screenplay, Horace Jackson, Robert H. Raff, Mike Rhodes; Photography, Mike Rhodes; Art Director, Haaga/Jacobsen; Music, Tom McIntosh; Assistant Directors, Ruben Watt, Ralph Sariego; In DeLuxe Color; 109 minutes; Rating GP; July release. CAST: Mike Simms (Billy), Stephanie Faulkner (Tanya), Burl Bullock (Michael), Tony Sweeting (Dobie), Jack Stillman (John), Sandra Reed (Miss Nickerson), Bob Brubaker (Chief Jackson), Morgan Jones (Tim), Dick Ryal (Corie), Eddie Kendrix, Juan Russell.

THE LAST REBEL (Columbia) Producer, Larry G. Spangler; Director, Denys McCoy; Story and Screenplay, Warren Kiefer; Photography, Carlo Carlini; Associate Producer, Fritz Mueller; Costumes, Gaia Romanini; Assistant Director, Victor Tourjansky; Music, Jon Lord, Tony Ashton; A Spangler Pictures Production in Color; 89 minutes; Rating GP; August release. CAST: Joe Namath (Burnside), Jack Elam (Matt), Woody Strode (Duncan), Ty Hardin (Sheriff), Victoria George (Pearl), Renato Romano (Virgil), Marina Coffa (Camelia), Annamaria Chio (Mme. Dupres), Mike Forrest (Cowboy), Bruce Eweka (Black Boy), Jessica Dublin (Ruby), Herb Andress (Lt.), Larry Laurence (Bedroom Man), Sebastian Segriff (Union Officer), Al Hassan (Barman), Art Johnson (Tall Soldier), Paul Sheriff (Old Soldier), Troy Patterson, Rick Wells (Ranchers), Dominic Barto (Stagecoach Agent), Jim Garbo, Thomas Rudy.

THE MARRIAGE OF A YOUNG STOCKBROKER (20th Century-Fox) Producer-Director, Lawrence Turman; Screenplay, Lorenzo Semple, Jr. from Charles Webb novel; Photography, Laszlo Kovacs; Music, Fred Karlin; Designer, Pato Guzman; Assistant Director, Dave Salven; In DeLuxe Color; 95 minutes; Rating R; August release. CAST: Richard Benjamin (William Alren), Joanna Shimkus (Lisa Alren), Elizabeth Ashley (Nan), Adam West (Chester), Patricia Barry (Psychiatrist), Tiffany Bolling (Girl in rain), Ed Prentiss (Broker).

**Julie Ege, Tony Bonner
in "Creatures the World Forgot"**

**Joanna Shimkus, Richard Benjamin
in "The Marriage of a Young Stockbroker"**

**Burgess Meredith, Marilyn Akin, Tom Stern
in "Clay Pigeon"**

**Karen Sperling
in "Make a Face"**

CLAY PIGEON (MGM) Producer, Tom Stern; Directors, Tom Stern, Lane Slate; Screenplay, Ronald Buck, Buddy Ruskin, Jack Gross, Jr.; Story, Buddy Ruskin, Jack Gross, Jr.; Executive Producers, Frank Avianca, Ronald Buck; Associate Producer, Clark L. Paylow; Music, Gavin Murrell; Photography, Alan Stensvold; A Tracom Production in MetroColor; 97 minutes; Rating R; August release. CAST: Telly Savalas (Frank), Robert Vaughn (Henry), John Marley (Police Captain), Burgess Meredith (Freedom), Ivan Dixon (Simon), Tom Stern (Joe), Jeff Corey (Doctor), Marilyn Akin (Angeline), Marlene Clark (Saddle), Belinda Palmer (Tracy), Mario Alcalde (Jason).

MAKE A FACE (Sperling) Producer-Director, Karen Sperling; Screenplay, Karen Sperling, Barbara Connell, Avraham Tau; Photography, Jeri Sopanen, Ken Van Sickle; Assistant Director, Virginia Ruffulo; Songs, Tony Cohan, John Jacobs; In DeLuxe Color; 90 minutes; August release. CAST: Karen Sperling (Nina), Paolo Patti (Dr. Davis), Davis Bernstein (Stranger), Nicolas Surovy (Larry), Joe Horan (George), Jackie Doroshow (Pucci lady), David Franciosi (Second Stranger), John Chin (Delivery boy).

JUMP (Cannon) Producer, Christopher C. Dewey; Director, Joe Manduke; Associate Producer, George Manasse; Screenplay, Richard Wheelwright; Photography, Greg Sandor; Assistant Director, Robert Koster; Presented by Christopher C. Dewey and Dennis Friedland; In DeLuxe Color; 97 minutes; Rating GP; August release. CAST: Tom Ligon (Chester Jump), Logan Ramsey (Babe), Collin Wilcox-Horne (April May), Sudie Bond (Ernestine), Conrad Bain (Lester), Norman Rose (Dutchman), Lada Edmund, Jr. (Enid), Bette Craig (Beulah), Vicki Lynn (Mercy), Jack Nance (Ace), Ron St. Germain (Billy Rae), Johnny Hicks (Starter) James Tallent (Young boy), The Kentucky Mountain Boys.

THE BROTHERHOOD OF SATAN (Columbia) Producers, L. Q. Jones, Alvy Moore; Director, Bernard McEveety; Associate Producer, Sheila Clague; Screenplay, William Welch; Story, Sean MacGregor; Music, Jaime Mendoza-Nava; Photography, John Arthur Morrill; Designer, Ray Boyle; Technical Director, James Bruner; An LQJAF Presentation in Techniscope and Technicolor; 92 minutes; Rating GP; August release. CAST: Strother Martin (Doc), L. Q. Jones (Sheriff), Charles Bateman (Ben), Ahna Capri (Nicky), Geri Reischl (Kiti), Charles Robinson (Priest), Alvy Moore (Tobey), Helene Winston (Dame Alice), Joyce Easton (Mildred), Debi Storm (Billy Jo), Jeff Williams (Stuart), Judy McConnell (Phyllis), Robert Ward (Mike), and John Barclay, Patrick Sullivan Burke, Ysabel MacCloskey, Cicely Walper, Phillis Coughlan, Anthony Jochim, Donald Journeaux, Elsie Moore, Lenore Shaenwise, Margaret Wheeler, Kevin McEveety, Alyson Moore, Sheila McEveety, Brian McEveety, Grant McGregor, Cindy Holden, Debbie Judith, Scott Aguilar, Jonathan Eisley, Robyn Grei, Linda Riffany.

REFINEMENTS IN LOVE (Hollywood International) Produced, Directed, and Written by Carlos Tobalina; In Color; 88 minutes; Rating X; August release. No other credits. CAST: Liz Renay (Hostess).

NO DRUMS, NO BUGLES (Cinerama) Produced, Directed, and Written by Clyde Ware; Photography, Richard McCarty; Music, Lyle Ritz; Theme sung by Shelby Flint; In Color; 85 minutes; Rating G; August release. CAST: Martin Sheen.

**Charles Bateman, Ahna Capri, Alvy Moore,
L. Q. Jones in "Brotherhood of Satan"**

**Martin Sheen
in "No Drums, No Bugles"**

**B. B. King
in "Medicine Ball Caravan"**

**Ike and Tina Turner
in "Soul to Soul"**

MEDICINE BALL CARAVAN (Warner Bros.) Producers, Francois Reichenbach, Tom Donahue; Director, Francois Reichenbach; From idea by Christian Haren; Associate Producer, Martin Scosese; Photography, Christian Odasso; Music, Joe Boyd; In Techniscope and Technicolor; 88 minutes; August release. 150 San Francisco youths in buses through Middle America to Washington.

SOUL TO SOUL (Cinerama) Executive Producer, Edward Mosk; Producers, Richard Bock, Edward Mosk; Director, Denis Sanders; Musical Director, Richard Bock; A Nigram-Aura Production presented by Josef Shaftel in Color; 96 minutes; August release. A documentary of Black American soul and gospel artists on a one week visit to Ghana.

THE JESUS TRIP (EMCO) Executive Producer, Saul Brandman; Producer, Joseph Feury; Director, Russ Mayberry; Screenplay, Dick Poston; Photography, Flemming Olsen; Music, Bernardo Segall; Art Direction, James Eric; Assistant Director, Bill Wilson; In DeLuxe Color; 84 minutes; Rating GP; August release. CAST: Elizabeth "Tippy" Walker (Sister Anna), Robert Porter (Waco), Billy "Green" Bush (Cop), Frank Orsati, Robert Tessier, Allan Gibbs (other police), Hanna Hertalanda (Older Nun), and gang members Diana Ivarson, Virgil Frye, Carmen Argenziano, Wally Strauss, Bebe Louie, Jenny Hecht.

JUD (Maron) Producer, Igo Kantor; Director, Screenplay, Gunther Collins; Photography, Isidore Mankofsky; Music, Stu Phillips; "One Too Many Mornings" by Bob Dylan; Sung by John Hartford; A Duque Films Production in Movielab Color; 87 minutes; Rating GP; August release. CAST: Jason Robards (Jud), Robert Deman (Bill), Alix Wyeth (Shirley), Norman Burton (Uncle), Claudia Jennings (Sunny), Maurice Sherbanee (Salvadore), Victor Dunlap (Vincent), Bonnie Bittner (Kathy).

THE PLEDGEMASTERS (Signature) Producer-Director, Photography, David P. Parrish; From an idea by Bruce Gregory, David Knapp; A Caracal Production in Metrocolor; 87 minutes; August release. CAST: Bruce Gregory, David Knapp (Pledgemasters), Michael Tremor (Pledge 1), James Palmer (Pledge 2), Trevor Tiffany (Pledge 3), Larry Kennedy (Pledge 4).

CLIMAX (Sherpix) Produced, Directed, Photographed by Jack Genaro; Screenplay, Jack Genaro, Rick Beaty; Story, Cal Dunn; Music, Bob Harvey; Art Direction, Bernie Lewis; A Reel Art Production in EastmanColor; 85 minutes; Rating X; August release. CAST: Lesley Conners (Kate), Richard Patrick (Perry), Susan Shaw (Erica), Marie Ario (CeCe), Rick Livermore (Bud), Maxine Langtree (Adriene), Jeff Patton (Henry), Julie Douglas (Daphney), Ivan Beaudell (Norman).

CUBA VA (Impact) Produced, Directed, Photographed, Narrated by Felix Greene; In EastmanColor; 76 minutes; September release. A documentary on conditions within Cuba at the present time.

BELIEVE IN ME (MGM) Producers, Robert Chartoff, Irwin Winkler; Director, Stuart Hagmann; Screenplay, Israel Horovitz; Photography, Dick Kratina, Richard C. Brooks; Art Director, Robert Gundlach; Music, Fred Karlin; Assistant Director, Terence Donnelly; In Metrocolor; 90 minutes; Rating R; September release. CAST: Michael Sarrazin (Remy), Jacqueline Bisset (Pamela), Jon Cypher (Alan), Allen Garfield (Stutter), Kurt Dodenhoff (Matthew), Marcia Jean Kurtz (Nurse), Kevin Conway (Clancy), Roger Robinson (Angel), Antonio Fargas (Boy), Milt Kamen (Physician), Susan Doukas (Ward Nurse), Suzannah Norstrand (Sylvia), Ultra Violet (Patient), William Abruzzi (Lecturer), Matthew Anton (David), Elizabeth Brown (Saleslady), Tony Capodilupo (Max), Tom Foral (Michael), Katherine Helmond (Saleslady), Tom Lacy (Manager), Barbara Thurston (Margaret), Larry Weber (Dr. Markham), Jan Saint (Morgue attendant).

**Jacqueline Bisset, Kevin Conway, Allen Garfield,
Michael Sarrazin in "Believe in Me"**

**Susan Kussman, Ivor Francis, Suzanne Charny,
Richard Benjamin in "The Steagle"**

**Richard Benjamin, Cloris Leachman
in "The Steagle"**

**John Phillip Law, Sylvia Miles, Samuel Fuller
in "The Last Movie"**

THE STEAGLE (AVCO Embassy) Executive Producer, Frank P. Rosenberg; Producer, Jim Di Gangi; Direction and Screenplay, Paul Sylbert; From novel of same name by Irvin Faust; Photography, Burnett Guffey; Music, Fred Myrow; A Joseph E. Levine Presentation in Color by Movielab; Rating R; 91 minutes; September release. CAST: Richard Benjamin (Harold), Chill Wills (Tall-Guy), Cloris Leachman (Rita), Jean Allison (Florence), Suzanne Charny (Marcy), Ivor Francis (Clergyman), Susan Tyrrell (Louise), Jack Bernardi (Marty).

FUNNYMAN (New Yorker) Producers, Hugh McGraw, Stephen Schmidt; Director, John Korty; Screenplay, John Korty; Music, Peter Schickele; Photography, John Korty; In Color and Black and White; 98 minutes; September release. CAST: Peter Bonerz (Perry), Sandra Archer (Sue), Carol Androsky (Sybil), Larry Hankin (Rodger), Barbara Hiken (Molly), Gerald Hiken (Mahlon), Nancy Fish (Jan), Budd Steinhilber (Vogel), Ethel Sokolow (Vera), Marshall Efron (Sid), George Ede (Ad Executive), Jane House (Bikini Girl), Herb Beckman (Watson), Manuela Ruecker (Heidi), Rodger Bowen (Lester), Mel Stewart (Phil), Dick Stahl (Zach), Stephen D. Newman (Ollie), Alan Myerson (Seymour), Jerry Mander (Arnie), Lucille Bliss (Girl of 1000 voices), Ellsworth Milburn (pianist), Anne Bowen (Lester's wife), Arthur Okamura (Arthur).

ANGELS HARD AS THEY COME (New World) Producer, Jonathan Demme; Director, Joe Viola; Screenplay, Jonathan Demme, Joe Viola; Photography, Steve Katz; Music, Richard Hieronymous; Assistant Director, Lorenzo Barzaghi; Art Director, Jack Fisk; In Metrocolor; 90 minutes; Rating R; September release. CAST: Scott Glenn (Long John), Charles Dierkop (General), Gilda Texter (Astrid), James Iglehart (Monk), Gary Littlejohn (Axe), Gary Busey (Henry), Janet Wood (Vicki), Don Carerra (Juicer), Brendan Kelly (Brain), Larry Tucker (Lucifer), Cheri Latimer (Cheri), Marc Seaton (Louie), John Taylor (Crab), Dennis Art (Rings), Niva Davis (Clean Sheila), Hal Marshall (Dr. Jagger), Steve Slauson (Magic).

THE LAST MOVIE (Universal) Executive Producer, Michael Gruskoff; Producer, Paul Lewis; Associate Producer, David Hopper; Director, Dennis Hopper; Screenplay, Stewart Stern; Story, Stewart Stern, Dennis Hopper; Photography, Laszlo Kovacs; Music, Kris Kristofferson; In Technicolor; 108 minutes; Rating R; September release. CAST: Julie Adams (Mrs. Anderson), Daniel Ades (Tomas Mercado), John Alderman (Jonathan), Michael Anderson, Jr. (Mayor's son), Rich Aguilar (Gaffer), Donna Baccala (Miss Anderson), Tom Baker (Member of Billy's gang), Toni Basil (Rose), Poupee Bocar (Singer), Anna Lynn Brown (Dance Hall Girl), Rod Cameron (Pat), Bernard Casselman (Doctor), James Contreras (Boomman), Eddie Donno (Stunt Man), Severn Darden (Mayor), Lou Donelan (Prop Man), Roy Engel (Anderson), Warren Finnerty (Banker), Peter Fonda (Sheriff), Fritz Ford (Citizen), Sam Fuller (Director), Stella Garcia (Maria), Michael Greene (Hired Gun), Samya Greene (Baby), William Gray (in Billy's Gang), Don Gordon (Neville), Dennis Hopper (Kansas), Al Hopson (Sheriff), Bud Hassink (in gang), George Hill (Key Grip), Henry Jaglom (Minister's son), Gray Johnson (Stunt Man), Clint Kimbrough (Minister), Kris Kristofferson (Minstrel Wrangler), John Phillip Law (Little Brother), Ted Markland (Big Brother), Victor Maymudes (in gang), Cynthia McAdams (Dance Hall Girl), Tomas Milian (Priest), Sylvia Miles (Script Clerk), Jim Mitchum (Art), Al Monroe (Citizen), Jorge Montoro (Jorge), Owen Orr (Hired Gun), Michelle Phillips (Banker's Daughter), Robert Rothwell (Citizen), Richard Rust (Pisco), John Stevens (Cameraman), Toni Stern (Dance Hall Girl), Dennis Stock (Still Man), Dean Stockwell (Billy), Russ Tamblyn (in gang), Alan Warnick (Assistant Director), John Buck Wilken (Minstrel Wrangler).

MILLHOUSE: A WHITE COMEDY (New Yorker) Producer-Director, Emile de Antonio; Photography, Ed Emshwiller, Mike Gray, Bruce Shah, Richard Kletter; Edited by Mary Lampson; 92 minutes; September release. A satiric documentary on Richard Milhous Nixon.

**Peter Bonerz
in "Funnyman"**

**Richard Milhous Nixon
in "Millhouse: A White Comedy"**

Brian Foley, Francesca Tu, Kevin O'Connor
in "Welcome to the Club"

Bruce Davison, Barry Primus
in "Been Down So Long. . . ."

WELCOME TO THE CLUB (Columbia) Producer-Director, Walter Shenson; Associate Producer, Leon Becker; Screenplay, Clement Biddle Wood; From his novel of the same name; Assistant Director, Niels Hoeje; Photography, Mikael Salomon; Art Director, Maurice Fowler; Music, Ken Thorne; "A Song for Them" composed and sung by Brian Foley; In Color; 88 minutes; Rating R; September release. CAST: Brian Foley (Andrew), Jack Warden (Gen. Strapp), Andy Jarrell (Fairfax), Kevin O'Connor (Harrison), Francesca Tu (Hogan), David Toguri (Hideki), Al Mancini (Marcantonio), Art Wallace (Col. Buonocure), Louis Quinn (Capt. Sigmus), Lionel Murton (Col. Ames), Marsha Hunte (Leah), Joyce Wilford (Shawna), Lon Satton (Marshall), Christopher Malcolm (Henry), John Dunne-Hill (O'Malley), Lee Meredith (Betsy).

GLEN AND RANDA (UMC) Director, Jim McBride; Screenplay, Lorenzo Mans, Rudolph Wurliter, Jim McBride; Photography, Alan Raymond; In Eastman-Color; 94 minutes; Rating X; September release. CAST: Steven Curry (Glen), Shelley Plimpton (Randa), Woodrow Chambliss (Sidney), Garry Goodrow (Magician), and Roy Rox, Robert Holmer, Hubert Powers, William Fratis, Alice Huffman, Ortega Sangster, Richard Frazier, Charles Huffman, Barbara Spiegel, Martha Furey, Leonard Johnson, Jack Tatarsky, Laura Hawbecker, Lucille Johnson, Dwight Tate, Mary Henry, Matthew Levine, Bud Thompson, Talmadge Holiday, James Nankerius, Winona Tomanoczy, David Woeller.

SWEET SAVIOUR (Trans World) Producer, Director, Story, Bob Roberts; Screenplay, Matt Cavanaugh; Photography, Victor Petroshevitz; Music, Jeff Barry, Gilbert Slavin; In DeLuxe Color; 90 minutes; September release. CAST: Troy Donahue (Moon), Renay Granville (Sandra), Francine Middleton (Faith), Talie Cochrane (Ruth), Matt Greene (Bull), Tobi Marsh (Fritzi), Lee Terri (Maggie), Joie Addison (Carol), Mark Curran (Chris), Alan Waters (Folk Singer), Perry Gewirtz (Pretzel Man), Joy Campbell (Elsa), Michelle Norris (Maggie's friend).

BEEN DOWN SO LONG IT LOOKS LIKE UP TO ME (Paramount) Producer, Robert M. Rosenthal; Director, Jeffrey Young; Screenplay, Robert Schlitt; From novel by Richard Farina; Photography, Urs Furrer; Music, Garry Sherman; Lyrics, Gene Pistilli; Art Director, William Molyneux; Assistant Director, Stanley Panesoff; In Movielab Color; 90 minutes; Rating R; September release. CAST: Barry Primus (Gnossos), Linda DeCoff (Kristin), David Downing (Heff), Susan Tyrrell (Jack), Philip Shafer (Calvin), Bruce Davison (Fitzgore), Zack Norman (Mojo), Raul Julia (Juan).

MAIDSTONE (Supreme Mix) Producers, Buzz Farber, Norman Mailer; Conceived and Directed by Norman Mailer; Photography, Jim Desmond, Richard Leacock, D. A. Pennebaker, Nick Proferes, Sheldon and Diane Rochlin, Jan Pieter Welt; In EastmanColor; 110 minutes; September release. CAST: Norman Mailer (Kingsley), Rip Torn (Raoul), and Beverly Bentley, Ultra Violet.

THE LATE LIZ (Dick Ross) Producer-Director, Dick Ross; Screenplay, Bill Rega; Based on Gert Behanna autobiography; Photography, Harry Stradling, Jr.; Music, Ralph Carmichael; Art Director, Bill Malley; Assistant Director, Arthur Levinson; In Metrocolor; 119 minutes; Rating GP; September release. CAST: Anne Baxter (Liz), Steve Forrest (Jim), James Gregory (Sam), Colleen Gray (Sue), Joan Hotchkis (Sally), Jack Albertson (Rev. Rogers), Eloise Hardt (Laura), Steve Dunne (Si), Reid Smith (Alan), Bill Katt (Peter), Ivor Francis (Dr. Murray), Gail Bonney (Maid), Jackson Bostwick (Randal).

HEAD ON (Leon) Producer, Michael Donovan O'Donnell; Executive Producer, Peter T. Steinmann; Directed and Written by Edward Lakso; Photography, William Davies; Music, William G. St. Pierre; In Movielab Color; 91 minutes; September release. CAST: Michael Witney (Steve), Michael Conrad (Mike), Lori Saunders (Millie), Art Lund (Koger), Kathleen Freeman (Nadine), Mickey Morton (Fred).

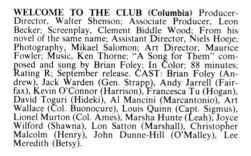

Jack Warden, Brian Foley
in "Welcome to the Club"

Sherry Miles, Michael Blodgett
in "The Velvet Vampire"

Barbara Bel Geddes, Robert F. Lyons
in "The Todd Killings"

Lee Van Cleef, Carroll Baker
in "Captain Apache"

YOU'VE GOT TO WALK IT LIKE YOU TALK IT OR YOU'LL LOSE THAT BEAT (JER) Produced, Directed, Written by Peter Locke; Photography, Stephen Bower; Music, Walter Becker, Donald Fagin, Billy Cunningham; Associate Producers, Gary Melhman, David Finfer, Ron Sullivan; Art Director, Linda Sampson; In Color; 85 minutes; Rating R; September release. CAST: Zalman King (Carter), Allen Garfield (Herby), Suzette Green (Susan), Richard Pryor (Wino), Bob Downey (Ad Agency Head), Liz Torres (Singer in men's room), Roz Kelly (Girl in park), Karen Ludwig (Erica), Billy Cunningham (Fat lady), Ruth Locke (Carter's mother), Daisy Locke (Old Woman), Stan Gottlieb (Fellestrio).

THE VELVET VAMPIRE (New World) Producer, Charles S. Swartz; Director, Stephanie Rothman; Screenplay, Maurice Jules, Charles S. Swartz, Stephanie Rothman; Assistant Director, Marty Katz; Photography, Daniel Lacambre; Music, Clancy B. Grass, Roger Dollarhide; In MetroColor; 82 minutes; Rating R; October release. CAST: Michael Blodgett (Lee), Sherry Miles (Susan), Celeste Yarnall (Diane), Jerry Daniels (Juan), Gene Shane (Carl), Paul Prokop (Cliff), Sandy Ward (Amos), Chris Woodley (Cliff's Girlfriend), Bob Thessier (Biker).

THE TODD KILLINGS (National General) Executive Producer, Walter Wood; Associate Producer, Robert Levy; Producer-Director, Barry Shear; Screenplay, Dennis Murphy, Joel Oliansky; Story, Mann Rubin; Photography, Harold E. Stine; Music, Leonard Rosenman; Assistant Director, John H. Roe; In Panavision and Technicolor; 93 minutes; Rating R; October release. CAST: Robert F. Lyons (Skipper), Richard Thomas (Billy), Belinda Montgomery (Roberta), Barbara Bel Geddes (Mrs. Todd), Sherry Miles (Amata), Joyce Ames (Haddie), Holly Near (Norma), James Broderick (Sam), Gloria Grahame (Mrs. Roy), Fay Spain (Mrs. Mack), Edward Asner (Fred), Michael Conrad (Detective).

BRAZIL: A REPORT ON TORTURE (New Yorker) Produced and Directed by Saul Landau with Haskell Wexler; October release. A Documentary.

CAPTAIN APACHE (Scotia International) Producers, Milton Sperling, Philip Yordan; Associate Producer, Irving Lerner; Director, Alexander Singer; Screenplay, Philip Yordan, Milton Sperling; Based on novel by S. E. Whitman; Photography, John Cabrera; Costumes, Tony Pueo; Music, Dolores Claman; Title song sung by Lee Van Cleef; In Technicolor and Cinemascope; 94 minutes; Rating GP; October release. CAST: Lee Van Cleef (Capt. Apache), Carroll Baker (Maude), Stuart Whitman (Griffin), Percy Herbert (Moon), Elisa Montes (Rosita), Tony Vogel (Snake), Charles Stalnaker (O'Rourke), Charlie Bravo (Sanchez), Faith Clift (Abigail), Dan Van Husen (Al), D. Pollock (Ben), Hugh McDermott (Gen. Ryland), George Margo (Sheriff), Jose Bodalo (General), Elsa Zabala (Witch), Allen Russell (Maitre D'), Luis Induni (Ezekiel), Vito Salier (Diablo), Fernando Sanchez Pollack (Guitarist).

SOME OF MY BEST FRIENDS ARE ... (American International) Executive Producer, Joseph Rhodes; Producers, Marty Richards, John Lauricella; Direction and Screenplay, Mervyn Nelson; Music, Gordon Rose; Color by Movielab; Presented by Bluebird Productions in association with Cutler Griffin Association; 109 minutes; Rating R; October release. CAST: Tom Bade (Tanny), David Baker (Clint), Paul Blake (Kenny), Gary Campbell (Terry), Carleton Carpenter (Miss Untouchable), Robert Christian (Eric), Candy Darling (Karen/Harry), Jeff David (Leo), Alan Dellay (Pete), Nick Denoia (Phil), Dan Drake (Lloyd), David Drew (Howard), Jim Enzel (Gable), Tommy Fiorello (Ernie), Fannie Flagg (Helen), Joe George (Al), Gil Gerard (Scott), Uva Harden (Michel), Rue McClanahan (Lita), Hector Martinez (Jose), Peg Murray (Mrs. Nabour), Dick O'Neil (Tim), Larry Reed (Louis), Gary Sandy (Jim), Lou Steele (Barrett), Clifton Steere (Giggling Gertie), Sylvia Syms (Sadie), Joe Taylor (Nebraska), Ben Yaffee (Marvin).

"Brazil. ..."

Nick Denoia (C)
in "Some of My Best Friends Are"

"The African Elephant"

Tina Turner
in "Superstars in Film Concert"

THE AFRICAN ELEPHANT (National General) Producers, William N. Graf, Monty C. Ruben; Direction and Photography, Simon Trevor; Story, Simon Trevor, Monty C. Ruben; Narration, Alan Landsburg; Spoken by David Wayne; Music, Laurence Rosenthal; Lyrics, Marilyn and Alan Bergman; A Cinema Center Films Presentation in Technicolor; 92 minutes; Rating G; October release. A documentary feature on African wildlife.

PUNISHMENT PARK (Sherpix) Producer, Susan Martin; Director, Peter Watkins; Photography, John Churchill; A Francoise Film; 88 minutes; October release. CAST: Jim Bohan (Captain), Van Daniels (Sheriff), Frederick Franklyn (Prof. Daly), Sanford Golden (Senator Harris), Harlan Green (Sheriff), Rodger Greene (Marshal).

THE PEACE KILLERS (Transvue) Producer, Joel B. Michaels; Director, Douglas Schwartz; Screenplay, Michael Berk; Story, Diana Maddox, Joel B. Michaels; Associate Producer, Diana Maddox; Music, Kenneth Wannberg; Songs composed and sung by Ruthann Friedman; Photography, Douglas Schwartz; Assistant Director, R. J. Louis; Designer, Carl Randall; A Damocles Production in DeLuxe Color; 88 minutes; Rating R; October release. CAST: Clint Ritchie (Rebel), Jess Walton (Kristy), Paul Prokop (Alex), Michael Ontkean (Jeff), Lavelle Roby (Black Widow), Nino Candido (Snatch), Jon Hill (Whitey), Gary Morgan (Gadget), John Raymond Taylor (Cowboy), Robert Cornthwaite (Ben), Kres Mersky (Carol), Albert Popwell (Blackjack), Joey Rosendo (Joey), Candace Dupuy (Linda), Jack Starr (Detective), Milt Gold (Hippie).

A TIME FOR DYING (Etoile) Producer, Audie Murphy; Directed and Written by Budd Boetticher; Photography, Lucien Ballard; Art Director, Les Thomas; Music, Harry Betts; A Fipco Production in DeLuxe Color; 67 minutes; October release. CAST: Richard Lapp (Cass), Anne Randall (Nellie), Audie Murphy (Jesse James), Victor Jory (Judge), Beatrice Kay (Mamie), Bob Random (Billy), Peter Brocco (Ed), Burt Mustin (Seth).

NIGHT OF DARK SHADOWS (MGM) Producer-Director, Dan Curtis; Screenplay, Sam Hall; Story, Sam Hall, Dan Curtis; Photography, Richard Shore; Music, Robert Cobert; Art Director, Trevor Williams; Assistant Director, Stanley Penesoff; In Metrocolor; 97 minutes; October release. CAST: David Selby (Quentin/Charles), Lara Parker (Angelique), Kate Jackson (Tracy), Grayson Hall (Carlotta), John Karlen (Alex), Nancy Barrett (Claire), James Storm (Gerard), Diana Millay (Laura), Christopher Pennock (Gabriel), Thayer David (Rev. Strack), Monica Rich (Sarah), Clarisse Blackburn (Mrs. Castle).

SUPERSTARS IN FILM CONCERT (National Cinema) Produced, Directed, and Photographed by Peter Clifton; In Color and Black and White; Presented by KDAY and Sam Riddle; 105 minutes; October release. CAST: The Rolling Stones, Mick Jagger, Ike and Tina Turner, The Animals, Eric Burdon, Donovan, Paul Jones, Zoot Money, Arthur Brown, Jimi Hendrix, Procul Harem, Ten Years After, Ted Jones, Otis Redding, Traffic, John Lennon, Yoko Ono, Jethro Tull, Joe Cocker.

THE TELEPHONE BOOK (Rosebud) Producer, Merwin Bloch; Associate Producer, Steve Sirkin; Directed and Written by Nelson Lyon; Photography, Leon Perer; Art Director, Jim Taylor; Music, Nate Sassover; "Something to Remember You By" (Howard Dietz, Arthur Schwartz) sung by Helen Morgan; In EastmanColor and Black and White; 89 minutes; Rating X; October release. CAST: Sarah Kennedy (Alice), Norman Rose (Smith), James Harder (Caller 1), Jill Clayburgh (Eyemask), Ondine (Narrator), Barry Morse (Har Poon), Ultra Violet (Whip Woman), Geri Miller (Dancer), Roger C. Carmel (Analyst), William Hickey (Man in bed), Matthew Tobin (Mugger), Jan Farrand (Woman in park), David Dozer (Caller 2), Lucy Lee Flippen (Caller 3), Dolph Sweet (Caller 4), Joan Ziehl (Young girl), Margaret Brewster (Old Lady), Arthur Haggerty (District Attorney).

Clint Ritchie
in "The Peace Killers"

David Selby, Kate Jackson, Grayson Hall
in "Night of Dark Shadows"

Jimi Hendrix
in "Superstars in Film Concert"

Candice Bergen, Peter Boyle
in "T. R. Baskin"

WEREWOLVES ON WHEELS (Fanfare) Producer, Paul Lewis; Director, Michel Levesque; Screenplay, David M. Kaufman, Michel Levesque; Photography, Isidore Mankofsky. Music, Don Gere; Art Director, Allen Jones; In DeLuxe Color; 85 minutes; Rating R; October release. CAST: Stephen Oliver (Adam), Severn Darden (High Priest), D. J. Anderson (Helen), Duece Berry (Tarot), Billy Gray (Bill), Gray Johnson (Movie), Barry McGuire (Scarf), Owen Orr (Mouse), Anna Lynn Brown (Shirley), Leonard Rogel (Gas Station Operator).

T. R. BASKIN (Paramount) Produced and Written by Peter Hyams; Director, Herbert Ross; Photography, Gerald Hirschfeld; Music, Jack Elliott; Art Director, Albert Brenner; Assistant Director, Don Kranze; In Technicolor; 90 minutes; October release. CAST: Candice Bergen (T. R.), Peter Boyle (Jack), James Caan (Larry), Marcia Rodd (Dayle), Erin O'Reilly (Kathy), Howard Platt (Arthur), William Wise (Gary).

THE SCAVENGERS (Aquarius) Produced and Written by R. W. Cresse; Director, R. L. Frost; Photography, Bob Maxwell; Music, Lee Frost, Paul Hunt; Lyrics, Tom Bowden, Jr., R. W. Cresse; Assistant Director, Don Baker; In EastmanColor; 111 minutes; October release. CAST: Jonathon Bliss, Maria Lease, Michael Divoka, Roda Spain, John Riazzi, Wes Bishop, Bruce Kemp, Sanford Mitchell, Tom Siegel, Jody Berry, Paul Wilmouth, Ushi Digart, James E. McIarty, Claudia Siefried, Karen Swanson, Warren James, Paul Hunt, James K. Shea, Freddy Mizrahi, Ben Adams, Tom Bowden, Jr., Fig Blackman, Ben Cadlett, Robert Jones, James Gorden.

COME TO YOUR SENSES (National General) Producer, Walt DeFaria; Executive Producer, Lee Mendelson; Director, Bernard Gunther; Photography, Al Niggemeyer; Music, Rod McKuen, Bernie Krause, Paul Beaver; Assistant Director, Ned Kopp; In DeLuxe Color; 90 minutes; Rating G; October release. A film for those infatuated by sensory awareness. No cast listed.

THE ANIMALS (Levitt-Pickman) Executive Producer, and Screenplay, Hy Mizrahi; Producer, Richard Bakalyan; Director, Ron Joy; Photography, Keith Smith; Music, Rupert Holmes; Lyrics, Danny Jordan; An XYZ Production in Techniscope and Technicolor; 88 minutes; Rating R; October release. CAST: Henry Silva (Chatto), Keenan Wynn (Pudge), Michele Carey (Alice), John Anderson (Sheriff Pierce), Joseph Turkel (Peyote), Pepper Martin (Jamie), Bobby Hall (Cat), Peter Hellmann (Karl), William Bryant (Sheriff Lord), Peggy Stewart (Emily).

BUSHMAN (American Film Institute) Produced, Directed, and Written by David Schickele; Photography, David Myers; In Black and White; 73 minutes; Documentary; October release. CAST: Paul Eyam, Nzie Okpokam, Elaine Featherstone, Timothy Near, Jack Nance, Ann Scofield.

IS THERE SEX AFTER DEATH (Abel-Child) Produced, Directed, and Written by Jeanne and Alan Abel; Associate Producer, Michael Rothschild; Photography, Gerald Cotts; In EastmanColor; 97 minutes; October release. CAST: Buck Henry (Dr. Manos), Alan Abel (Dr. Rogers), Marshall Efron (Vince), Holly Woodlawn (Herself), Robert Downey (Himself), Jim Moran (Dr. Elevenike), Rubin Carson (Himself), Earle Doud (Merkin the Magician), Larry Wolf (Announcer), Iris Brooks (Breast School Student), Jim Dixon (Richard Nixon), Roger Jon Diamond (Attorney).

JACK JOHNSON (Big Fights Inc.) Producer, Jim Jacobs; Director, William Cayton; Screenplay, Al Bodian; Photography, Larry Garinger; Music, Miles Davis; Narration, Kevin Kennedy; Narrated by Brock Peters; Black and White Documentary; 90 minutes; October release.

James Caan, Candice Bergen
in "T. R. Baskin"

Buck Henry
in "Is There Sex after Death"

Judy Brown, Roberta Collins, Pam Grier, Brooke Mills, Pat Woodell in "The Big Doll House"

Reni Santoni, Clint Eastwood in "Dirty Harry"

THE BIG DOLL HOUSE (New World) Executive Producer, Eddie Romero; Producer, Jane Schaffer; Director, Jack Hill; Screenplay, Don Spencer; Photography, Freddie Conde; Music, Hall Daniels; Assistant Director, Maria S. Abelardo; Designer, Ben Otico; In DeLuxe Color; 93 minutes; Rating R; November release. CAST: Judy Brown (Collier), Roberta Collins (Alcott), Pam Grier (Grear), Brooke Mills (Harrad), Pat Woodell (Bodine), Sid Haig (Harry), Christiane Schmidtmer (Miss Dietrich), Kathryn Loder (Lucian), Jerry Franks (Fred), Jack Davis (Dr. Phillips), Gina Stuart (Ferina), Letty Mirasol (Leyte), Shirley De Las Alas (Guard).

JENNIFER ON MY MIND (United Artists) Producer, Bernard Schwartz; Director, Noel Black; Screenplay, Erich Segal; Based on novel "Heir" by Roger L. Simon; Photography, Andy Lazlo; Music, Stephen J. Lawrence; Art Director, Ben Edwards; Associate Producer, Philip Hazleton; Costumes, Joseph Aulis; Assistant Director, Steve Barnett; In DeLuxe Color; 90 minutes; Rating R; November release. CAST: Michael Brandon (Marcus), Tippy Walker (Jenny), Lou Gilbert (Max), Steve Vinovich (Ornstein), Peter Bonerz (Sergei), Renee Taylor (Selma), Chuck McCann (Sam), Bruce Kornbluth (Dolci), Barry Bostwick (Nanki), Jeff Conaway (Hanki).

THREE LIVES (Impact) Producers, Louva Irvine, Susan Kleckner, Bici Forbes, Ann Sheppard; Directors, Louva Irvine, Susan Kleckner, Robin Mide; Photography, Lenore Bode; A Women's Liberation Cinema Co. Production in Color and Black and White; 70 minutes; documentary; November release. CAST: Mallory Millet-Jones (Mallory), Lillian Shreve (Lillian), Robin Mide (Robin).

THE RESURRECTION OF ZACHARY WHEELER (Vidtronics) Producer, Robert Stabler; Director, Robert Wynn; Screenplay, Jay Simms, Tom Rolf; Photography, Bob Boatman; Music, Marlin Skiles; Assistant Director, George Fenaja; In Technicolor; 100 minutes; Rating G; November release. CAST: Leslie Nielsen (Harry), Bradford Dillman (Sen. Wheeler), James Daly (Dr. Redding), Angie Dickinson (Dr. Johnson), Robert J. Wilke (Hugh), Jack Carter (Dwight), Don Haggerty (Jake), and Jim Healy, Lou Brown, Pat O'Moore, Richard Schuyler, Richard Simmons, Ruben Moreno, Peter Mamakos, Jill Jaress, Jim Healey, Lee Giroux.

HONKY (Jack H. Harris) Producers, Will Chaney, Ron Roth; Director, William A. Graham; Screenplay, Will Chaney; Based on novel "Sheila" by Gunard Selberg; Photography, Ralph Woolsey; Music, Quincy Jones; Art Director, Frank Sylos; Assistant Director, Edward Teets; A Getty-Fromkess & Stonehenge Production in DeLuxe Color; 92 minutes; November release. CAST: Brenda Sykes (Sheila), John Nielson (Honky), Maia Danziger (Sharon), John Lasell (Archer), William Marshall (Dr. Smith).

EROTICON (Adelphia) Producer, Bernard L. Sackett; Director, Richard Lacey; Screenplay, Bernard L. Sackett, Richard Lacey; Photography, Richard Lacey, Peter Vanadia; In EastmanColor; 91 minutes; Rating X; November release. A documentary look at America's erotic explosion with interviews involving Bernard Sackett, Al Goldstein, James Buckley, Dr. Albert Ellis, Tommi Angerer.

Clint Eastwood in "Dirty Harry"

Tommy Moore in "Boys in the Sand"

Harry Guardino, Reni Santoni, Clint Eastwood
in "Dirty Harry"

Beau Bridges, Maud Adams
in "The Christian Licorice Store"

CALLIOPE (Moonstone) Producer, Harry Korshak; Director, Matt Cimber; Screenplay, Beth Keele; Music, Tommy Oliver; In Color; 81 minutes; Rating R; November release. CAST: Sherry Miles (Groupie), Mark Gottlieb (Rock musician), Sherry Bain (Clerk), Marty Huston (Boss), Dwen Van Dam (Housewife), Lou Epton (Husband), Diana Jones (Cultist), Shelly Fisher (Black Revolutionary), Choo Choo Collins (Actress), Borah Silver (Producer), Marjorie Bennett (Snoopy Lady), Stan Rose (Chauffeur).

LENNY BRUCE WITHOUT TEARS (Baker) A Fred Baker Production in Black and White; 85 minutes; No other credits; November release. Compilation of Lenny Bruce film clips.

MARCO (Kartemquin) Producers, Vaile Scott, Louis Marrone; Directors, Gerald Temaner, Gordon Quinn; Photography, Gordon Quinn; In Black and White; 83 minutes; November release. A documentary on natural childbirth.

PRISM (Corn King) Producers, Bob Silverstein, Jay Freund, Anitra Pivnick; Executive Producer, Leo Pivnick; Direction and Screenplay, Anitra Pivnick; Photography, Jay Freund; Music, Tom Manoff; In DuArt Color; 80 minutes; November release. CAST: Paul Geier (Ben), Dale Soules (Eva), Nancy Volkman (Sally), Ozzie Tortora (Peter), Frank Geraci (Larry), Robert Root (Heckler).

FAR OUT, STAR ROUTE (Lipton) Production by Lenny Lipton and collaborators in Color; 70 minutes; November release. No other credits. A documentary of a commune in Oregon.

THE CHRISTIAN LICORICE STORE (National General) Producers, Michael S. Laughlin, Floyd Mutrux; Director, James Frawley; Screenplay, Floyd Mutrux; Photography, David Butler; Music, Lalo Schifrin; Songs, Tim Buckley, Tim McIntire, David Byron; Art Director, Dale Hennessy; Assistant Directors, James Brown, Tom Konig, Bruce Chevillat; Cinema Center Films Presentation in DeLuxe Color; 90 minutes; Rating GP; November release. CAST: Beau Bridges (Franklin), Maud Adams (Cynthia), Gilbert Roland (Jonathan), Alan Arbus (Monroe), Anne Randall (Texas), Monte Hellman (Joseph), Jaclyn Hellman (Mary), "Butch" Bucholtz (Tennis opponent), Walter Barnes (P.C.), McLean Stevenson (Smallwood), Howard Storm (McGhee), Greg Mullavey (Robin), Larry Gelman (Assistant director), Louis De Farra (Mime), Gary Rose (Evans), Billy James, Rusty Durrell (Reporters), Dawn Cleary (Hostess), Joanna Phillips, Barbara Leigh (Starlets), James Jeter (Texas man), Nina Varela (Parking lady), Bruce Graziano (Tall sailor), Harold Keller (Short Sailor), Toni Clayton (Mercedes girl), Dido and Jean Renoir (Themselves).

DIRTY HARRY (Warner Bros.) Producer-Director, Don Siegel; Executive Producer, Robert Daley; Screenplay, Harry Julian Fink, R. M. Fink, Dean Riesner; Story, The Finks; Photography, Bruce Surtees; Music, Lalo Schifrin; Art Director, Dale Henessy; Assistant Director, Robert Rubin; In Technicolor; 102 minutes; Rating R; December release. CAST: Clint Eastwood (Harry), Harry Guardino (Lt. Bressler), Reni Santoni (Chico), John Vernon (Mayor), John Larch (Chief), Andy Robinson (Killer).

BOYS IN THE SAND (Poolemar) Conceived, Directed, and Photographed by Wakefield Poole; In Color; 90 minutes; Rating R; December release. CAST: Casey Donovan, Peter Fisk, Danny Di Cioccio, Tommy Moore.

Gilbert Roland, Beau Bridges
in "The Christian Licorice Store"

Peter Fisk, Casey Donovan
in "Boys in the Sand"

Jo Van Fleet, Herve Villechaize in
"The Gang that Couldn't Shoot Straight"

Ernie Kovacs
in "Kovacs"

THE GANG THAT COULDN'T SHOOT STRAIGHT (MGM) Producers, Robert Chartoff, Irwin Winkler; Director, James Goldstone; Screenplay, Waldo Salt from novel by Jimmy Breslin; Photography, Owen Roizman; Art Director, Robert Gundlach; Music, Dave Grusin; Assistant Director, William Gerrity; In Metrocolor; 96 minutes; Rating GP; December release. CAST: Jerry Orbach (Kid Sally), Leigh Taylor-Young (Angela), Jo Van Fleet (Big Momma), Lionel Stander (Baccala), Robert De Niro (Mario), Irving Selbst (Big Jelly), Herve Villechaize (Beppo), Joe Santos (Ezmo), Carmine Caridi (Tony), Frank Campanella (Water Buffalo), Harry Basch (De-Lauria), Sander Vanocur (Commentator), Phil Bruns (Gallagher), Roy Shuman (Mayor), Alice Hirson (Mayor's wife), and Jack Kehoe, Despo, Sam J. Coppola, James J. Sloyan, Paul Benedict, Louis Criscuolo, George Loros, Harry Davis, Burt Young, Jackie Vernon, Ted Beniades, Fat Thomas Rand, Michael Gazzo, Robert Gerringer, Walter Flanagan, Dan Morgan, Dorothi Fox, Johnny Addie, Robert Weil, Leopold Badia, Fran Stevens, Florence Tarlow, Alisha Fontaine, Lorrie Davis, Rita Karin, Tom Lacy, William H. Boesen, Gary Melkonian, Sully Boyar, Gustave Johnson, George Stefans, Frank Jourdano, Elsa Raven, Gloria LeRoy.

HAROLD AND MAUDE (Paramount) Producers, Colin Higgins, Charles B. Mulvehill; Executive Producer, Mildred Lewis; Director, Hal Ashby; Screenplay, Colin Higgins; Photography, John Alonzo; Music, Cat Stevens; Designer, Michael Haller; Assistant Director, Michael Dmytryk; In Technicolor; 90 minutes; Rating GP; December release. CAST: Ruth Gordon (Maude), Bud Cort (Harold), Vivian Pickles (Mrs. Chasen), Cyril Cusack (Sculptor), Charles Tyner (Uncle Victor), Ellen Geer (Sunshine), Eric Christmas (Priest), G. Wood (Psychiatrist), Judy Engles (Candy), Shari Summers (Edith), M. Borman (Motorcycle cop).

B. J. PRESENTS (Maron) Producer, Charles Brent; Direction and Screenplay, Yabo Yablonsky; From story by John Durin; A CoBurt Production; 85 minutes; Rating R; December release. CAST: Mickey Rooney (B. J.), Luana Anders (Carlotta), Keenan Wynn (Old Man).

CACTUS IN THE SNOW (General Film Corp.) Producer, Lou Brandt; Direction and Screenplay, Martin Zweiback; Photography, Wilbur Grossman; Music, Joe Parnello; Associate Producer, Maurie M. Suess; A Rudy Durand Production in Technicolor; 90 minutes; Rating GP; December release. CAST: Richard Thomas (Harley), Mary Layne (Cissy), Lucille Benson (Mrs. Sawyer), Oscar Beregi (Mr. Albert), Jan Burrell (Pharmacist), Ruby Dake (Dolores), Joseph Di Reda (Mr. Harris), Dennis Fimple (Mr. Murray), Corey Fischer (Bartender), Hugh Fischer (Drill Instructor), Dan Halleck (Seymour), Stan Kamber (Cal), Maggie King (Rhoda), Tiger Joe Marsh (Cab driver), Gregory Mead (Joe), Christopher Mitchum (George), Beatriz Monteil (Valerie), Tani Phelps (Mrs. Harris).

KOVACS (Stone-Galanoy) Producers, B. Ziggy Stone, Terry Galanoy; Director, B. Ziggy Stone; Screenplay, Terry Galanoy with assistance of Edie Adams; Photography, Scott Gibbs; Narration, Jack Mogulescu; In Black and White; 84 minutes; December release. A documentary on Ernie Kovacs made up of blackouts and sketches from his tv years.

ANDY WARHOL'S WOMEN (Warhol) Producer, Andy Warhol; Directed and Photographed by Paul Morrissey; In Color; 90 minutes; Rating X; December release. No other credits. CAST: Candy Darling, Jackie Curtis, Holly Woodlawn.

TOGETHER (Hallmark) Producers, Sean S. Cunningham, Roger Murphy; Director, Sean S. Cunningham; Photography, Roger Murphy; Music, Manny Bardi; Assistant Producer, Wes Craven; Narrator, Jan Peter Welt; In Color; 70 minutes; Rating X; December release. No cast listing.

Bud Cort, Ruth Gordon
in "Harold and Maud"

Holly Woodlawn
in "Andy Warhol's Women"

PROMISING PERSONALITIES OF 1971

SANDY DUNCAN

BRUCE DAVISON

ARTHUR GARFUNKEL

JENNIFER O'NEILL

KEN HOWARD

JO ANN PFLUG

CYBILL SHEPHERD

TOM LIGON

AL PACINO

TRISH VAN DEVERE

KRISTOFFER TABORI

KITTY WINN

PATTON

(20th CENTURY-FOX) Producer, Frank McCarthy; Director, Franklin J. Schaffner; Screen Story and Screenplay, Francis Ford Coppola, Edmund H. North; Based on factual material by Ladislas Farago, and Omar N. Bradley; Music, Jerry Goldsmith; Photography, Fred Koenekamp; Assistant Directors, Eli Dunn, Jose Lopez Rodero; Associate Producer, Frank Caffey; In Dimension 150 and Deluxe Color; 170 minutes; February release.

CAST

Gen. George S. Patton, Jr.	George C. Scott
Gen. Omar N. Bradley	Karl Malden
Capt. Chester B. Hansen	Stephen Young
Brig. Gen. Hobart Carver	Michael Strong
Gen. Bradley's driver	Cary Loftin
Moroccan Minister	Albert Dumortier
Lt. Col. Henry Davenport	Frank Latimore
Capt. Richard N. Jenson	Morgan Paull
Field Marshal Erwin Rommel	Karl Michael Vogler
Gen. Patton's driver	Bill Hickman
1st Lt. Alexander Stiller	Patrick J. Zurica
Sgt. William G. Meeks	James Edwards
Col. Gaston Bell	Lawrence Dobkin
Lt. Gen. Harry Buford	David Bauer
Air Vice-Marshal Sir Arthur Coningham	John Barrie
Col. Gen. Alfred Jodl	Richard Muench
Capt. Oskar Steiger	Siegfried Rauch
Field Marshal Sir Bernard L. Montgomery	Michael Bates
Lt. Col. Charles R. Codman	Paul Stevens
Air Chief Marshal Sir Arthur Tedder	Gerald Flood
Gen. Sir Harold Alexander	Jack Gwillim
Maj. Gen. Walter Bedell Smith	Edward Binns
Col. John Welkin	Peter Barkworth
Third Army Chaplain	Lionel Murton
Clergyman	David Healy
Correspondent	Sandy Kevin
Maj. Gen. Francis de Guingand	Douglas Wilmer
Maj. Gen. Lucian K. Truscott	John Doucette
Soldier who gets slapped	Tim Considine
Willy	Abraxas Aaran
Tank Captain	Clint Ritchie
British Briefing Officer	Alan MacNaughtan

Left: Michael Strong, George C. Scott, Paul Stevens, Michael Bates Above: George C. Scott, Karl Malden

George C. Scott

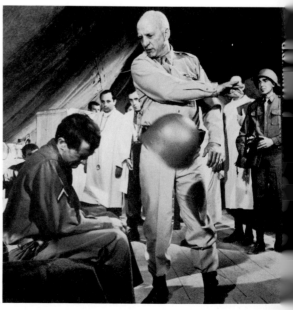

Tim Considine, George C. Scott

1970 "Oscars" for Best Film, Best Director, Best Story and Screenplay, Best Editing, Best Sound, Best Art Direction, Best Set Decoration, and Best Actor George C. Scott

GEORGE C. SCOTT
in "Patton"
BEST PERFORMANCE BY AN ACTOR IN 1970

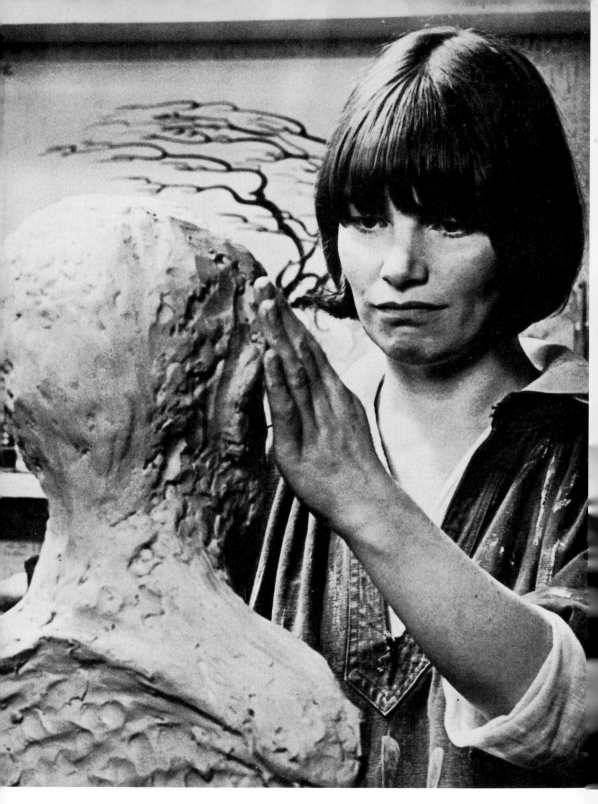

GLENDA JACKSON
in "Women in Love"
BEST PERFORMANCE BY AN ACTRESS IN 1970

JOHN MILLS
in "Ryan's Daughter"
BEST SUPPORTING PERFORMANCE BY AN ACTOR IN 1970

HELEN HAYES
in "Airport"
BEST SUPPORTING PERFORMANCE BY AN ACTRESS IN 1970

INVESTIGATION OF A
CITIZEN ABOVE SUSPICION

(COLUMBIA) Producer, Daniele Senatore; Director Elio Petri; Story and Screenplay, Ugo Pirro, Elio Petri; Photography, Luigi Kuveiller; Assistant Director, Antonio Gabrielli; Music, Ennio Morricone; A Vera Film in Color; 115 minutes; December release.

CAST

Police Inspector	Gian Maria Volonte
Augusta Terzi	Florinda Bolkan
Plumber	Salvo Randone
Police Commissioner	Gianni Santuccio
Mangani	Arturo Dominici
Biglia	Orazio Orlando
Antonio Pace	Sergio Tramonti
Augusta's Husband	Massimo Foschi
Homicide Functionary	Aldo Rendine

Left: Gian Maria Volonte (L)

Florinda Bolkan, Gian Maria Volonte
Above: Gian Maria Volonte

BEST FOREIGN LANGUAGE FILM OF 1970

| Julie Andrews | Red Buttons | Kim Hunter | George Chakiris | Lila Kedrova |

PREVIOUS ACADEMY AWARD WINNERS
(1) Best Picture, (2) Actor, (3) Actress, (4) Supporting Actor, (5) Supporting Actress, (6) Director, (7) Special Award, (8) Best Foreign Language Film

1927-28: (1) "Wings", (2) Emil Jannings in "The Way Of All Flesh", (3) Janet Gaynor in "Seventh Heaven", (6) Frank Borzage for "Seventh Heaven", (7) Charles Chaplin.

1928-29: (1) "Broadway Melody", (2) Warner Baxter in "Old Arizona", (3) Mary Pickford in "Coquette", (6) Frank Lloyd for "The Divine Lady".

1929-30: (1) "All Quiet On The Western Front", (2) George Arliss in "Disraeli", (3) Norma Shearer in "The Divorcee", (6) Lewis Milestone for "All Quiet On The Western Front".

1930-31: (1) "Cimarron", (2) Lionel Barrymore in "A Free Soul", (3) Marie Dressler in "Min and Bill", (6) Norman Taurog for "Skippy".

1931-32: (1) "Grand Hotel", (2) Fredric March in "Dr. Jekyll and Mr. Hyde", (3) Helen Hayes in "The Sin of Madelon Claudet", (6) Frank Borzage for "Bad Girl".

1932-33: (1) "Cavalcade", (2) Charles Laughton in "The Private Life of Henry VIII", (3) Katharine Hepburn in "Morning Glory", (6) Frank Lloyd for "Cavalcade".

1934: (1) "It Happened One Night", (2) Clark Gable in "It Happened One Night", (3) Claudette Colbert in "It Happened One Night", (6) Frank Capra for "It Happened One Night", (7) Shirley Temple.

1935: (1) "Mutiny On The Bounty", (2) Victor McLaglen in "The Informer", (3) Bette Davis in "Dangerous", (6) John Ford for "The Informer", (7) D. W. Griffith.

1936: (1) "The Great Ziegfeld", (2) Paul Muni in "The Story of Louis Pasteur", (3) Luise Rainer in "The Great Ziegfeld", (4) Walter Brennan in "Come and Get It", (5) Gale Sondergaard in "Anthony Adverse", (6) Frank Capra for "Mr. Deeds Goes To Town".

1937: (1) "The Life of Emile Zola", (2) Spencer Tracy in "Captains Courageous", (3) Luise Rainer in "The Good Earth", (4) Joseph Schildkraut in "The Life of Emile Zola", (5) Alice Brady in "In Old Chicago", (6) Leo McCarey for "The Awful Truth", (7) Mack Sennett, Edgar Bergen.

1938: (1) "You Can't Take It With You", (2) Spencer Tracy in "Boys' Town", (3) Bette Davis in "Jezebel", (4) Walter Brennan in "Kentucky", (5) Fay Bainter in "Jezebel", (6) Frank Capra for "You Can't Take It With You", (7) Deanna Durbin, Mickey Rooney, Harry M. Warner, Walt Disney.

1939: (1) "Gone With The Wind", (2) Robert Donat in "Goodbye, Mr. Chips", (3) Vivien Leigh in "Gone With The Wind", (4) Thomas Mitchell in "Stagecoach", (5) Hattie McDaniel in "Gone With The Wind", (6) Victor Fleming for "Gone With The Wind", (7) Douglas Fairbanks, Judy Garland.

1940: (1) "Rebecca", (2) James Stewart in "The Philadelphia Story", (3) Ginger Rogers in "Kitty Foyle", (4) Walter Brennan in "The Westerner", (5) Jane Darwell in "The Grapes of Wrath", (6) John Ford for "The Grapes of Wrath", (7) Bob Hope.

1941: (1) "How Green Was My Valley", (2) Gary Cooper in "Sergeant York", (3) Joan Fontaine in "Suspicion", (4) Donald Crisp in "How Green Was My Valley", (5) Mary Astor in "The Great Lie", (6) John Ford for "How Green Was My Valley", (7) Leopold Stokowski, Walt Disney.

1942: (1) "Mrs. Miniver", (2) James Cagney in "Yankee Doodle Dandy", (3) Greer Garson in "Mrs. Miniver", (4) Van Heflin in "Johnny Eager", (5) Teresa Wright in "Mrs. Miniver", (6) William Wyler for "Mrs. Miniver", (7) Charles Boyer, Noel Coward.

1943: (1) "Casablanca", (2) Paul Lukas in "Watch On The Rhine", (3) Jennifer Jones in "The Song of Bernadette", (4) Charles Coburn in "The More The Merrier", (5) Katina Paxinou in "For Whom The Bell Tolls", (6) Michael Curtiz for "Casablanca".

1944: (1) "Going My Way", (2) Bing Crosby in "Going My Way", (3) Ingrid Bergman in "Gaslight", (4) Barry Fitzgerald in "Going My Way", (5) Ethel Barrymore in "None But The Lonely Heart", (6) Leo McCarey for "Going My Way", (7) Margaret O'Brien, Bob Hope.

1945: (1) "The Lost Weekend", (2) Ray Milland in "The Lost Weekend", (3) Joan Crawford in "Mildred Pierce", (4) James Dunn in "A Tree Grows in Brooklyn", (5) Anne Revere in "National Velvet", (6) Billy Wilder for "The Lost Weekend", (7) Walter Wanger, Peggy Ann Garner.

1946: (1) "The Best Years of Our Lives", (2) Fredric March in "The Best Years of Our Lives", (3) Olivia de Havilland in "To Each His Own", (4) Harold Russell in "The Best Years of Our Lives", (5) Anne Baxter in "The Best Years of Our Lives", (6) Laurence Olivier, Harold Russell, Ernst Lubitsch, Claude Jarman, Jr.

1947: (1) "Gentleman's Agreement", (2) Ronald Colman in "A Double Life", (3) Loretta Young in "The Farmer's Daughter", (4) Edmund Gwenn in "Miracle On 34th Street", (5) Celeste Holm in "Gentleman's Agreement", (6) Elia Kazan for "Gentleman's Agreement", (7) James Baskette, (8) "Shoe Shine."

1948: (1) "Hamlet", (2) Laurence Olivier in "Hamlet", (3) Jane Wyman in "Johnny Belinda", (4) Walter Huston in "The Treasure of The Sierra Madre", (5) Claire Trevor in "Key Largo", (6) John Huston for "The Treasure of The Sierra Madre", (7) Ivan Jandl, Sid Grauman, Adolph Zukor, Walter Wanger, (8) "Monsieur Vincent".

1949: (1) "All The King's Men", (2) Broderick Crawford in "All The King's Men", (3) Olivia de Havilland in "The Heiress", (4) Dean Jagger in "Twelve O'Clock High", (5) Mercedes McCambridge in "All The King's Men", (6) Joseph L. Mankiewicz for "A Letter To Three Wives", (7) Bobby Driscoll, Fred Astaire, Cecil B. DeMille, Jean Hersholt, (8) "The Bicycle Thief."

1950: (1) "All About Eve", (2) Jose Ferrer in "Cyrano de Bergerac", (3) Judy Holliday in "Born Yesterday", (4) George Sanders in "All About Eve", (5) Josephine Hull in "Harvey", (6) Joseph L. Mankiewicz for "All About Eve", (7) George Murphy, Louis B. Mayer, (8) "The Walls of Malapaga".

1951: (1) "An American in Paris", (2) Humphrey Bogart in "The African Queen", (3) Vivien Leigh in "A Streetcar Named Desire", (4) Karl Malden in "A Streetcar Named Desire", (5) Kim Hunter in "A Streetcar Named Desire", (6) George Stevens for "A Place In The Sun", (7) Gene Kelly, (8) "Rashomon."

Rex Harrison

Dorothy Malone

Danny Kaye

Rita Moreno

George Kennedy

1952: (1) "The Greatest Show On Earth", (2) Gary Cooper in "High Noon", (3) Shirley Booth in "Come Back, Little Sheba", (4) Anthony Quinn in "Viva Zapata", (5) Gloria Grahame in "The Bad and the Beautiful", (6) John Ford for "The Quiet Man", (7) Joseph M. Schenck, Merian C. Cooper, Harold Lloyd, Bob Hope, George Alfred Mitchell, (8) "Forbidden Games."

1953: (1) "From Here To Eternity", (2) William Holden in "Stalag 17", (3) Audrey Hepburn in "Roman Holiday", (4) Frank Sinatra in "From Here To Eternity", (5) Donna Reed in "From Here To Eternity", (6) Fred Zinnemann for "From Here To Eternity", (7) Pete Smith, Joseph Breen.

1954: (1) "On The Waterfront", (2) Marlon Brando in "On The Waterfront", (3) Grace Kelly in "The Country Girl", (4) Edmond O'Brien in "The Barefoot Contessa", (5) Eva Marie Saint in "On The Waterfront", (6) Elia Kazan for "On The Waterfront", (7) Greta Garbo, Danny Kaye, Jon Whitely, Vincent Winter, (8) "Gate of Hell."

1955: (1) "Marty", (2) Ernest Borgnine in "Marty", (3) Anna Magnani in "The Rose Tattoo", (4) Jack Lemmon in "Mister Roberts", (5) Jo Van Fleet in "East of Eden", (6) Delbert Mann for "Marty", (8) "Samurai."

1956: (1) "Around The World in 80 Days", (2) Yul Brynner in "The King and I", (3) Ingrid Bergman in "Anastasia", (4) Anthony Quinn in "Lust For Life", (5) Dorothy Malone in "Written On The Wind", (6) George Stevens for "Giant", (7) Eddie Cantor, (8) "La Strada."

1957: (1) "The Bridge On The River Kwai", (2) Alec Guinness in "The Bridge On The River Kwai", (3) Joanne Woodward in "The Three Faces of Eve", (4) Red Buttons in "Sayonara", (5) Miyoshi Umeki in "Sayonara", (6) David Lean for "The Bridge On The River Kwai", (7) Charles Brackett, B. B. Kahane, Gilbert M. (Bronco Billy) Anderson, (8) "The Nights of Cabiria."

1958: (1) "Gigi", (2) David Niven in "Separate Tables", (3) Susan Hayward in "I Want to Live", (4) Burl Ives in "The Big Country", (5) Wendy Hiller in "Separate Tables", (6) Vincente Minnelli for "Gigi", (7) Maurice Chevalier, (8) "My Uncle."

1959: (1) "Ben-Hur", (2) Charlton Heston in "Ben-Hur", (3) Simone Signoret in "Room At The Top", (4) Hugh Griffith in "Ben-Hur", (5) Shelley Winters in "The Diary of Anne Frank", (6) William Wyler for "Ben-Hur", (7) Lee de Forest, Buster Keaton, (8) "Black Orpheus."

1960: (1) "The Apartment", (2) Burt Lancaster in "Elmer Gantry", (3) Elizabeth Taylor in "Butterfield 8", (4) Peter Ustinov in "Spartacus", (5) Shirley Jones in "Elmer Gantry", (6) Billy Wilder for "The Apartment", (7) Gary Cooper, Stan Laurel, Hayley Mills, (8) "The Virgin Spring."

1961: (1) "West Side Story", (2) Maximilian Schell in "Judgment At Nuremberg", (3) Sophia Loren in "Two Women", (4) George Chakiris in "West Side Story", (6) Robert Wise for "West Side Story", (7) Jerome Robbins, Fred L. Metzler, (8) "Through A Glass Darkly."

1962: (1) "Lawrence of Arabia", (2) Gregory Peck in "To Kill A Mockingbird", (3) Anne Bancroft in "The Miracle Worker", (4) Ed Begley in "Sweet Bird of Youth", (5) Patty Duke in "The Miracle Worker", (6) David Lean for "Lawrence of Arabia", (8) "Sundays and Cybele."

1963: (1) "Tom Jones", (2) Sidney Poitier in "Lilies of The Field", (3) Patricia Neal in "Hud", (4) Melvyn Douglas in "Hud", (5) Margaret Rutherford in "The V.I.P.'s", (6) Tony Richardson for "Tom Jones", (8) "8½".

1964: (1) "My Fair Lady", (2) Rex Harrison in "My Fair Lady", (3) Julie Andrews in "Mary Poppins", (4) Peter Ustinov in "Topkapi", (5) Lila Kedrova in "Zorba The Greek", (6) George Cukor for "My Fair Lady", (7) William Tuttle, (8) "Yesterday, Today and Tomorrow."

1965: (1) "The Sound Of Music", (2) Lee Marvin in "Cat Ballou", (3) Julie Christie in "Darling", (4) Martin Balsam in "A Thousand Clowns", (5) Shelley Winters in "A Patch Of Blue", (6) Robert Wise for "The Sound of Music", (7) Bob Hope, (8) "The Shop On Main Street".

1966: (1) "A Man For All Seasons", (2) Paul Scofield in "A Man For All Seasons", (3) Elizabeth Taylor in "Who's Afraid of Virginia Woolf?", (4) Walter Matthau in "The Fortune Cookie", (5) Sandy Dennis in "Who's Afraid of Virginia Woolf?", (6) Fred Zinnemann for "A Man For All Seasons", (8) "A Man and A Woman".

1967: (1) "In The Heat Of The Night", (2) Rod Steiger in "In The Heat Of The Night", (3) Katharine Hepburn in "Guess Who's Coming To Dinner", (4) George Kennedy in "Cool Hand Luke", (5) Estelle Parsons in "Bonnie and Clyde", (6) Mike Nichols for "The Graduate", (8) "Closely Watched Trains."

1968: (1) "Oliver!", (2) Cliff Robertson in "Charly", (3) Katharine Hepburn in "The Lion in Winter" and Barbra Streisand in "Funny Girl", (4) Jack Albertson in "The Subject Was Roses", (5) Ruth Gordon in "Rosemary's Baby", (6) Carol Reed for "Oliver!", (7) Onna White for "Oliver!" choreography, John Chambers for "Planet of the Apes" make-up, (8) "War and Peace."

1969: (1) "Midnight Cowboy", (2) John Wayne in "True Grit", (3) Maggie Smith in "The Prime of Miss Jean Brodie", (4) Gig Young in "They Shoot Horses, Don't They?", (5) Goldie Hawn in "Cactus Flower", (6) John Schlesinger for "Midnight Cowboy", (7) Cary Grant, (8) "Z."

1970: (1) "Patton", (2) George C. Scott in "Patton", (3) Glenda Jackson in "Women in Love", (4) John Mills in "Ryan's Daughter," (5) Helen Hayes in "Airport," (6) Franklin J. Schaffner for "Patton," (7) Lillian Gish, Orson Welles, (8) "Investigation of a Citizen above Suspicion."

Estelle Parsons

Maximilian Schell

Simone Signoret

Frank Sinatra

Miyoshi Umeki

WUTHERING HEIGHTS

(AMERICAN INTERNATIONAL) Producers, Samuel Z. Arkoff, James H. Nicholson; Executive Producer, Louis M. Heyward; Director, Robert Fuest; Associate Producer, John Pellatt; Screenplay, Patrick Tilley; From novel by Emily Bronte; Music, Michel LeGrand; Photography, John Coquillon; Assistant Director, Ted Lewis; Movielab Color; Rating G; 105 minutes; January release.

CAST

Catherine	Anna Calder-Marshall
Heathcliff	Timothy Dalton
Mr. Earnshaw	Harry Andrews
Mrs. Linton	Pamela Browne
Nellie	Judy Cornwell
Mr. Linton	James Cossins
Mrs. Earnshaw	Rosalie Crutchley
Isabella	Hilary Dwyer
Hindley	Julian Glover
Dr. Kenneth	Hugh Griffith
Frances	Morag Hood
Edgar	Ian Ogilvy
Mr. Shielders	Peter Sallis
Joseph	Aubrey Woods

Right: Anna Calder-Marshall, Harry Andrews, Timothy Dalton

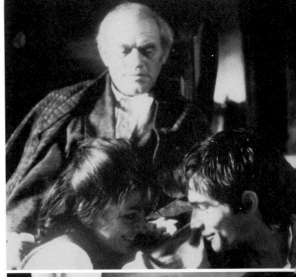

Timothy Dalton, Anna Calder-Marshall Above: Pamela Browne, Ian Ogilvy, Judy Cornwell, Anna Calder-Marshall

Aubrey Woods, Rosalie Crutchley Above: Morag Hood, Julian Glover

THE LAST VALLEY

(CINERAMA) Produced, Directed, and Written by James Clavell; Photography, John Wilcox; Music, John Barry; A Seamaster Production in Eastman-Color; 126 minutes; Rating GP; January release.

CAST

The Captain	Michael Caine
Vogel	Omar Sharif
Erica	Florinda Bolkan
Gruber	Nigel Davenport
Father Sebastian	Per Oscarsson
Hoffman	Arthur O'Connell
Inge Hoffman	Madeline Hinde
Pirelli	Yorgo Voyagis
Julio	Miguel Alejandro
Andreas	Christian Roberts
Graf	Ian Hogg
Hansen	Michael Gothard
Korski	Brian Blessed
Vornez	George Innes
Frau Hoffman	Irene Prador
Mathias	Vladek Sheybal
Geddes	John Hallam
Shutz	Andrew McCulloch
Eskesen	Jack Shepherd
Czeraki	Leon Lissek
Svenson	Chris Chittell
Tsarus	Kurt Christian
Sernen	Mark Edwards

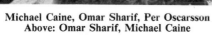

Michael Caine, Omar Sharif, Per Oscarsson
Above: Omar Sharif, Michael Caine

Florinda Bolkan, Michael Caine Above: Omar
Sharif Top: Michael Caine, Omar Sharif

123

BED AND BOARD

(COLUMBIA) Producer-Director, Francois Truffaut; Executive Producer, Marcel Berbert; Screenplay, Francois Truffaut, Claude De Givray, Bernard Revon; Assistant Director, Suzanne Schiffman; Photography, Nestor Almendros; Art Director, Jean Mandaroux; A Co-Production of Les Films du Carrosse-Valoria Films, Fida Cinematofrafic; 95 minutes; Rating GP; January release.

CAST

Antoine	Jean-Pierre Leaud
Christine	Claude Jade
Kyoko	Hiroko Berghauer
Executive Secretary	Barbara Laage
Monsieur Darbon	Daniel Ceccaldi
Madame Darbon	Claire Duhamel
The "Sneerer"	Pierre Fabre
Strangler	Claude Vega
American Customer	Bill Kearns
Tenor	Daniel Boulanger
Tenor's Wife	Silvana Blasi
Servant	Daniele Gerard
Bistro Landlord	Jacques Jouanneau
Housekeeper	Marie Irakane
Unknown Person	Serge Rousseau
Customer in bistro	Pierre Maguelon
Mother of young violinist	Annick Asty
Pensioner	Rispal
String-puller	Christian De Tiliere
"Hotel" Owner	Ada Lonati

Jean-Pierre Leaud, Claude Jade
Top Left: Jean-Pierre Leaud, Claude Jade

124

Jean-Pierre Leaud, Claude Jade

LUPO

(CANNON) Executive Producers, Dennis Friedland, Christopher C. Dewey; Producers, Yoram Globus, Ami Artzi; Direction and Screenplay, Menahem Golan; Music, Nurit Hirsch; Photography, Yechiel Neeman; Songs, Enud Manor; Sung by The Lions; In Eastmancolor; Rating G; 100 minutes; January release.

CAST

Lupo	Yuda Barkan
Albert	Gabi Amrani
Mathilda	Esther Greenberg
Mr. Goldwasser	Yuda Efroni
Mrs. Goldwasser	Lia Konig
Rachel	Avirama Golan
Noam	Moti Giladi
Esther	Shoshik Shani
Elimelech	Jacob Ben-Sira
Sgt-Major Goldberg	Arik Lavi
Major	Pinhas Koren
Sgt. Gabriella	Tzipi Zavit
Military Police	Pshik Levi
Ruthie	Naomi Golan
Aliza	Tikva Azziz
Tzipi	Shulamit Nativ
Yoske	David Smadar
Adivi	Shlomo Barshavit

Right: Yuda Barkan, Avirama Golan

Esther Greenberg, Yuda Barkan Above: Gabi Amrani, Yuda Barkan

Yuda Barkan, Gabi Amrani Above: Lia Konig, Yuda Efroni, Avirama Golan, Yuda Barkan, Moti Giladi

THE MUSIC LOVERS

(UNITED ARTISTS) Producer-Director, Ken Russell; Executive Producer, Roy Baird; Screenplay, Melvyn Bragg; Based on "Beloved Friend" by Catherine Drinker Bowen and Barbara Von Meck; Photography, Douglas Slocombe; Costumes, Shirley Russell; Choreographer, Terry Gilbert; Assistant Director, Jonathan Benson; Music of Tchaikovsky conducted by Andre Previn; In Panavision and DeLuxe Color; Rating R; 122 minutes; January release.

CAST

Tchaikovsky	Richard Chamberlain
Nina	Glenda Jackson
Rubenstein	Max Adrian
Count Anton Chiluvsky	Christopher Gable
Modeste	Kenneth Colley
Madame Von Meck	Izabella Telezynska
Nina's Mother	Maureen Pryor
Sasha	Sabina Maydelle
Davidov	Andrew Faulds
Alexei	Bruce Robinson
Lieutenant	Ben Aris
Koyola	Xavier Russell
Vladimir	Dennis Myers
Anatole	John Myers
Olga Bredska	Joanne Brown
Dimitri Shubelov	Alex Jawdokinov
Doctor	Clive Gazes
Odile in 'Swan Lake'	Georgina Parkinson
Prince in 'Swan Lake'	Alain Dubreuil
Prince Balukin	Graham Armitage
Tchaikovsky's Mother	Consuela Chapman
Bobyek	James Russell
Headwaiter	Ernest Bale
Tatiana	Victoria Russell
Young Tchaikovsky	Alex Brewer
Madame Von Meck's Son	Alexander Russell

Richard Chamberlain, Glenda Jackson Above: Richard Chamberlain (also top), Christopher Gable

Top: Richard Chamberlain, Glenda Jackson
Below: Glenda Jackson (L)

THE STATUE

(CINERAMA) Producer, Josef Shaftel; Director, Rod Amateau; Screenplay, Alec Coppel, Denis Norden; Based on story by Alec Coppel; Photography, Piero Portalupi; Art Director, Bruno Avesani; Music, Riz Ortolani; Assistant Director, Rae Mottola; In Humphries Color; 84 minutes; Rating R; January release.

CAST

Alex	David Niven
Rhonda	Virna Lisi
Ray	Robert Vaughn
Pat	Ann Bell
Joachim	Mircha Carven
Harry	John Clees
Dunhill	Bettine Milne
Sanders	Derek Francis
Hillcrest	Tim Brooke-Taylor
Mr. Southwick	Desmond Walter-Ellis
Mrs. Southwick	Susan Travers
Mr. Euston	David Mills
Mrs. Euston	Zoe Sallis
Mr. Westbury	David Allister
Mrs. Westbury	Maureen Lane
Chuck	Granville Van Dusen
Hunter	Tony Gardner
Sir Geoffrey	Hugh Burden
Mouser	Eric Chitty
Jacques	Gianni Musi
Melinda	Katarina Lidfeldt
Larry Patten	Troy Patterson

Tolis Karachalios (Greek guide), Hazel Hoskins (C.I.A.), Aldo De Carellis (Martinello), Sergio Silverio, Antonio D'Acquisto (Marines), Lorenzo Fineschi (Mike), F. L. Greaves (Herbert), Edward Danko (Harold), Dough Parish (Philip), Julian Jenkins, Mike Atkinson, Ron Hepher (Detectives), John Frederick (Adviser), Bill Vanders (Lawyer), Jack Repp (Air Force Officer), Robert Pomeroy (Navy Officer), Marne Maitland (Sec. General), John Stacy (Commentator), Pistillo Antonio (Piet), Graham Chapman (Newsreader), John Wregg (Policeman), Marco Gobbi (Hank), Kiko Concalves (Consul), Mario Guizzardi (George), Nicolette Le Pelley (Caroline), Bruno Erba (Maurice)

**Virna Lisi, David Niven
(also at top)**

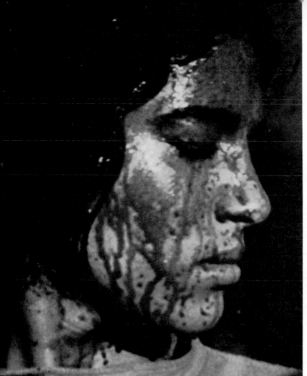

RAMPARTS OF CLAY

(CINEMA V) Producer-Director, Jean-Louis Bertucelli; Screenplay, Jean Duvignaud; Based on his book "Change at Chebika"; Adapted by Jean-Louis Bertucelli; Photography, Andreas Winding; Assistant Director, Mohamed Bouamari; Berber songs collected and sung by Taos Amrouche; Rating GP; 85 minutes; In Color; February release.

CAST

Rima .... Leila Schenna
and inhabitants of Tehouda, a village in Algeria

Leila Schenna, also at top and right

CLAIRE'S KNEE

(COLUMBIA) Producer, Pierre Cottrell; Direction and Screenplay, Eric Rohmer; French with subtitles; A Les Films du Losange Production in Color; 103 minutes; Rating GP; February release.

CAST

Jerome	Jean-Claude Brialy
Aurora	Aurora Cornu
Laura	Beatrice Romand
Claire	Laurence De Monaghan
Mme. Walter	Michele Montel
Gilles	Gerard Falconetti
Vincent	Fabrice Luchini

Voted best film of 1971 by National Society of Film Critics.

Aurora Cornu, Laurence DeMonaghan, Jean-Claude Brialy

Jean-Claude Brialy, Laurence DeMonaghan
Top: (R) Beatrice Romand (L) Gerard Falconetti (L)

131

JULIUS CAESAR

(AMERICAN INTERNATIONAL) Executive Producers, Henry T. Weinstein, Anthony B. Unger; Producer, Peter Snell; Director, Stuart Burge; Screen adaptation by Robert Furnival from play by William Shakespeare; Photography, Ken Higgins; Music, Michael Lewis; Designer, Julia Trevelyan Oman; Art Director, Maurice Pelling; Costumes, Robin Archer; Associate Producer, James Swann; Assistant Directors, Christopher Dryhurst, Tony McWhirter, Tony Buck, Peter MacGregor Scott; In Panavision and Technicolor; A Commonwealth United Production; 117 minutes; Rating G; February release.

CAST

Mark Antony	Charlton Heston
Brutus	Jason Robards
Julius Caesar	John Gielgud
Cassius	Richard Johnson
Casca	Robert Vaughn
Octavius Caesar	Richard Chamberlain
Portia	Diana Rigg
Calpurnia	Jill Bennett
Artemidorus	Christopher Lee
Marullus	Alan Browning
Titinius	Norman Bowler
Volumnius	Andrew Crawford
Lepidus	David Dodimead
Cinna the Poet	Peter Eyre
Publius	Edwin Finn
Decius Brutus	Derek Godfrey
Metellus Cimber	Michael Gough
Messala	Paul Hardwick
Carpenter	Laurence Harrington
Flavius	Thomas Heathcote
Strato	Ewan Hooper
Lucilius	Robert Keegan
Cicero	Andre Morell
Cinna the Conspirator	David Neal

and Preston Lockwood (Trebonius), John Moffatt (Popilius), Steven Pacey (Lucius), Ron Pember (Cobbler), John Tate (Clitus), Damien Thomas (Pindarus), Liz Geghardt (Calpurnia's Maid)

Front: Richard Chamberlain, Charlton Heston, Jason Robards
Above: Richard Johnson, Robert Vaughn, Diana Rigg, John Gielgud, Jill Bennett

Richard Chamberlain

Charlton Heston

Robert Vaughn, John Gielgud, Jason Robards
Top: Jill Bennett, John Gielgud, Charlton Heston

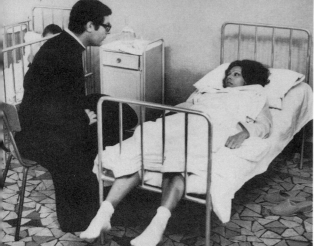

THE PRIEST'S WIFE

(WARNER BROS.) Executive Producers, Pio Angeletti, Andriano De Micheli; Producer, Carlo Ponti; Director, Dino Risi; Screenplay, Ruggero Maccari, Bernardino Zapponi; Costumes, Gianni Polidori; Music Armando Trovajoli; Assistant Director, Renato Rizzuto; An Italo-French Co-Production in Technicolor; Rating GP; 106 minutes; February release.

CAST

Valeria Villi	Sophia Loren
Don Marco	Marcello Mastroianni
Maurizio	Venantino Venantini
Jimmy Guitar	Jacques Stany
Valeria's Father	Pippo Starnazza
Monsignor Caldana	Augusto Mastrantoni
Davide Libretti	Guiseppe Maffioli
Valeria's Mother	Miranda Campa
Don Filippo	Gino Cavalieri
Caldana's Secretary	Gino Lazzari
Lucia	Dana Ghia

Left: Marcello Mastroianni, Sophia Loren

Sophia Loren, Marcello Mastroianni
Above: Venantino Venantini, Sophia Loren

Marcello Mastroianni, Sophia Loren,
also above with Miranda Campa

Curt Jurgens, Orson Welles, Above: Sergei
Bondarcuk Top: Yul Brynner

BATTLE OF NERETVA

(AMERICAN INTERNATIONAL) Executive Producers, Henry T. Weinstein, Anthony B. Unger, Steve Previn; Director, Veljko Bulajic; Screenplay, Ugo Pirro, Ratko Djurovic, Stevo Bulajic, Veljko Bulajic; English Adaptation, Alfred Hayes; Music, Bernard Herrmann; Played by London Philharmonic; Photography, Tomislav Pinter; A Commonwealth United presentation in Technicolor and Panavision; Rating G; 102 minutes; February release.

CAST

Vlado	Yul Brynner
Martin	Sergei Bondarcuk
General Lohring	Curt Jurgens
Danica	Silva Koscina
Colonel Kranzer	Hardy Kruger
Captain Riva	Franco Nero
Senator	Orson Welles
Novak	Ljubisa Samardjic
Ivan	Lojze Rozman
Nada	Milena Dravic
Nikola	Oleg Vidov
Stole	Bata Zivojinovic
Mad Bosko	Fabijan Sovagovic
Stipe	Boris Dvornik
Jordan	Pavle Vuisic
General Morelli	Anthony Dawson
Sergeant Mario	Howard Ross
Djuka	Charles Millot

Top: Silva Koscina
Below: Hardy Kruger

SUDDEN TERROR

(NATIONAL GENERAL) Producer, Paul Maslansky; Executive Producer, Irving Allen; Director, John Hough; Screenplay, Ronald Harwood; From novel "Eyewitness" by Mark Hebden; Photography, David Holmes; Assistant Director, John O'Connor; Music, Fairfield Parlour; Additional Music, David Whittaker; An Anglo-Emi Film in Technicolor; Rating GP; 95 minutes; February release.

CAST

Ziggy	Mark Lester
Colonel	Lionel Jeffries
Pippa	Susan George
Tom	Tony Bonner
Galleria	Jeremy Kemp
Paul	Peter Vaughan
Victor	Peter Bowles
Madame Robiac	Betty Marsden
Tacherie	Anthony Stamboulieh
Boutique Boy	John Allison
Local Station Sergeant	Joseph Furst
H. Q. Sergeant	Robert Russell
Waiter	Jonathan Burn
First Policeman	Christopher Robbie
Monk	Jeremy Young
President	Tom Eytle
Policeman in Jeep	David Lodge
Anne Marie	Maxine Kalli

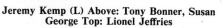

Jeremy Kemp (L) Above: Tony Bonner, Susan George Top: Lionel Jeffries

Maxine Kalli, Peter Bowles Above: Susan George, Mark Lester

136

MELODY

(LEVITT-PICKMAN) Executive Producer, Ronald S. Cass; Associate Producer, Adrian Gaye; Producer, David Puttnam; Director, Waris Hussein; Story and Screenplay, Alan Parker; Music, Bee Gees; A Hemsdale/Sagittarius Production in association with Goodtimes Enterprises; In Color; Rating G; 103 minutes; Sound Track Album on Atlantic Records; March release.

CAST

Ornshaw	Jack Wild
Daniel	Mark Lester
Melody	Tracy Hyde
Mrs. Latimer	Sheila Steafel
Mr. Latimer	Keith Barron
Headmaster	James Cossins
Mr. Perkins	Roy Kinnear
Mrs. Perkins	Kate Williams

Top: Mark Lester, Jack Wild
Below: Tracy Hyde, Jack Wild

Jack Wild, Mark Lester (C) Above: Mark Lester, Tracy Hyde, James Cossins Top: Mark Lester, Jack Wild

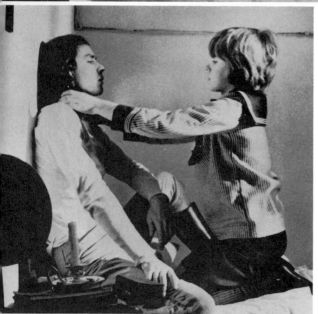

THE CONFORMIST

(PARAMOUNT) Producer, Maurizio Lodi-Fe; Director, Bernardo Bertolucci; Screenplay, Mr. Bertolucci; Based on novel by Alberto Moravia; Music, Georges Delerue; Costumes, Gitt Magrini; Photography, Vittorio Storaro; Executive Producer, Giovanni Bertolucci; Assistant Director, Aldo Lado; Co-Production of Mars Film and Marianne Productions; In Technicolor. Rating R; 110 minutes; March release.

CAST

Marcello	Jean Louis Trintignant
Giulia	Stefania Sandrelli
Anna Quadri	Dominique Sanda
Nino Seminara	Pierre Clementi
Manganiello	Gastone Moschin
Prof. Quadri	Enzo Tarascio
Italo	Jose Quaglio
Marcello's Mother	Milly
Marcello's Father	Giuseppe Addobbati
Giulia's Mother	Yvonne Sanson
Colonel	Fosco Giachetti
Minister	Benedetto Benedetti
Secretary	Gio Vagni Luca
Raoul	Christian Alegny
Priest	Antonio Maestri
Gypsy	Christian Belegue
Marcello as a child	Pasquale Fortunato
Marcello's Daughter	Marta Lado
Male Nurse	Pierangelo Givera
Hired Killers	Carlo Gaddi
Franco Pellerani, Claudio Cappelli, Umberto Silvestri	

Pierre Clementi, Pasquale Fortunato Top: Jean Louis Trintignant, Stefania Sandrelli, Enzo Tarascio, Dominique Sanda

Jean Louis Trintignant (also top), Stefania Sandrelli

Jean Louis Trintignant, Dominique Sanda
Top: Stefania Sandrelli, Dominique Sanda

THE BUTTERCUP CHAIN

(COLUMBIA) Producers, John Whitney, Philip Waddilove; Executive Producer, Leslie Gilliat; Director, Robert Ellis Miller; Screenplay, Peter Draper; From novel by Janice Elliott; Photography, Douglas Slocombe; Music, Richard Rodney Bennett; In Panavision and Color; 95 minutes; Rating R; March release.

CAST

France	Hywel Bennett
Manny	Leigh Taylor-Young
Margaret	Jane Asher
Fred	Sven-Bertil Taube
George	Clive Revill
Chauffeur	Michael Elphick

Left: Hywel Bennett, Leigh Taylor-Young

Leigh Taylor-Young, Jane Asher, Sven-Bertil Taube, Hywel Bennett

WATERLOO

(PARAMOUNT) Producer, Dino De Laurentiis; Director, Sergei Bondarchuk; Screenplay, H.A.L. Craig, Sergei Bondarchuk; Associate Producer, Thomas Carlile; Photography, Armando Nannuzzi; Assistant Directors, Vladimir Dostal, Allan Elledge; Designer, Mario Garbuglia; Music, Nino Rota; Costumes, Maria De Matteis, Ugo Pericoli; An Italian-Soviet Co-production in Panavision and Technicolor; 123 minutes; Rating G; March release.

CAST

Napoleon	Rod Steiger
Wellington	Christopher Plummer
Louis XVIII	Orson Welles
General Picton	Jack Hawkins
Duchess of Richmond	Virginia McKenna
Marshal Ney	Dan O'Herlihy
Sir William Ponsonby	Michael Wilding
Lord Uxbridge	Terence Alexander
Pvt. O'Connor	Donal Donnelly
Lord Gordon	Rupert Davies
Marshal Soult	Ivo Garrani
General Drouot	Gianni Garko
Cambronne	Eughenj Samoilov
William De Lancey	Ian Ogilvy
Marshal Blucher	Sergei Zakhariadze
Le Bedoyere	Philippe Forquet
Sauret	Andrea Checchi
Maria	Irina Skobzeva
General Muffling	John Savident
Sarah	Susan Wood
Lord Richard Hay	Peter Davies
Tomlinson	Oleg Vidov
Grouchy	Charles Millot
Gerard	Vladimir Druzhnikov
Duke of Richmond	Andre Esterhazy
Constant	Orazio Orlando
Colborne	Jeffry Wickham
Capt. Ramsay	Willoughby Gray
Capt. Normyle	Adrian Brine
Duncan	Roger Green

and Karl Liepinsc, Richard Heffer, Colin Watson, Charles Borromel, Franco Fantasia, Giorgio Sciolette, Jean Louis, Vasili Livanov, Victor Murganov, Veronica de Laurentiis, Rodolfo Lodi, Giuliano Raffaelli, Filippo Perego, Valentin A. Koval, Boris Molcianov, Attilio Severini, Massimo Della Torre, Ghennadj Judin, Andrei Jurenev, Aldo Cecconi, Vasili Plaksin, Valentino Skulme, Camillo A. Rota, Fred Jackson, Rotislav Jankowski, Oleg Machajlov, Lev Poliakov, Christian Janakiev, Armando Bottin, Gheorghy B. Rybakov, Vaslav Bledis, Sergei Testori, Antonio Anelli, Franco Ceccarelli, Felix Eynas, Guglielmo Ambrosi, William Slater, Alan Elledge, Volodia Levcenko, Alexander Paromenko, Guidarino Guidi, Valerij Gurjev, Paul Butkevic, Igor Jasulovic, Isabella Albonico, Andrea Dosne, Ivan Milanov, Vladimir Butenko, Rino Bellini.

**Top: (L) Jack Hawkins, Christopher Plummer
(R) Dan O'Herlihy, Rod Steiger**

**Rod Steiger
Above: Orson Welles (L)**

A SEVERED HEAD

(COLUMBIA) Producer, Alan Ladd, Jr.; Director, Dick Clement; Screenplay, Frederic Raphael; Based on novel and play of same name by Iris Murdoch and J. B. Priestley; Associate Producer, Denis Holt; Music, Stanley Myers; Designer, Richard Macdonald; Costumes, Sue Yelland; Assistant Director, Peter Bolton; Photography, Austin Dempster; A Jerry Gershwin/Elliot Kastner Production in EastmanColor; 96 minutes; Rating R; April release.

CAST

Antonia Lynch-Gibbon	Lee Remick
Palmer Anderson	Richard Attenborough
Martin Lynch-Gibbon	Ian Holm
Honor Klein	Claire Bloom
Georgie Hands	Jennie Linden
Alexander Lynch-Gibbon	Clive Revill
Rosemary Lynch-Gibbon	Ann Firbank
Miss Seelhaft	Rosamunde Greenwood
Miss Hernshaw	Constance Lorne
Winking Patient	Robert Gillespie
Nurse	Katerine Parr
Women at party	Ann Jameson, Yvette Rees

Right: Ian Holm, Jennie Linden, Claire Bloom

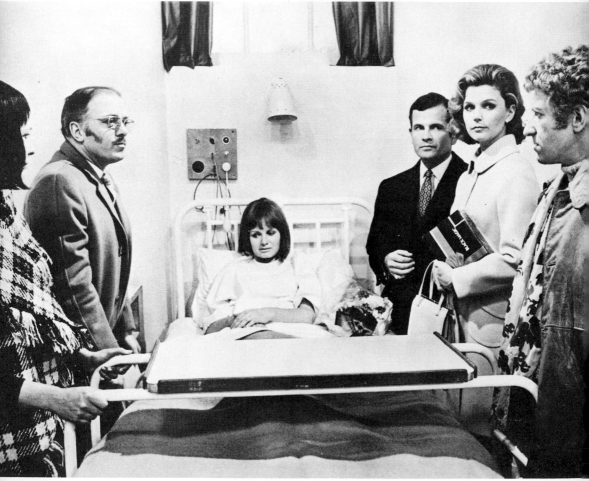

Claire Bloom, Richard Attenborough, Jennie Linden, Ian Holm, Lee Remick, Clive Revill

FLIGHT OF THE DOVES

(COLUMBIA) Producer-Director, Ralph Nelson; Screenplay, Frank Gabrielson, Ralph Nelson; Based on book by Walter Macken; A Rainbow Production in Color; 105 minutes, Rating G, April release.

CAST

Hawk Dove	Ron Moody
Finn Dove	Jack Wild
Granny O'Flaherty	Dorothy McGuire
Judge Liffy	Stanley Holloway
Derval Dove	Helen Raye
Tobias Cromwell	William Rushton
Shiela	Dana
Rabbi	James Barclay
Club Manager	Brendan Cauldwell
Michael	Brendan O'Reilly

Right: Dorothy McGuire (L)

Brendan O'Reilly, Ron Moody, Helen Raye, William Rushton, Dorothy McGuire, Jack Wild

AND SOON THE DARKNESS

(LEVITT-PICKMAN) Producers, Albert Fennel, Brian Clemens; Director, Robert Fuest; Story and Screenplay, Brian Clemens, Terry Nation; Music, Laurie Johnson; An Associated British Production for Anglo-Emi in Technicolor; Rating GP; 98 minutes; April release.

CAST

Jane	Pamela Franklin
Cathy	Michele Dotrice
Paul	Sandor Eles
Gendarme	John Nettleton
Schoolmistress	Clare Kelly
Madame Lassal	Hana-Maria Pravda
Old Man	John Franklyn
Lassal	Claude Bertrand
Renier	Jean Carmet

Michele Dotrice
Top: Pamela Franklin, Sandor Eles

LA COLLECTIONNEUSE

(PATHE) Producers, Barbet Schroeder, Georges de Beauregard; Direction and Screenplay, Eric Rohmer; Photography, Nestor Almendros; In EastmanColor; 88 minutes; April release.

CAST

Adrien	Patrick Bauchau
Haydee	Haydee Politoff
Daniel	Daniel Pommereulle
Writer	Alain Jouffroy
Carol	Mijanou Bardot
Sam	Seymour Herzberg

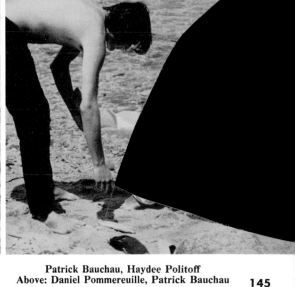

Haydee Politoff Above: Patrick Bauchau, Mijanou Bardot Top: Haydee Politoff, Patrick Bauchau

Patrick Bauchau, Haydee Politoff Above: Daniel Pommereuille, Patrick Bauchau

ONE DAY IN THE LIFE OF IVAN DENISOVICH

(CINERAMA) Producer-Director, Casper Wrede; Screenplay, Ronald Harwood; From Gillion Aitken's translation of Alexander Solzhenitsyn's novel; Executive Producers, Richard Pack, Howard G. Barnes, Erik Borge; Photography, Sven Nykvist; Assistant Director, Allan Ousby; Art Director, Per Schwab; Music, Arne Nordheim; In EastmanColor; 100 minutes; Rating G; May release.

CAST

Ivan Denisovich	Tom Courtenay
Tiurin	Espen Skjonberg
Captain	James Maxwell
Alyosha	Alfred Burke
Tsezar	Eric Thompson
Pavlo	John Cording
Kilgas	Mathew Guiness
Fetiukov	Alf Malland
Senka	Friman Falck Clausen
Gopchick	Jo Skjonberg
Eino	Odd Jan Sandsdalen
Vaino	Torstein Rustdal

James Maxwell, Tom Courtenay
Top Left: Tom Courtenay

Tom Courtenay
Top: (L) Tom Courtenay (R) James Maxwell, Tom Courtenay

10 RILLINGTON PLACE

(COLUMBIA) Producers, Martin Ransohoff, Leslie Linder; Director, Richard Fleischer; Associate Producer, Basil Appleby; Screenplay, Clive Exton; Based on novel by Ludovic Kennedy; Photography, Dennys Coop; Music, John Dankworth; Assistant Director, Terry Marcel; In Color; 109 minutes; Rating GP; May release.

CAST

John Reginald Christie	Richard Attenborough
Beryl Evans	Judy Geeson
Timothy John Evans	John Hurt
Mrs. Ethel Christie	Pat Heywood
Alice	Isobel Black
Baby Geraldine	Miss Riley
Muriel Eady	Phyllis McMahon
Workman Willis	Ray Barron
Workman Jones	Douglas Blackwell
Mrs. Lynch	Gabrielle Daye
Mr. Lynch	Jimmy Gardner
Detective Inspector	Edward Evans
Detective Sergeant	Tenniel Evans
Constables	David Jackson, Jack Carr, George Lee, Richard Coleman
Judge Lewis	Andre Morell
Malcolm Morris	Robert Hardy
Christmas Humphreys	Geoffrey Chater
Medical Board	Basil Dignam, Norman Henry, Edward Burnham
Hangman	Edwin Brown
Woman in cafe	Norma Shebbeare
Furniture dealer	Sam Kydd
Tramp	Reg Lye
West Indians	Rudolph Walker, Tommy Ansah

148 Top: Judy Geeson, Richard Attenborough
Below: Richard Attenborough, Edward Evans

Richard Attenborough, and above with
Judy Geeson Top: Judy Geeson, John Hurt

THE CROOK

(UNITED ARTISTS) Producer, Alexandre Mnouchkine; Director, Claude Lelouch; Screenplay, Claude Lelouch, Pierre Uytterhoeven, Claude Pinoteau; Music, Francis Lai; Assistant Director, Claude Pinoteau; Photography, Jean Collomb; In DeLuxe Color; Rating GP; 120 minutes; May release.

CAST

Simon	Jean-Louis Trintignant
Janine	Daniele Delorme
Monsieur Gallois	Charles Denner
Martine	Christine Lelouch
Bill	Amidou
Martine's Husband	Pierre Zimmer
Charles	Charles Gerard
Madame Gallois	Judith Magre
Inspector	Yves Robert
Daniel Gallois	Vincent Roziere

and guest star Sacha Distel

Right: Jean-Louis Trintignant, Vincent Roziere

Jean-Louis Trintignant (C)

149

UNE FEMME DOUCE

(NEW YORKER) Producer, Mag Bodard; Direction and Screenplay, Robert Bresson; Adapted from "The Gentle Woman" by Dostoyevsky; 87 minutes; May release.

CAST

She .... Dominique Sanda
He .... Guy Frangin
Anna .... Jane Lobre

Dominique Sanda, and above
with Guy Frangin

Dominique Sanda, Guy Frangin,
and also at top Above: Dominique Sanda

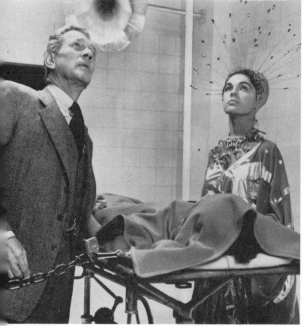

Vincent Price, Virginia North Above: Joseph
Cotten, Virginia North Top: Terry-Thomas,
Virginia North

THE ABOMINABLE
DR. PHIBES

(AMERICAN INTERNATIONAL) Producers,
Louis M. Heyward, Ron Dunas; Director, Robert
Fuest; Screenplay, James Whiton, William Goldstein;
Assistant Director, Frank Ernst; Photography, Nor-
man Warwick; Designer, Brian Eatwell; Music, Basil
Kirchen, Jack Nathan; Color by Movielab; Rating
GP; 90 minutes; May release.

CAST

Dr. Phibes	Vincent Price
Dr. Vesalius	Joseph Cotten
Rabbi	Hugh Griffith
Dr. Longstreet	Terry-Thomas
Vulnavia	Virginia North
Goldsmith	Audrey Woods
Nurse Allan	Susan Travers
Dr. Hargreaves	Alex Scott
Dr. Dunwoody	Edward Burnham
Dr. Kitaj	Peter Gilmore
Trout	Peter Jeffrey
Dr. Whitcombe	Maurice Kaufman
Schenley	Norman Jones
Waverley	John Cater
Crow	Derek Godfrey
Lem	Sean Bury
Ross	Walter Horsbrugh
Mrs. Frawley	Barbara Keogh
Police Officials	Dallas Adams, Alan Zipson

Top: Vincent Price

Victoria Chaplin

THE CLOWNS

(LEVITT-PICKMAN) Producers, Elio Scardamaglia, Ugo Guerra; Director, Federico Fellini; Screenplay, Federico Fellini, Bernardino Zapponi; Music, Nino Rota; Photography, Dario Di Palma; Costumes, Danilo Donati; Assistant Director, Maurizio Mein; Soundtrack on CBS Records; In Technicolor; 90 minutes; Rating G; June release.

CAST

The Clowns   Billi, Scotti, Fanfulla, Rizzo, Pistoni, Furia, Reder, Valentini, 14 Colombaioni, Merli, I Martana, Maggio, Sbarra, Carini, Terzo, Vingelli, Fumagalli, Zerbinati, Janigro, Maunsell, Peverello, Sorrentino, Valdemaro, Bevilacqua

The Troupe .... Maya Morin, Lina Albert, Alvaro Vitali, Gasparino

French Clowns .... Alex, Bario, Pere Loriot, Ludo, Mais, Nino

Animal Trainer .... Franco Migliorini and Anita Ekberg, Pierre Etaix, Annie Fratellini, Gustav Fratellini, Baptiste, Tristan Remy, Liana, Rinaldo, Nando, Orfei

Top Left to Right: Fumagalli, Mio Mao, Fanfulla

DEATH IN VENICE

(WARNER BROS.) Producer-Director, Luchino Visconti; Screenplay, Luchino Visconti, Nicola Badalucco; From novel by Thomas Mann; Photography, Pasquale De Santis; Costumes, Piero Tosi; Assistant Directors, Albino Cocco, Paolo Pietrangeli; Executive Producer, Mario Gallo; Associate Executive Producer, Robert Gordon Edwards; Music, Gustav Mahler; In Panavision and Technicolor; 130 minutes; Rating GP; June release.

CAST

Aschenbach	Dirk Bogarde
Hotel Manager	Romolo Valli
Alfred	Mark Burns
Governess	Nora Ricci
Mrs. Aschenbach	Marisa Berensen
Esmeralda	Carol Andre
Tadzio	Bjorn Andresen
His Mother	Silvana Mangano
Singer	Masha Predit
Travel Agent	Leslie French
Barber	Franco Fabrizi
Polish Youth	Sergio Garafanolo
Scapegrace	Luigi Battaglia
Hotel Clerk	Ciro Cristofoletti

Luigi Battaglia, Dirk Bogarde Above: Mark Burns, Dirk Bogarde Top: Marisa Berenson, Dirk Bogarde

Silvana Mangano, Bjorn Andresen Above: Dirk Bogarde, Marisa Berensen

154

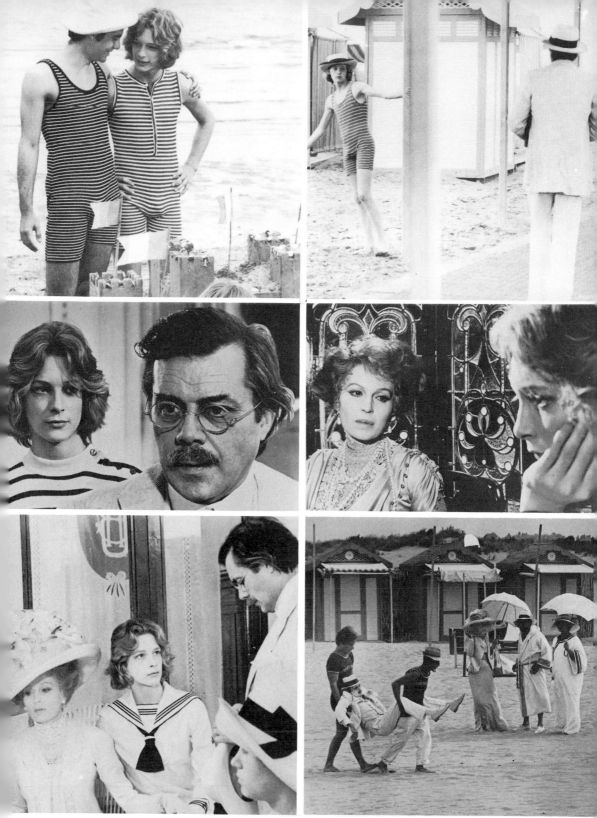

Silvana Mangano, Bjorn Andresen, Dirk Bogarde
Above: Bjorn Andresen, Dirk Bogarde Top: Sergio
Garfagnoli, Bjorn Andresen

Dirk Bogarde Above: Silvana Mangano, Bjorn
Andresen Top: Bjorn Andresen, Dirk Bogarde

UNMAN, WITTERING AND ZINGO

(PARAMOUNT) Producer, Gareth Wigan; Director, John Mackenzie; Screenplay, Simon Raven; Based on play by Giles Cooper; Music, Michael J. Lewis; Photography, Geoffrey Unsworth; Costumes, Judy Moorcroft; Assistant Director, Scott Wodehouse; A Mediarts Production in association with David Hemmings; In EastmanColor; 100 minutes; Rating GP; June release.

CAST

John Ebony	David Hemmings
Headmaster	Douglas Wilmer
Cary Garthingale	Anthony Haygarth
Silvia Ebony	Carolyn Seymour
Mr. Winstanley	Hamilton Dyce
Mrs. Winstanley	Barbara Lott
Stretton	Donald Gee
Clackworthy	David Jackson
Blisterine	Hubert Rees
Lower Five B:	
Aggeridge	David Auker
Ankerton	Tom Morris
Borby	Richard Gill
Bungabine	Michael Kitchen
Cloistermouth	Nicholas Hoye
Cuthbin	Tom Owen
Hogg	Toby Simpson
Lipstrob	James Wardroper
Muffett	Clive Gray
Munn Major	Rodney Paulden
Orris	Keith Janess
Root	Christopher Moran
Terhew	Michael Cashman
Trimble	Paul Aston
Unman	Michael Howe
Wittering	Colin Barrie

**Top: Tom Owen, Nicholas Hoye, David Hemmings
Below: David Hemmings, Anthony Haygarth**

**David Hemmings, Douglas Wilmer
Top: David Hemmings, Carolyn Seymour**

156

FIGURES IN A LANDSCAPE

(NATIONAL GENERAL) Producer, John Kohn; Director, Joseph Losey; Executive Producer, Sir William Piggott-Brown; Assistant Directors, David Tringham, Julio Sempere Parrondo; Costumes, Susan Yelland; Based on novel by Barry England; Adapted by Robert Shaw, Joseph Losey; A Cinecrest Production in Panavision and EastmanColor; 111 minutes; Rating GP; July release.

CAST

MacConnachie	Robert Shaw
Ansell	Malcolm McDowell
Helicopter Pilot	Henry Woolf
Helicopter Observer	Christopher Malcolm
The Widow	Pamela Brown
Soldiers	Andrew Bradford, Warwick Sims, Roger Lloyd Pack, Robert East, Tariq Younus

Right: Malcolm McDowell, Robert Shaw

Malcolm McDowell, Robert Shaw
(also above)

THE GO-BETWEEN

(COLUMBIA) Executive Producer, Robert Velaise; Producers, John Heyman, Norman Priggen; Director, Joseph Losey; Screenplay, Harold Pinter; Based on novel by L. P. Hartley; Music, Michel Legrand; Photography, Gerry Fisher; Costumes, John Furniss; Assistant Director, Richard Dalton; In Technicolor; 116 minutes; Rating GP; July release.

CAST

Marian-Lady Trimingham	Julie Christie
Ted Burgess	Alan Bates
"Leo" Colston	Dominic Guard
Mrs. Maudsley	Margaret Leighton
Leo Colston	Michael Redgrave
Mr. Maudsley	Michael Gough
Hugh Trimingham	Edward Fox
Marcus	Richard Gibson
Denys	Simon Hume-Kendall

Julie Christie, Dominic Guard
Top Left: Alan Bates, Dominic Guard

Julie Christie, Alan Bates
Top: (L) Dominic Guard, Margaret Leighton (R) Michael Redgrave

ADRIFT

(MPO) Executive Producer, Judd L. Pollock; Director, Jan Kadar; Producer, Julius Potocsny; Associate Director, Elmar Klos; Photography, Vladimir Novotny; Music; Zdenek Liska; Screenplay, Imre Gyongyossy, Jan Kadar, Elmar Klos; Based on novel "Something Is Adrift in the Water" by Lajos Zilahy; Designer, Karel Skvor; Color by Magyar Film Laboratories; A Studio Barrandov Production; 102 minutes; Rating R; July release.

CAST

Yanos	Rade Markovic
Zuzka	Milena Dravic
Anada	Paula Pritchett
Stutterer	Josef Kroner
Helmsman	Vlado Muller
Balthazar	Gustav Valach
Kristof	Ivan Darvas
Father-in-law	Jaroslav Marvan
Peter	Janko Boldis
Doctor	Dezso Kiraly

Right: Rade Markovic, Milena Dravic

Paula Pritchett, Rade Markovic

HOA-BINH

(TRANSVUE) Producer, Gilbert de Goldschmidt; Direction and Screenplay, Raoul Coutard; Based on novel "The Column of Ashes" by Francoise Lorrain; Music, Michel Portal; Photography, Georges Liron; Assistant Directors, Pierre Roubaud, Nguyen Van Han; A Gilbert de Goldschmidt-Allen A. Funt Production in EastmanColor; 93 minutes; Rating GP; August release.

CAST

Hung	Phi Lan
Xuan	Huynh Cazenas
Mother	Xuan Ha
Father	Le Quynh
Cousin	Lan Phuong
Tran Thi Ha	Bui Thi Thanh
Political Commissioner	Tran Van Lich
Vietcong Officer	Anh Tuan
Vietnamese Nurse	Kieu Anh

Right: Huynh Cazenas, Phi Lan

Le Quynh

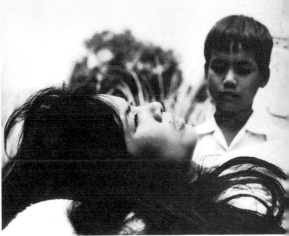

Xuan Ha, Phi Lan

Glenda Jackson, Murray Head Above: Bessie
Love Top: Murray Head, Peter Finch

SUNDAY BLOODY SUNDAY

(UNITED ARTISTS) Producer, Joseph Janni, Director, John Schlesinger; Associate Producer, Teddy Joseph; Screenplay, Penelope Gilliatt; Assistant Director, Simon Relph; Photography, Billy Williams; Designer, Luciana Arrighi; Costumes, Jocelyn Rickards; In DeLuxe Color; 110 minutes; Rating R; September release.

CAST

Alex Greville	Glenda Jackson
Dr. Daniel Hirsh	Peter Finch
Bob Elkin	Murray Head
Mrs. Greville	Peggy Ashcroft
Mr. Harding	Tony Britton
Mr. Greville	Maurice Denham
Answering Service	Bessie Love
Alva Hodson	Vivian Pickles
Bill Hodson	Frank Windsor
Prof. Johns	Thomas Baptiste
Daniel's Father	Harold Goldblatt
Daniel's Mother	Hannah Norbert
Middle-aged Patient	Richard Pearson
Woman Patient	June Brown
Rowing Woman	Caroline Blakiston
Her Husband	Peter Halliday
Man at Party	Douglas Lambert
Aunt Astrid	Marie Burke
Tony	Richard Loncraine
Scotsman	Jon Finch
Alex as a child	Cindy Burrows
Lucy Hodson	Kimi Tallmadge
Timothy Hodson	Russell Lewis
Tess Hodson	Emma Schlesinger
Baby John Stuart Hodson	Patrick Thornberry

Top: Murray Head, Glenda Jackson,
and below with Tony Britton

Glenda Jackson, Murray Head (also top)
Above: Glenda Jackson, Tony Britton

Peter Finch, Murray Head, and above
with Glenda Jackson Top: Glenda Jackson

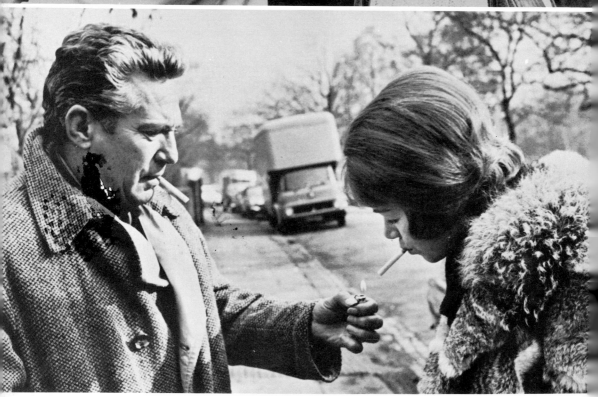

Peter Finch, Glenda Jackson
Top: Peter Finch, Murray Head, Glenda Jackson
in "Sunday Bloody Sunday"

FRAGMENT OF FEAR

(COLUMBIA) Producer, John R. Sloan; Director, Richard C. Sarafian; Screenplay, Paul Dehn; Associate Producer, Paul Dehn; Photography, Oswald Morris, Assistant Director, Bill Cartlidge; Based on novel by John Bingham; Music, Johnny Harris; In Color; 96 minutes; Rating GP; September release.

CAST

Tom Brett	David Hemmings
Juliet	Gayle Hunnicutt
Lucy Dawson	Flora Robson
Mr. Copsey	Wilfrid Hyde-White
Major Ricketts	Daniel Massey
Mr. Vellacot	Roland Culver
Bardoni	Adolfo Celi
Mrs. Gray	Mona Washbourne
"Bunface"	Mary Wimbush
Priest	Bernard Archard
C.I.D. Superintendent	Glyn Edwards
Sgt. Matthews	Derek Newark
Mr. Nugent	Arthur Lowe
Mrs. Ward-Cadbury	Yootha Joyce
Mrs. Baird	Patricia Hayes
Uncle Stanley	John Rae
Bruno	Angelo Infanti
Miss Dacey	Hilda Barry
Mario	Massimo Sarchielli
C.I.D. Sergeant	Philip Stone
Kenny	Edward Kemp
Joe	Kenneth Cranham
Rocky	Michael Rothwell
Nino	Kurt Christian
Pop Singer	Richard Kerr
American Matrons	Jessica Dublin, Louise Cambert
Schoolgirls	Georgina Moon, Petra Markham, Lois Hyett

Right and Top: Gayle Hunnicutt, David Hemmings

Massimo Sarchielli, David Hemmings

David Hemmings, Derek Newark

SEE NO EVIL

(COLUMBIA) Producers, Martin Ransohoff, Leslie Linder; Director, Richard Fleischer; Associate Producer, Basil Appleby; Screenplay, Brian Clemens; Photography, Gerry Fisher; Music, Elmer Bernstein; Assistant Director, Terry Marcel; A Filmways Presentation in Color; 89 minutes; Rating GP; September release.

CAST

Sarah	Mia Farrow
Betty Rexton	Dorothy Alison
George Rexton	Robin Bailey
Sandy Rexton	Diane Grayson
Barker	Brian Rawlinson
Steve Reding	Norman Eshley
Jacko	Paul Nicholas
Frost	Christopher Matthews
Gypsy Mother	Lila Kaye
Gypsy Jack	Barrie Houghton
Gypsy Tom	Michael Elphick
Doctor	Donald Bisset
Steve's Men	Max Faulkner, Scott Fredericks, Reg Harding

Top: Mia Farrow, Dorothy Alison

Mia Farrow, Michael Elphick Above: Mia Farrow, Dorothy Alison Top: Diane Grayson, Mia Farrow

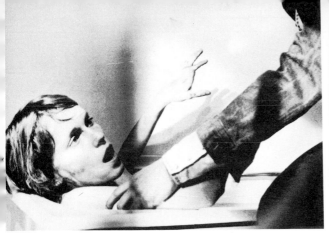

Mia Farrow, Norman Eshley Above: Diane Grayson, Mia
Farrow Top: Mia Farrow

Mia Farrow, Diane Grayson
Top: Mia Farrow

LONG AGO, TOMORROW

(CINEMA 5) Producer, Bruce Cohn Curtis; Direction and Screenplay by Bryan Forbes; Based on novel "The Raging Moon" by Peter Marshall; Photography, Tony Imi; Music, Stanley Myers; Assistant Director, Dickie Bamber; Title Song by Burt Bacharach, Hal David; Sung by B. J. Thomas; 100 minutes; Rating GP; September release.

CAST

Bruce	Malcolm McDowell
Jill	Nanette Newman
Sarah	Georgia Brown
Uncle Bob	Bernard Lee
Rev. Corbett	Gerald Sim
Clarence Marlow	Michael Flanders
Matron	Margery Mason
Bill	Barry Jackson
Harold	Geoffrey Whitehead
Terry	Christopher Chittell
Bruce's father	Jack Woolgar
Dr. Mathews	Norman Bird
Mrs. Mathews	Constance Chapman
Geoffrey	Michael Lees
Mr. Latbury	Geoffrey Gayldon
Bruce's mother	Patsy Smart
Gladys	Theresa Watson
Celia	Sylvia Coleridge
Hugh Collins	Brook Williams
Arnold Foster	Richard Moore
George	George Hilsdon
Margaret	Nellie Hanham
Alice	Aimee Delamain
Gladys' mother	Anne Dyson
Gladys' father	Norman Tyrrell
Mary	Petra Markham
Mrs. Hetherington	Winifride Shelley
Fete Guest	John Savident
Mr. Thomas	Michael Nightingale
Edna	Jackie Agrique
Doctor	Paul Darrow
Wedding Singer	Lee Carter
Bridesmaids	Sarah Forbes, Emma Forbes

Nanette Newman, Malcolm McDowell
Top Left: Nanette Newman

Nanette Newman, Malcolm McDowell
(also at top)

THE TROJAN WOMEN

(CINERAMA) Producers, Michael Cacoyannis, Anis Nohra; Director, Michael Cacoyannis; Screenplay, Mr. Cacoyannis; Adapted from Edith Hamilton's English translation of the Euripides play; Photography, Alfio Contini; Music, Mikis Theodorakis; Art Director, Nicholas Georgiadis; A Josef Shaftel Presentation in EastmanColor; 102 minutes; Rating GP; September release.

CAST
Hecuba	Katharine Hepburn
Andromache	Vanessa Redgrave
Cassandra	Genevieve Bujold
Helen	Irene Papas
Talthybius	Brian Blessed
Menelaus	Patrick Magee
Atsyanax	Alberto Sanz

Right: Patrick Magee, Irene Papas

Katharine Hepburn, Irene Papas

Vanessa Redgrave, Alberto Sanz
Top: Vanessa Redgrave (C)

Patrick Magee, Katharine Hepburn, Irene Papas
Top: Katharine Hepburn
in "The Trojan Women"

CATLOW

(MGM) Producer, Euan Lloyd; Director, Sam Wanamaker; Screenplay, Scot Finch, J. J. Griffith; From novel by Louis L'Amour; Photography, Ted Sciafe; Music, Roy Budd; Art Director, Herbert Smith; Assistant Director, Jose Maria Ochoa; In Metrocolor; 101 minutes; October release.

CAST

Catlow	Yul Brynner
Cowan	Richard Crenna
Miller	Leonard Nimoy
Rosita	Daliah Lavi
Christina	Jo Ann Pflug
Merridew	Jeff Corey
Rio	Michael Delano
Recalde	Julian Mateos
Caxton	David Ladd
Mrs. Frost	Bessie Love

(Photos not supplied)

1000 CONVICTS AND A WOMAN

(AMERICAN INTERNATIONAL) Producer, Philip N. Krasne; Director, Ray Austin; Screenplay, Oscar Brodney; Music, Peter J. Elliott; Photography, Gerald Moss; In DeLuxe Color; 91 minutes; Rating R; October release.

CAST

Angela Thorne	Alexandra Hay
Paul	Sandor Eles
Carl	Harry Baird
Warden Thorne	Neil Hallett
Ralph	Robert Brown
Forbus	Frederick Abbott
Gribney	David Bauer
Matthews	Peter J. Elliott
Linda	Tracy Reed
Mrs. Jackson	Stella Tanner

Alexandra Hay, Neil Hallett, Harry Baird, David Bauer
Top Right: Alexandra Hay, Sandor Eles Below: Sandor Eles, Frederick Abbott

IT ONLY HAPPENS TO OTHERS

(GSF) Executive Producer, Claude Pinoteau; Producer, Films 13/Claude Lelouch; Direction and Screenplay, Nadine Trintignant; Photography, William Lubtchansky; Assistant Director, Alain Corneau; Costumes, Gitt Magrini; Music, Michel Polnareff; Lyrics, Jean Loupdabadie; English subtitles, Sonya Friedman; Color by Movielab; 88 minutes; Rating G; October release.

CAST

Marcello	Marcello Mastroianni
Catherine	Catherine Deneuve
Xavier	Serge Marquand
Marguerite	Dominique Labourier
Woman in the park	Catherine Allegret
Marcello's mother	Daniele Lebrun

and Marc Eyraud, Rosa Chira Magrini, Benoit Ferreux, Marie Trintignant, Edouard Niermans, Michel Gudin, Andree Damant

Marcello Mastroianni, Catherine Deneuve
(also above and top)

Catherine Deneuve, Marcello Mastroianni
Above: Dominique Labourier, Catherine Deneuve

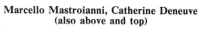

Marcello Mastroianni, Catherine Deneuve,
also Top Left, and Right with Serge Marquand

THE RAILWAY CHILDREN

(UNIVERSAL) Producer, Robert Lynn; Direction and Screenplay, Lionel Jeffries; From novel by E. Nesbit; Photography, Arthur Ibbetson; Music, Johnny Douglas; Technical Adviser, Robert Cryer; Assistant Director, Richard Dalton; In Technicolor; 109 minutes; Rating G; October release.

CAST

Mother	Dinah Sheridan
Perks	Bernard Cribbins
Old Gentleman	William Mervyn
Father	Iain Cuthbertson
Bobbie	Jenny Agutter
Phyllis	Sally Thomsett
Peter	Gary Warren
Doctor	Peter Bromilow
Russian	Gordon Whiting
Ruth	Ann Lancaster
Aunt Emma	Beatrix Mackey
Mrs. Perks	Deddie Davis
Jim	Christopher Witty
Bandmaster	David Lodge
Mrs. Viney	Brenda Cowling
Cart Man	Paddy Ward
Maid	Sally James
Photographer	Erik Chitty
C. I. D. Man	Dominic Allen

Top: Gary Warren, Dinah Sheridan, Sally Thomsett, Jenny Agutter

Sally Thomsett, Jenny Agutter, Bernard Cribbins

Jenny Agutter, Sally Thomsett Top: Gary Warren, Jenny
Agutter, Christopher Witty

Jenny Agutter, Sally Thomsett, Gary Warren

MURMUR OF THE HEART

(WALTER READE) Executive Producers, Vincent Malle, Claude Nedjar; Producer, Direction and Screenplay, Louis Malle; Assistant Director, Ghislain Uhry; Designers, Jean Jacques Caziot, Philippe Turlure; Assistant Directors, Fernand Moscowitz, Rita Drais; Music, Charlie Parker; A Minerva Film in Color; 118 minutes; October release.

CAST

Clara	Lea Massari
Laurent	Benoit Ferreux
Father	Daniel Gelin
Marc	Marc Winocourt
Thomas	Fabien Ferreus
Father Henri	Michel Lonsdale
Augusta	Ave Ninchi
Freda	Gila Von Weitershausen
Aunt Claudine	Micheline Bona
Uncle Leonce	Henri Poirier
Helene	Jacqueline Chauveau
Daphne	Corinne Kersten
Hubert	Francoise Werner
Fernande	Liliane Sorval
Father Superior	Yvon Lee
Mothers	Nicole Carriere, Lia Wanjtal, Hughette Faget
Disquaire	Michel Charrel
Maitre d'hotel	Eric Burnelli
Cook	Annie Savarin
Soldier	Jean-Pierre Pessoz
Man at party	Rene Bouloc
Madeleine	Isabelle Kloucowsky

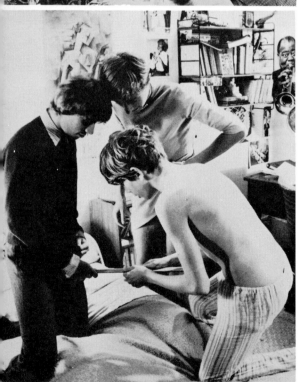

Marc Winocourt, Fabien Ferreus, Benoit Ferreux, also at top and above with Lea Massari, Daniel Gelin

Lea Massari, Benoit Ferreux

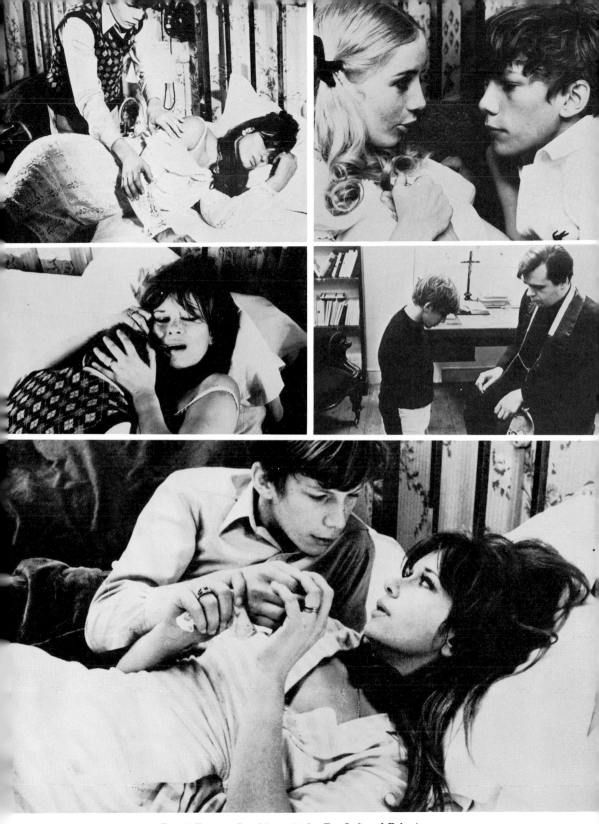

Benoit Ferreux, Lea Massari (also Top Left and Below)
Top Right: Corinne Kersten, Benoit Ferreux Below: Benoit Ferreux, Michel Lonsdale

KING LEAR

(ALTURA) Producer, Michael Birkett; Director, Peter Brook; Screenplay by Mr. Brook adapted from play by William Shakespeare; Photography, Henry Kristiansen; Designer, George Wakhevitch; A Filmways presentation in association with Royal Shakespeare Company; 137 minutes; November release.

CAST

King Lear	Paul Scofield
Goneril	Irene Worth
Fool	Jack MacGowran
Duke of Gloucester	Alan Webb
Duke of Albany	Cyril Cusack
Duke of Cornwall	Patrick Magee
Edgar	Robert Lloyd
Earl of Kent	Tom Fleming
Regan	Susan Engel
Cordelia	Annelise Gabold
Edmund	Ian Hogg
Oswald	Barry Stanton
Duke of Burgundy	Soren Elung Jensen

Right: Paul Scofield

Jack MacGowran, Paul Scofield

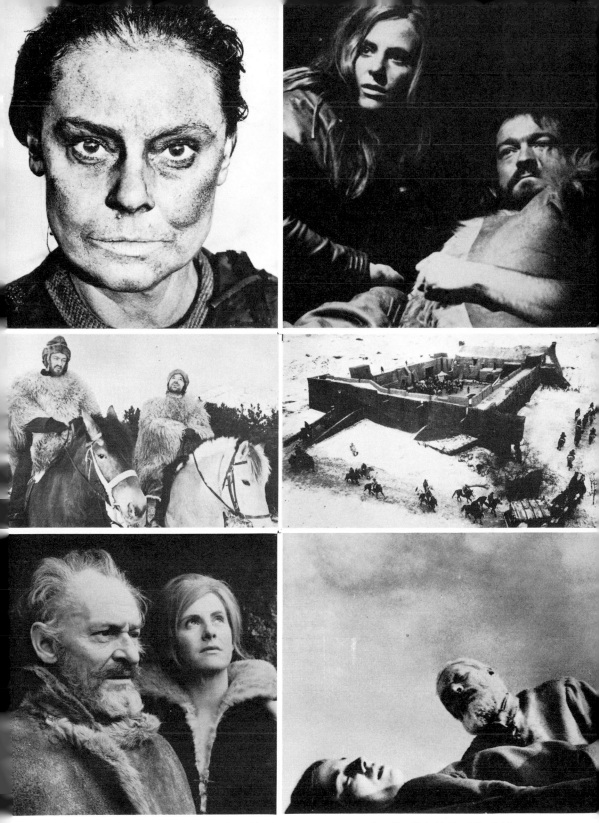

Alan Webb, Susan Engel Above: Ian Hogg, Robert Lloyd
Top: Irene Worth

Annelise Gabold, Paul Scofield
Top: Susan Engel, Ian Hogg

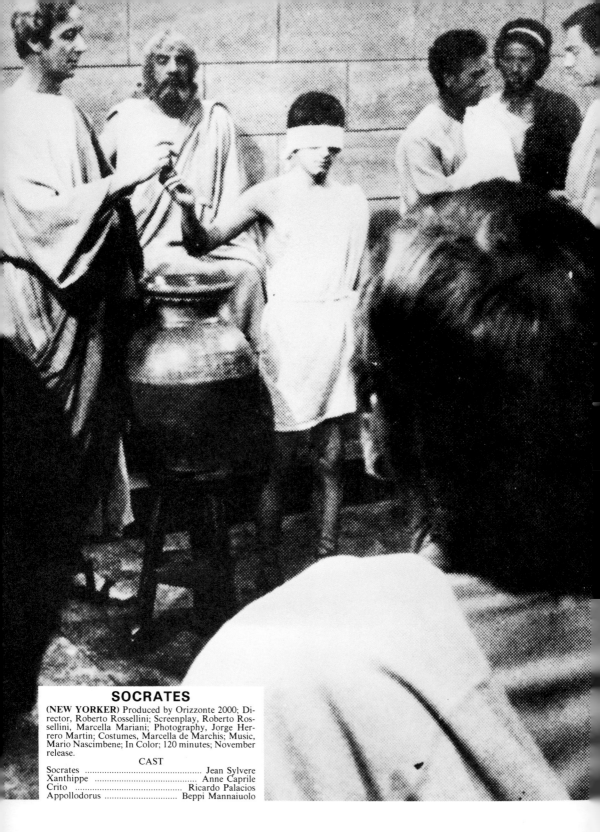

SOCRATES

(**NEW YORKER**) Produced by Orizzonte 2000; Director, Roberto Rossellini; Screenplay, Roberto Rossellini, Marcella Mariani; Photography, Jorge Herrero Martin; Costumes, Marcella de Marchis; Music, Mario Nascimbene; In Color; 120 minutes; November release.

CAST

Socrates .... Jean Sylvere
Xanthippe .... Anne Caprile
Crito .... Ricardo Palacios
Appollodorus .... Beppi Mannaiuolo

WHO SLEW AUNTIE ROO?

(AMERICAN INTERNATIONAL) Producers, Samuel Z. Arkoff, James H. Nicholson; Executive Producer, Louis M. Heyward; Associate Producer, John Pellatt; Director, Curtis Harrington; Screenplay, Robert Blees, James Sangter; Story, David Osborn; Photography, Desmond Dickinson; Music, Kenneth V. Jones; Art Director, George Provis; A Hemdale Production in Movielab Color; 89 minutes; Rating GP; December release.

CAST

Auntie Roo (Mrs. Forrest)	Shelley Winters
Christopher	Mark Lester
Katy	Chloe Franks
Mr. Benton	Ralph Richardson
Inspector Willoughby	Lionel Jeffries
Pigman (Mr. Harrison)	Hugh Griffith
Miss Henley	Rosalie Crutchley
Dr. Mason	Pat Heywood
Clarine	Judy Cornwell
Albie	Michael Gothard
Angela	Jacqueline Cowper
Peter	Richard Beaumont
Katherine	Charlotte Sayce
Miss Wilcox	Marianne Stone

Right: Mark Lester, Shelley Winters, Chloe Franks

**Chloe Franks, Shelley Winters
Above: Ralph Richardson, Shelley Winters**

**Judy Cornwell, Michael Gothard Above:
Hugh Griffith, Chloe Franks, Mark Lester**

KIDNAPPED

(AMERICAN INTERNATIONAL) Producer, Frederick H. Brogger; Director, Delbert Mann; Associate Producer, Hugh Attwooll; Screenplay, Jack Pulman; Based on Robert Louis Stevenson's "Kidnapped" and "David Balfour"; Photography, Paul Beeson; Music, Roy Budd; Art Director, Vetchinsky; Costumes, Olga Lehmann; "For All My Days" sung by Mary Hopkin; An Omnibus Production in Panavision and Movielab Color; 100 minutes; Rating G; December release.

CAST

Alan Breck	Michael Caine
Lord Advocate Grant	Trevor Howard
Captain Hoseason	Jack Hawkins
Ebenezer Balfour	Donald Pleasence
Charles Stewart	Gordon Jackson
Catriona	Vivien Heilbron
David Balfour	Lawrence Douglas
Cluny	Freddie Jones
James Stewart	Jack Watson
Andrew	Andrew McCulloch
Doctor	Eric Woodburn
Duke of Cumberland	Roger Booth
Lord Advocate's Secretary	Russell Waters
Simon Campbell	John Hughes
Barbara Grant	Claire Nielson
Lt. Duncansby	Geoffrey Whitehead
Riach	Peter Jeffrey
Mungo Campbell	Terry Richards

Left: Vivien Heilbron, Lawrence Douglas

Jack Watson, Vivien Heilbron, Michael Caine, Lawrence Douglas

Lawrence Douglas, Vivien Heilbron
Above: Michael Caine Top: Jack Hawkins, Donald
Pleasence, Lawrence Douglas

Vivien Heilbron, Michael Caine

A CLOCKWORK ORANGE

(WARNER BROS.) Produced, Directed, and Written by Stanley Kubrick; From novel by Anthony Burgess; Executive Producers, Max L. Raab, Si Litvinoff; Photography, John Alcott; Designer, John Barry; Art Director, Russell Hagg; Music, Walter Carlos; Assistant Directors, Derek Cracknell, Dusty Symonds, Bill Welch; In Color; 137 minutes; Rating X; December release.

CAST

Alex	Malcolm McDowell
Mr. Alexander	Patrick Magee
Mrs. Alexander	Adrienne Corri
Deltold	Aubrey Morris
Georgie	James Marcus
Dim	Warren Clarke
Pete	Michael Tarn
Mum	Sheila Raynor
Dad	Philip Stone
Cat Lady	Miriam Karlin
Chaplain	Godfrey Quigley
Chief Guard	Michael Bates
Stage Actor	John Clive
Dro. Brodsky	Carl Duering
Tramp	Paul Farrell
Lodger	Clive Francis
Prison Governor	Michael Gover
Dr. Branum	Madge Ryan
Conspirator	John Savident
Minister	Anthony Sharp
Psychiatrist	Pauline Taylor
Conspirator	Margaret Tyzack

and Steven Berkoff, Lindsay Campbell, David Prowse, Barrie Cookson, Jan Adair, Gaye Brown, Peter Burton, John J. Carney, Vivienne Chandler, Richard Connaught, Prudence Drage, Carol Drinkwater, Lee Fox, Cheryl Grunwald, Gillian Hills, Craig Hunter, Shirley Jaffe, Barbara Scott, Virginia Weatherell, Neil Wilson, Katya Wyeth

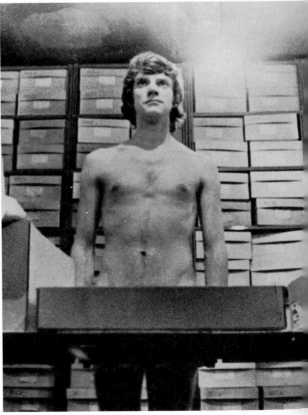

Warren Clarke, Adrienne Corri, Malcolm McDowell
Above: Malcolm McDowell (C)

Malcolm McDowell, also
at top

Malcolm McDowell
Top: Michael Bates (L), Malcolm McDowell (R)

Warren Clarke, Malcolm McDowell, James Marcus
(also at top)
in "A Clockwork Orange"

DIAMONDS ARE FOREVER

(UNITED ARTISTS) Producers, Albert R. Broccoli, Harry Saltzman; Director, Guy Hamilton; Screenplay, Richard Maibaum, Tom Mankiewicz; Based on Ian Fleming story; Photography, Ted Moore; Music, John Barry; Designer, Ken Adams; Assistant Directors, Derek Cracknell, Jerome M. Siegel; In Technicolor; 119 minutes; Rating GP; December release.

CAST

James Bond	Sean Connery
Tiffany Case	Jill St. John
Blofeld	Charles Gray
Plenty O'Toole	Lana Wood
Willard Whyte	Jimmy Dean
Saxby	Bruce Cabot
Wint	Bruce Glover
Kidd	Putter Smith
Felix Leiter	Norman Burton
'M'	Bernard Lee
'Q'	Desmond Llewelyn
Shady Tree	Leonard Barr
Mrs. Whistler	Margaret Lacey
Miss Moneypenny	Lois Maxwell
Peter Franks	Joe Robinson
Bambi	Donna Garratt
Thumper	Trina Parks
Klaus Hergersheimer	Edward Bishop
Barker	Larry Blake
Dentist	Henry Rowland
Doorman	Nicky Blair
Aide to Metz	Constantin De Goguel

Sean Connery (L) and Top Right

NICHOLAS AND ALEXANDRA

(COLUMBIA) Producer, Sam Spiegel; Director, Franklin J. Schaffner; Screenplay, James Goldman; From book by Robert K. Massie; Designer, John Box; Photography, Freddie Young; Music, Richard Rodney Bennett; Associate Producer, Andrew Donally; Costumes, Yvonne Blake, Antonio Castillo; Assistant Director, Jose Lopez Rodero; Music performed by New Philharmonia Orchestra of London conducted by Marcus Dods; An Horizon Film in Panavision and Color; 183 minutes plus intermission; Rating GP; December release.

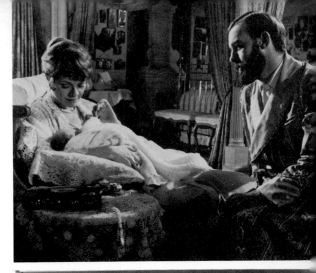

CAST

The Royal Family:
Nicholas	Michael Jayston
Alexandra	Janet Suzman
Alexis	Roderic Noble
Olga	Ania Marson
Tatiana	Lynne Frederick
Marie	Candace Glendenning
Anastasia	Fiona Fullerton
Grand Duke Nicholas	Harry Andrews
Queen Mother Marie Fedorovna	Irene Worth

Royal Household:
Rasputin	Tom Baker
Count Fredericks	Jack Hawkins
Dr. Botkin	Timothy West
Tegleva	Katharine Schofield
Gilliard	Jean-Claude Drouot
Nagorny	John Hallam
Dr. Fedorov	Guy Rolfe
Col. Kobylinsky	John Wood

Statesmen:
Count Witte	Laurence Olivier
Stolypin	Eric Porter
Sazonov	Michael Redgrave
Kokovtsov	Maurice Denham
Rodzianko	Ralph Truman
Guchkov	Gordon Gostelow
Kerensky	John McEnery

Revolutionaries:
Lenin	Michael Bryant
Mme. Krupskaya	Vivian Pickles
Trotsky	Brian Cox
Stalin	James Hazeldine
Martov	Stephen Greif
Pankratov	Steven Berkoff
Plekhanov	Eric Chapman
Yakovlev	Ian Holm
Yurevsky	Alan Webb
Avadeyev	Leon Lissek
Goloshchekin	David Giles

Other Characters:
General Alexiev	Roy Dotrice
Prince Yussoupcv	Martin Potter
Grand Duke Dmitri	Richard Warwick
Dr. Lazovert	Vernon Dobtcheff
American Ambassador Root	Alexander Knox
British Ambassador Buchanan	Ralph Neville
French Ambassador Paleologue	Jorge Rigaud
German Consul Sklarz	Curt Jergens
Gapon	Julian Glover
Petya	John Shrapnel
Sonya	Diana Quick

**Janet Suzman, Michael Jayston,
also Top Right Below: Janet Suzman, Tom Baker**

**Michael Redgrave, Jaime DeMora y Aragon, Maurice Denha
Michael Jayston, Laurence Olivier, Harry Andrews,
John Forbes-Robertson**

Academy Awards for Best Costumes, and Best Set and Art Direction in 1971

John McEnery Top: Candace Glendenning, Janet Suzman,
Roderic Noble, Lynne Frederick, Ania Marson,
Michael Jayston, Fiona Fullerton

Michael Bryant

191

MACBETH

(COLUMBIA) Producer, Andrew Braunsberg; Director, Roman Polanski; Executive Producer, Hugh M. Hefner; Screenplay, Roman Polanski, Kenneth Tynan; Based on play by William Shakespeare; Associate Producer, Timothy Burrill; Photography, Gil Taylor; Designer, Anthony Mendleson; Costumes, Anthony Mendleson; Music, The Third Ear Band; Assistant Executive Producer, Victor Lownes; Assistant Director, Simon Relph; Choreographer, Sally Gilpin; A Playboy Production in Todd-AO 35; 140 minutes; Rating R; December release.

CAST

Macbeth	Jon Finch
Lady Macbeth	Francesca Annis
Banquo	Martin Shaw
Duncan	Nicholas Selby
Ross	John Stride
Malcolm	Stephan Chase
Donalbain	Paul Shelley
Macduff	Terence Bayler
Lennox	Andrew Laurence
Mentieth	Frank Wylie
Angus	Bernard Archard
Caithness	Bruce Purchase
Fleance	Keith Chegwin
Seyton	Noel Davis
Young Witch	Noelle Rimmington
Blind Witch	Maisie MacFarquhar
First Witch	Elsie Taylor
Cawdor	Vic Abbott
King's Groom 1	Bill Drysdale
King's Groom 2	Roy Jones
Gentlewoman	Patricia Mason
First Minor Thane	Ian Hogg
Second Minor Thane	Geoffrey Reed
Third Minor Thane	Nigel Ashton
Macduff's son	Mark Dightam
Lady Macduff	Diane Fletcher
Doctor	Richard Pearson
Porter	Sydney Bromley
Young Seyward	William Hobbs
Old Seyward	Alf Joint
First Murderer	Michael Balfour
Second Murderer	Andrew McCulloch
First Old Soldier	Howard Lang
Second Old Soldier	David Ellison
Soldier	Terence Mountain
Boy Apprentice	Paul Hennen

Dancers .... Beth Owen, Maxine Skelton, Janie Kells, Olga Anthony, Roy Desmond, Pam Foster, John Gordon, Barbara Grimes, Aud Johansen, Dickie Martyn, Christina Paul, Don Vernon, Anna Willoughby

Jon Finch, Francesca Annis
(also at top)

Top: Francesca Annis, Patricia Mason

192

Jon Finch, Francesca Annis

MARY, QUEEN OF SCOTS

(UNIVERSAL) Producer, Hal B. Wallis; Director, Charles Jarrott; Screenplay, John Hale; Photography, Christopher Challis; Designer, Terry Marsh; Costumes, Margaret Furse; Music, John Barry; Assistant Director, Simon Relph; In Technicolor and Panavision; 128 minutes; Rating GP; December release.

CAST

Mary, Queen of Scots	Vanessa Redgrave
Queen Elizabeth	Glenda Jackson
James Stuart	Patrick McGoohan
Henry, Lord Darnley	Timothy Dalton
Lord Bothwell	Nigel Davenport
William Cecil	Trevor Howard
Robert Dudley	Daniel Massey
David Riccio	Ian Holm
Ruthven	Andrew Keir
Father Ballard	Tom Fleming
Catherine de Medici	Katherine Kath
Mary Seton	Beth Harris
Mary Fleming	Frances White
Morton	Bruce Purchase
Huntly	Brian Coburn
Duc de Guise	Vernon Dobtcheff
Cardinal de Guise	Raf De La Torre
Walsingham	Richard Warner
Lady Bothwell	Maria Aitken
Andrew	Jeremy Bulloch
John Knox	Robert James
Francis, King of France	Richard Denning

Daniel Massey, Glenda Jackson, Trevor Howard
Top Right: Vanessa Redgrave

Vanessa Redgrave, and above with Timothy Dalton
Top: Vanessa Redgrave, Ian Holm, Patrick McGoohan

Glenda Jackson, and above
with Daniel Massey

THE BOY FRIEND

(MGM) Produced, Directed, and Written by Ken Russell; Based on Sandy Wilson's musical of same name; Photographer, David Watkin; Designer, Tony Walton; Assistant Director, Graham Ford; In Metrocolor; 110 minutes; Rating G; December release.

CAST

Polly Browne	Twiggy
Tony Brockhurst	Christopher Gable
Madame Dubonnet	Moyra Fraser
Max (Lord Brockhurst)	Max Adrian
Percy	Bryan Pringle
Lady Brockhurst	Catherine Wilmer
Alphonse	Murray Melvin
Fay	Georgina Hale
Nancy	Sally Bryant
De Thrill	Vladek Sheybal
Tommy	Tommy Tune
Rita	Glenda Jackson
Masie	Antonia Ellis
Dulcie	Caryl Little
Michael	Graham Armitage
Peter	Brian Murphy
Mrs. Peter	Ann Jameson
Chauffeur	Robert LaBassiere
Hortense	Barbara Windsor

Left: Christopher Gable, Twiggy

Twiggy, Tommy Tune
Above: Max Adrian, Twiggy

Moyra Fraser, Twiggy
Above: Antonia Ellis, Caryl Little,
Sally Bryant, Georgina Hale

Caryl Little, Antonia Ellis, Twiggy
Above: Moyra Fraser, Bryan Pringle, Christopher Gable,
Twiggy, Max Adrian Top: Gable, Twiggy

Christopher Gable, Caryl Little, Twiggy
Above: Antonia Ellis, Tommy Tune

STRAW DOGS

(CINERAMA) Producer, Daniel Melnick; Director, Sam Peckinpah; Screenplay, Sam Peckinpah, David Zelag Goodman; Based on Gordon Williams' novel "Siege at Trencher's Farm"; Photography, John Coquillon; Music, Jerry Fielding; An ABC Pictures presentation in EastmanColor; 113 minutes; December release.

CAST

David	Dustin Hoffman
Amy	Susan George
Tom Hedden	Peter Vaughan
Major Scott	T. P. McKenna
Venner	Del Henney
Scutt	Ken Hutchison
Rev. Hood	Colin Welland
Cawsey	Jim Norton
Janice	Sally Thomsett
Riddaway	Donald Webster
Bobby Hedden	Len Jones
Bertie Hedden	Michael Mundell
John Niles	Peter Arne
Harry Ware	Robert Keegan
Mrs. Hedden	June Brown
Emma Hedden	Chloe Franks
Mrs. Hood	Cherina Mann

Ken Hutchison, Dustin Hoffman, Susan George, Del Heeney

Top: Peter Vaughan, Del Heeney, Dustin Hoffman, Robert Keegan

Dustin Hoffman, Susan George

THE GARDEN OF THE FINZI-CONTINIS

(CINEMA V) Producers, Gianni Hecht, Lucari, and Arthur Cohn; Director, Vittorio De Sica; Screenplay, Cesare Zavattini, Vittorio Bonicelli, Ugo Pirro; Based on novel by Giorgio Bassani; Music, Manuel De Sica; 95 minutes; Rating R; December release.

CAST
Micol .... Dominique Sanda
Giorgio .... Lino Capolicchio
Alberto .... Helmut Berger
Malnate .... Fabio Testi
Giorgio's father .... Romolo Valli

Left: Dominique Sanda

Dominique Sanda, Lino Catolicchio
Academy Award for Best Foreign Language Film in 1971

Dominique Sanda, Lino Catolicchio

**Dominique Sanda (also top)
in "The Garden of the Finzi-Continis"**

LE BOUCHER

(CINERAMA) Producer, Andre Genevoese; Direction and Screenplay, Claude Chabrol; Photography, Jean Rabier; Music, Pierre Jansen; Costumes, Joseph Poulard; A Franco-Italian Co-Production in Color; 93 minutes; December release.

CAST

Helene	Stephane Audran
Popaul the butcher	Jean Yanne
Angelo	Antonio Passallia
Leon Hamel	Mario Beccaria
Pere Cahrpy	Pasquale Ferone
Police Inspector	Roger Rudel
Charles	William Gerrault

Stephane Audran, Jean Yanne
(also top right)

**Adrienne LaRussa, Rossano Brazzi
in "Psychout for Murder"**

**Patrick Allen, Lorna Wilde
in "The Body Stealers"**

THE RECKONING (Columbia) Producer, Ronald Shedlo; Director, Jack Gold; Screenplay, John McGrath; Based on novel "The Harp That Once" by Patrick Hall; Photography, Geoffrey Unsworth; Music, Malcolm Arnold; Art Director, Ray Simm; Associate Producer, Hugh Perceval; Assistant Director, Douglas Hermes; In Technicolor; 111 minutes; Rating R; January release. CAST: Nicol Williamson (Michael), Rachel Roberts (Joyce), Paul Rogers (John), Zena Walker (Hilda), Ann Bell (Rosemary), Douglas Wilmer (Moyle), Gwen Nelson (Michael's mother), Christine Hargreaves (Michael's sister), Tom Kempinski (Brunzy), J. G. Devlin (Cocky).

PSYCHOUT FOR MURDER (Times) Producer, Oscar Brazzi; Directors, Edward Ross, Ted Kneeland; Music, Benedetto Ghiglia; An International Co-Productions Films in Eastmancolor and Wide Screen; Rating R; 88 minutes; January release. CAST: Adrienne La Russa (Licia), Rossano Brazzi (Daddy), Nino Castelnuovo (Mario), Paola Pitagora (Giovanna), Alberto De Mendoza (Francesco), Idelma Carlo (Laura), Renzo Petretto (Paterlini), Nestor Garay (Politician).

BEAST OF BLOOD (Marvin) Executive Producer, Kane W. Lynn; Producer-Director, Eddie Romero; Associate Director, Armando Herrera; Screenplay, Eddie Romero; Story, Beverly Miller; Music, Tito Arevalo; Photography, Justo Paulino; Assistant Director, Maria Abelardo; A Sceptre Production in Color; Rating GP; 90 minutes; January release. CAST: John Ashley (Bill), Celeste Yarnell (Myra), Alfonso Carvajal (Ramu), Lisa Belmonte (Laida), Bruno Punzalan (Razak), Eddie Garcia (Dr. Lorca) and Angel Buenaventura, Beverly Miller, Johnny Long.

FROM EAR TO EAR (Cinemation) Director, Louis Soulanes; Music, Clay Pitts; Co-Production by Les Activites Cinegraphiques/Claude Capra; Presented by Jerry Gross; in DeLuxe Color and Wide Screen; Rating X; 81 minutes; January release. CAST: Nicole Debonne (Elisa), Solange Pradel (Lucile), Daniele Argence (Josine), Liliane Bert (Beatrice), Robert Lombard (Borco), Jean Gavin (Bruno), Alain Doutey (Andre).

CURSE OF THE VAMPIRES (Marvin) Executive Producer, Amalia Muhlach; Director, Gerardo De Leon; Screenplay, Ben Feleo, Pierre L. Salas; Story, Ben Feleo; Music, Tito Arevalo; Lyrics, Robert Aravelo; Photography, Mike Accion; Assistant Director, Dik Trofeo; In Eastman Color; Rating GP; 90 minutes; January release. CAST: Amalia Fuentes, Romeo Vasquez, Eddie Garcia, Johnny Monteiro, Rosario Del Pilar, Mary Walter, Francisco Cruz, Paquito Salcedo, Quiel Mendoza, Andres Benitez, Luz Angeles, Tessie Hernandez, Linda Rivers.

THE BODY STEALERS (Allied Artists) Producer, Tony Tenser; Director, Gerry Levy; Photography, Peter Henry; A Tigon British-Saggittarius Production in Color; Rating R; January release. CAST: George Sanders (Armstrong), Maurice Evans (Matthews), Patrick Allen (Bob), Neil Connery (Jim), Robert Flemyng (Baldwin), Lorna Wilde (Lorna), Alan Cuthbertson (Hindsmith), Carl Rigg (Briggs), Hilary Dwyer (Julie), Sally Faulkner (Joanna), Michael Culver (Bailes), Carol Ann Hawkins (Paula), Shelagh Fraser (Mrs. Thatcher), Jan Miller (Sally).

THE BRIDGE IN THE JUNGLE (United Artists) Produced, Directed and Written by Pancho Kohner; Screenplay based on novel by B. Traven; Photography, Javier Cruz; Music, Leroy Holmes; In Color; January release. CAST: John Huston (Sleigh), Charles Robinson (Gales), Katy Jurado (Angela), and Elizabeth Guadalupe Chauvet, Jose Angel Espinoza, Enrique Lucero, Jorge Martinez de Hoyo, Xavier Mark, Aurora Clavel, Chano Urueta, Teddy Stauffer, Eduardo Lopez Rojas, Jose Chavez Trow, Sergio Calderon, Enrique de Pena, Ramiro Ramirez, Carlos Beriochoa, Juan Antonio Edwards, Elizabeth Dupeyron, Gilberto Ramos Atayde.

THE BODY (Anglo-Emi) Producer, Tony Garnett; Director, Roy Battersby; Photography, Tony Imi; Music, Ron Geesin, Roger Waters; Commentary, Adrian Mitchell, with extracts from the writings of William Blake; Voices of Vanessa Redgrave, Frank Finlay; A Kestrel Film in Technicolor; Presented by Nat Cohen; 111 minutes; Rating R; February release.

**Daniele Argence, Solange Pradel
in "From Ear to Ear"**

**Katy Jurado, John Huston (R)
in "The Bridge in the Jungle"**

**Victoria Vetri, Robin Hawdon
in "When Dinosaurs Ruled the Earth"**

**Jean Simmons, Leonard Whiting
in "Say Hello to Yesterday"**

WHEN DINOSAURS RULED THE EARTH (Warner Bros.) Producer, Aida Young; Direction and Screenplay, Val Guest; Photography, Dick Bush; Music, Mario Nascimbene; Costumes, Carl Toms; Assistant Director, John Stoneman; A Hammer Film in Technicolor; Rating G; 96 minutes; February release. CAST: Victoria Vetri (Sanna), Robin Hawdon (Tara), Patrick Allen (Kingsor), Drewe Henley (Khaku), Sean Caffrey (Kane), Magda Konopka (Ulido), Imogen Hassall (Ayak), Patrick Holt (Ammon), Jan Rossini (Rock Girl), Carol-Anne Hawkins (Yani), Maria O'Brien (Omah), Connie Tilton (Sand Mother), Maggie Lynton (Rock Mother), Jimmy Lodge (Fisherman), Billy Cornelius, Ray Ford (Hunters).

RELATIONS (Cambist) Producer, Sam Lomberg; Direction and Screenplay, Hans Abramson; Photography, Mikael Salomon; Music, Made in Sweden; Costumes, Evy Mark; A Forbes Ltd-Cineworld Production in Color; Rating R; 91 minutes; February release. CAST: Gertie Jung (Sonja), Bjorn Puggaard Muller (Papa), Paul Glargard (Egon), Dorthea Ross (Rigmor).

SOME GIRLS DO (United Artists) Producer, Betty E. Box; Director, Ralph Thomas; Screenplay, David Osborne, Liz Charles-Williams; Associate Producer, James Ware; Assistant Director, Simon Relph; Costumes, Yvonne Caffin; A Rank Production in DeLuxe Color; February release. CAST: Richard Johnson (Hugh), Daliah Lavi (Helga), Beba Loncar (Pandora), James Villiers (Carl), Vanessa Howard (#7), Sydne Rome (Flicky), Maurice Denham (Mortimer), Robert Morley (Miss Mary), Ronnie Stevens (Carruthers), Virginia North (#9), Adrienne Posta (Angela), Florence Desmond (Lady Manderley).

LA HORA DE LOS HORNOS (The Hour of the Furnaces) (Third World Cinema) Produced, Directed, Written by Fernando Ezequiel Solanas, Photography, Juan Carlos de Sanzo, Mr. Solanas; 90 minutes; February release. A documentary on politics in Argentina.

SAY HELLO TO YESTERDAY (Cinerama) Producer, Josef Shaftel; Director, Alvin Rakoff; Screenplay, Alvin Rakoff, Peter King; Photography, Geoffrey Unsworth; Assistant Directors, Anthony Waye, Russel Wolnough; Designer, Wilfrid Shingleton; Music, Riz Ortolani; In EastmanColor; 91 minutes; Rating GP; February release. CAST: Jean Simmons (Woman), Leonard Whiting (Roy), Evelyn Laye (Woman's mother), John Lee (Woman's husband), Jack Woolgar (Boy's father), Constance Chapman (Boy's mother), Gwen Nelson (Char), Richard Pescaud (Labor Exchange Official), Laraine Humphreys (Teenager), Nen Aris (Floorwalker), Nora Nicholson (Aged lady), Jimmy Gardner (Balloon seller), Carla Challoner (Au Pair girl).

THE NIGHT VISITOR (UMC) Producer, Mel Ferrer; Director, Laslo Benedek; Screenplay, Guy Elmes; From story by Samuel Rosecca; Photography, Henning Kristiansen; Music, Henri Mancini; In EastmanColor; 102 minutes; Rating GP; February release. CAST: Max Von Sydow (Salem), Trevor Howard (Inspector), Liv Ullmann (Esther), Per Oscarsson (Dr. Jenks), Rupert Davies (Clemens), Andrew Keir (Dr. Kemp), Arthur Hewlett (Pop), Jim Kennedy (Carl), Hanne Bork (Emmie), Bjorn Watt Boolsen (Tokens), Lottie Freddie (Britt).

THE MAN WHO HAD POWER OVER WOMEN (AVCO Embassy) Executive Producer, Leonard Lightstone; Producer, Judd Bernard; Director, John Krish; Screenplay, Alan Scott, Chris Bryant; From novel by Gordon Williams; Associate Producer, Patricia Casey; Photography, Gerry Turpin; Costumes, Brian Cox; Music, John Mandell; Lyrics, Hal David; Assistant Director, Barry Langley; A Kettledrum Production in EastmanColor; Presented by Joseph E. Levine; Rating R; 89 minutes; March release. CAST: Rod Taylor (Peter), Carol White (Jody), James Booth (Val), Penelope Horner (Angela), Charles Korvin (Felix), Alexandra Stewart (Frances), Keith Barron (Jake), Clive Francis (Barry), Marie-France Boyer (Maggie), Magali Noel (Mrs. Franchetti), Geraldine Moffat (Lydia), Wendy Hamilton (Mary), Ellis Dale (Norman), Sara Booth (Sarah), Matthew Booth (Mark).

**Daliah Lavi, Richard Johnson
in "Some Girls Do"**

**Rod Taylor, Marie-France Boyer
in "The Man Who Had Power over Women"**

"THX 1138"

"Beyond Love and Evil"

THE GARDEN OF DELIGHTS (Perry/Fleetwood) Producer, Elias Querieta; Director, Carlos Saura; Screenplay, Ragael Azcona, Carlos Saura; Photography, Luis Quadrado; Music, Luis de Pablo; 99 minutes; Rating GP; February release. CAST: Jose Luis Lopez Vasquez (Antonio), Luchy Soto (Luchy), Francisco Pierra (Don Pedro), Charo Soriano (Actress), Lina Canalejas (Aunt), Julia Pena (Julia), Mayrata O'Wisledo (Nurse), Esperanza Roy (Nicole), Alberto Alonso (Tony).

THX 1138 (Warner Bros.) Producer, Lawrence Sturhahn; Director, George Lucas; Screenplay, Geroge Lucas, Walter Murch; Story, George Lucas; Photography, Dave Meyers, Albert Kihn; Music, Lalo Schifrin; In Color; 88 minutes; Rating GP; March release. CAST: Robert Duvall (THX), Donald Pleasence (SEN), Maggie McOmie (LUH), Don Pedro Colley (SRT).

BEYOND LOVE AND EVIL (Allied Artists) Director, Jacques Scandelari; Screenplay, Jean Stuart, Jean Pierre Deloux, Jacques Scandelari; Photography, Jean Marc Ripert; Music, Jean Claude Pelletier; Costumes, Jean Bouquin; Comptoir Francais du Film Production in Color; 89 minutes; Rating X; March release. CAST: Souchka (Xenia), Lucas de Chabanieux (Zenoff), Fred Saint-James (Yalo), Marc Coutant (Young Man), Sabrina (Himself), Serge Halsdorf (Worlac), Michel Lablais (Ladies' Man), Milarka Nervi (Initiator), Dorsi Thon (Panther Woman), Nicole Huc (Driven-out-woman), Nadia Kempf (Lolita), Ursule Pauly (25 year old woman).

FRIENDS (Paramount) Producer-Director, Lewis Gilbert; Screenplay, Jack Russell, Vernon Harris; Music, Elton John, Bernie Taupin; Associate Producer, Geoffrey Helman; Photography, Andreas Winding; Assistant Director, William Cartlidge; In Technicolor; 102 minutes; Rating R; March release. CAST: Sean Bury (Paul), Anicee Alvina (Michelle), Pascale Roberts (Annie), Sady Rebbot (Pierre), Ronald Lewis (Harrison), Toby Robins (Mrs. Gardner), Joan Hinkson (Lady in bookshop), and natives of Camargue, France.

CHIKAMATZU MONOGATARI ("The Crucified Lovers") (New Line Cinema) Producer, Masaichi Nagata; Director, Kenji Mizoguchi; Screenplay, Yoshikota Yoda, Matsutaro Kwaguchi; After a Kabuki drama; Photography, Kazuo Miyagawa; Music, Fumio Hayasaka, Famezo Mochizuki, Gyiro Toyrsawa; 100 minutes; A Daiei Production; March release. CAST: Kazuo Hasegawa (Mohei), Kyrko Kogowa (Osan), Yoko Minamida (Otama), Eitaro Shindo (Ishun), Sakal Ozawa (Sukeyemon), Chieko Naniwa (Oko), Ichiro Sugai (Genebei), Haru Tanaka (Doki), Tatsuya Isheguro (Ison).

THE TENDER MOMENT (Maron) Producer, Francis Cosne; Director, Michel Boisrond; Screenplay, Claude Brule, Annette Wademanf, Michel Boisrond; Photography, Jean-Marc Ripert; Music, Francis Lai; In Color; Rating GP; March release. CAST: Renaud Verley (Olivier), Nathalie Delon (Frederique), Robert Hossein (Enrico), Bernard LeCoq (Jean-Pierre), Katia Cristina (Christine).

GET CARTER (MGM) Producer, Michael Klinger; Direction and Screenplay, Mike Hodges; Based on novel "Jack's Return Home" by Ted Lewis; Music, Roy Budd; Lyrics, Jack Fishman; Photography, Wolfgang Suschitzky; Designer, Asheton Gorton; Assistant Director, Keith Evans; Costumes, Vangie Harrison; In MetroColor; 111 minutes; Rating R; March release. CAST: Michael Caine (Jack Carter), Ian Hendry (Eric), Britt Ekland (Anna), John Osborne (Kinnear), Tony Beckley (Peter), George Sewell (Con), Geraldine Moffatt (Glenda), Dorothy White (Margaret), Rosemarie Dunham (Edna), Petra Markham (Doreen), Alun Armstrong (Keith), Bryan Mosley (Brumby), Glynn Edwards (Albert), Bernard Hepton (Thorpe), Terence Rigby (Gerald), John Bindon (Sid), Godfrey Quigley (Eddie), Kevin Brennan (Harry), Maxwell Dees (Vicar), Liz McKenzie (Mrs. Bumbry), Kitty Attwood (Old Woman), Denea Wilde (Pub Singer), and John Hussey, Ben Aris, Geraldine Sherman, Joy Merlyn, Yvonne Michaels, Alan Hockey.

**Sean Bury, Anicee Alvina
in "Friends"**

**Michael Caine
in "Get Carter"**

**John Marley, James Garner
in "A Man Called Sledge"**

**Christopher Lee, Nyree Dawn Porter
in "The House that Dripped Blood"**

A MAN CALLED SLEDGE (Columbia) Producer, Dino De Laurentiis; Director, Vic Morrow; Screenplay, Vic Morrow, Frank Kowalski; Photography, Luigi Kuveiller; Music, Giani Ferrio; In Color; 90 minutes; Rating R; March release. CAST: James Garner (Sledge), Dennis Weaver (Ward), Claude Akins (Hooker), John Marley (Old Man), Laura Antonelli (Ria), Wayne Preston (Ripley), Ken Clark (Floyd), Tony Young (Mallory).

THE HOUSE THAT DRIPPED BLOOD (Cinerama) Executive Producers, Paul Ellsworth, Gordon Wescourt; Producers, Max J. Rosenberg, Milton Subotsky; Director, Peter Duffell; Screenplay, Robert Bloch; Photography, Ray Parslow; Music, Michael Dress; Art Director, Tony Curtis; Assistant Director, Peter Beale; An Amicus Picture in EastmanColor; 101 minutes; Rating GP; March release. CAST: Denholm Elliott (Charles), Joanna Dunham (Alice), Tom Adams (Dominick), Robert Lang (Psychiatrist), Peter Cushing (Philip), Joss Ackland (Rogers), Wolfe Morris (Waxworks Owner), Christopher Lee (Reid), Nyree Dawn Porter (Ann), Chloe Franks (Jane), Jon Pertwee (Paul), Ingrid Pitt (Carla), Geoffrey Bayldon (Von Hartmann), John Bennett (Holloway), John Bryans (Stoker).

FIDELIO (Beta) Director, Gustav Rudolf Sellner; Libretto, Josef Sonnleithner, Goerge Friedrich Treitschke; Photography, Ernst Wild; Music, Ludwig Van Beethoven; Conductor, Karl Bohm; Chorus and Orchestra of Deutsche Oper Berlin; Sung in German; A Unitel-Neue Thalia-Beta Film production in Color; 115 minutes; March release. CAST: Gwyneth Jones (Leonore), James King (Florestan), Gustav Neidlinger (Don Pizzaro), Josef Greindl (Rocco), Donald Grobe (Jacquino), Martti Talvela (Don Fernando), Olivera Miljakovic (Marzelline), Barry McDaniel (Prisoner).

THIS TRANSIENT LIFE (Toho) Producer, Jossoji Productions; Director, Akio Jissoji; Screenplay, Yashiro Ishido; Photography, Yozo Inagaki; Music, Toru Fuyuki; 140 minutes; March release. CAST: Ryo Tamura (The Boy), Michiko Tsukasa (His Sister), Eiji Okada (Sculptor).

SILENCE HAS NO WINGS (Toho) Producer, Nippon Shinsha; Director, Kazuo Kuroki; Screenplay, Yasuo Matasukawa, Hisaya Iwasa, Kazuo Kuroki; Photography, Tatsuo Suzuki; Music, Teizo Matsumara; 103 minutes; March release. CAST: Mariko Kaga, Fumio Watanabe, Hiroyuki Nagato, Toshie Kumura, Kunie Tanaka.

INNOCENCE UNPROTECTED (Grove Press) Directed and Written by Dusan Makavejev; Photography, Branko Perak, Stevan Miskobic; An Avala Film; 75 minutes; March release. CAST: Dragoliub Aleksic (Dragoliub), Ana Milosavljevic (Orphan Nada), Vera Jovanovic (Stepmother), Bratoljub Gligorijevic (Petrovic), Ivan Zirkovic (Brother), Pera Milosavljevic (Servant).

DEAD OF SUMMER (Plaza) Producer-Director, Nelo Risi; Story and Screenplay, Anna Gobbi, Nelo Risi, Roger Mauge; Based on novel by Dana Moseley; Photography, Giulio Albonico; Music, Peppino De Luca, Carlo Pas; 89 minutes; March release. CAST: Jean Seberg (Joyce), Luigi Pistilli (Dr. Volterra), Paolo Modugno (Ali), Lilia Nguyen (Maid), Gianni Belfiore (Cherif), Franco Acampora (Bianchi), Stefano Oppedisano (Consul Mayer).

DOUBLE SUICIDE (Toho) Producers, Masayuki Nakajima, Masahiro Shinoda; Director, Masahiro Shinoda; Screenplay, Taeko Tomioka, Masahiro Shinoda, Toru Takemitsu; Based on play by Monzaemon Chikamatsu; Photography, Toichiro Narushima; Music, Toru Takemitsu; Art Director, Kiyoshi Awazu; Black and White; 104 minutes; March release. CAST: Kichiemon Nakamura (Jihei), Shima Iwashita (Koharu/Osan), Hosei Komatsu (Magoemon), Kamatari Fujiwara (Owner of Yamatoya), Yoshi Kato (Gosaemon), Shisue Kawarazaki (Osan's mother), Tokie Hidari (Osugi).

KAMA SUTRA (Trans America) Producer-Directors, Kobi Jaeger, Richard R. Rimmel; Music, Irmin Schmidt; In Color; 90 minutes; March release. No other credits. CAST: Haydee Politoff, Corrado Pani.

**Renaud Verley, Katia Cristina
in "The Tender Moment"**

"Double Suicide"

Flora Robson, Beryl Reid
in "The Beast in the Cellar"

Anna Gael
in "Nana"

I WANT TO BE A SHELLFISH (Toho) Direction and Screenplay, Shinobu Hashimoto; Based on writings of Tetsutaro Kato; Photography, Asaichi Nakai; Music, Masaru Sato; 113 minutes; Black and White; March release. CAST: Furanki Sakai (Toyomatsu), Michiyo Aratama (His wife), Akio Suano (Son), Kumi Mizuno (Toshiko), Daisuke Kato (Takeuchi), Susumu Fujita (General), Kamatari Fujiwara (Adachi), Chishu Ryu (Komiyo).

THE BEAST IN THE CELLAR (Cannon) Producer, Graham Harris; Direction and Screenplay, James Kelly; Associate Producer, Christopher Neame; Photography, Harry Waxman; Assistant Director, Dominic Fulford; Music, Tony Macauley; A Tigon British Production in association with Leander Films; In Color; Rating R; 100 minutes; April release. CAST: Beryl Reid (Ellie), Flora Robson (Joyce), John Hamill (Alan), Tessa Wyatt (Nurse), T. P. McKenna (Det. Paddick), John Kelland (Sgt. Young), David Dodimead (Dr. Spencer), Vernon Dodtcheff (Newsmath), Dafydd Havard (Stephen), Gail Lidstone (Young Ellie), Elisabeth Choice (Young Joyce), Merlin Ward (Young Stephen), Christopher Chittell (Baker), Anthony Heaton (Anderson), Peter Craze (Roy), Anabel Littledale (Gloria), Howard Rawlinson (Young Soldier), Roberta Tovey (Paper Girl), Robert Wilde (Soldier), Reg Lever (Ambulance Man).

THE BLOOD ON SATAN'S CLAW (Cannon) Executive Producer, Tony Tenser; Producers, Peter Andrews, Malcolm Heyworth; Director, Piers Haggard; Screenplay, Robert Wynne Simmons; Photography, Dick Bush; Assistant Director, Stephen Christian; Music, Marc Wilkinson; A Tigon British/Chilton Film Production in Color; Rating R; 100 mins; April release. CAST: Patrick Wymark (Judge), Linda Hayden (Angel), Barry Andrews (Ralph), Michele Dotrice (Margaret), Wendy Padbury (Cathy), Anthony Ainley (Rev. Fallowfield), Charlotte Mitchell (Ellen), Tamara Ustinov (Rosalind), Simon Williams (Peter), James Hayter (Middleton), Howard Goorney (Doctor), Avice Landon (Isobel), Robin Davies (Mark).

NANA (Distinction) Producer, Tore Sjoberg; Direction and Screenplay, Mac Ahlberg; Based on Emile Zola's novel "Nana"; Photography, Andreas Winding; Designer, Togo Esben; Music, George Riedel; A Minerva International Film in Technicolor; 99 minutes; Rating X; April release. CAST: Anna Gael (Nana), Gillian Hills (Tina), Lars Lunoe (Haupt), Keve Hjelm (Werner), Gerard Berner (Georges), Rikki Septimus (Rikki), Hans Ernback (Hoffman), Peter Bonke (Forman), Keith Bradfield (Photographer), Poul Glargaard (Leon), Erik Holme (Pallin), Fritz Ruzicka (Bond), Simon Rosenbaum (Otis), Willy Peters (Prince), Elsa Jackson (Ginny), Yvonne Ekman (Diana), Helli Louise (Simone), Bonnie Ewans (Clara).

THE DESERTER (Paramount) Producers, Norman Baer, Ralph Serpe; Director, Burt Kennedy; Screenplay, Clair Huffaker; Associate Producer, Guy Luongo; Designer, Mario Chiari; Music, Piero Piccioni; Costumes, Elio Micheli; Photography, Aldo Tonti; Assistant Director, Jose Lopez Rodero; An Italo-Yugoslav Co-production; In Panavision and Technicolor; 99 minutes; Rating GP; April release. CAST: Bekim Fehmiu (Victor Kaleb), John Huston (Gen. Miles), Richard Crenna (Maj. Brown), Chuck Connors (Reynolds), Ricardo Montalban (Natchai), Ian Bannen (Crawford), Brandon De Wilde (Ferguson), Slim Pickens (Tattinger), Albert Salmi (Schmidt), Woody Strode (Jackson), Patrick Wayne (Bill), Fausto Tozzi (Orozco), John Alderson (O'Toole), Mimo Palmara (Mangus), Larry Stewart (John), Remo D'Angelis (Mark), Gianni Vanicola (Jeff), Lucio Rosato (Jed), Roberto Simmi (Justin), Giancarlo Zampetti (Indian Prisoner), Doc Greaves (Scott).

VLADIMIR AND ROSA (Grove Press) Director, Jean-Luc Godard for Dziga-Vertov Filmmakers Cooperative; In Color; 106 minutes; April release. No other credits. CAST: Jean-Luc Godard, Jean-Pierre Gorin, Anne Wiazemsky, Juliette Bertho, Claude Nedjar.

Linda Hayden
in "The Blood on Satan's Claw"

Albert Salmi, Bekim Fehmiu, Richard Crenna, John Huston
in "The Deserter"

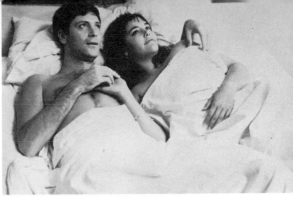

**Gina Lollobrigida
in "That Splendid November"**

**Oded Teomi, Levana Finkelstein
in "Margo"**

THAT SPLENDID NOVEMBER (United Artists) Producer-Director, Mauro Bolognini; Screenplay, Lucia Dridi Demby, Antonio Altoviti, Henry Vaughn; Based on novel by Ercole Patti; Music, Ennio Morricone; Photography, Armando Nannuzzi; Costumes, Cesare Rovatti; Assistant Director, Fabrizio Gianni; A Franco-Italian Co-Production in Color; Rating GP; 93 minutes; April release. CAST: Gina Lollobrigida (Cettina), Paolo Turco (Nino), Gabriele Ferzetti (Biago), Danielle Godet (Elisa), Isabella Savona (Giulietta), Margareta Lozano (Amalia), Pasquale Fortunato (Umberto), Corrado Gaipa (Uncle Alfio), Ileana Rigano (Rosario), Grazia Di Marza (Assunta), Jean Maucorps (Mimi), Franco Abbina (Enzo), Ettore Ribotta (Concetto), Maria Di Benedetto (Aunt Tecla), Vanni Castellani (Turiddu), Amalia Troiani (Aunt Maria), Maria Rosa Amato (Juzza), Giuseppe Naso (Uncle Nicola).

PERCY (MGM) Producer, Betty E. Box; Director, Ralph Thomas; Screenplay, Hugh Leonard; From novel by Raymond Hitchcock; Additional material, Terence Feely; Music and Lyrics, Ray Davies; Played by The Kinks; Photography, Ernest Steward; Assistant Director, Derek Whitehurst; Costumes, Emma Porteus; An Anglo-Emi Film; Rating R; 100 minutes; April release. CAST: Hywel Bennett (Edwin), Denholm Elliott (Emmanuel), Elke Sommer (Helga), Britt Ekland (Dorothy), Cyd Hayman (Moira), Janet Key (Hazel), Tracey Crisp (Miss Elder), Antonia Ellis (Rita), Tracy Reed (Mrs. Penney), Patrick Mower (James), Pauline Delaney (Sister), Adrienne Posta (Maggie), Julia Foster (Marilyn), Sheila Steafel (Mrs. Gold), Arthur English (M.C.), Angus MacKay (TV Producer), Rita Webb (Mrs. Hedges), Charles Hodgson (TV Interviewer), Sue Lloyd (Bernice), Denise Coffey (Operator). Photos not supplied.

MARGO (Cannon) Producer, Yoram Globus; Direction and Screenplay, Menahen Golan; Photography, Ya'acov Kalach; Music, Dov Seltzer; Title Song Lyrics, Uriel Ofek; Sung by Yehoran Gaon; A Noah Films Presentation; Rating R; 90 minutes; April release. CAST: Levana Finklstein (Margo), Oded Teomi (Talmor), Baracha Ne'eman (Shoshana), Ayner Hizkyahu (Dr. Davido), Joseph Shiloach (Hotel Manager), Avraham Ronay (Professor), Lia Dolitzkaya (Mrs. Levinhartz), and Arik Lavi, Tova Pardo, Ya'acov Bodo.

CHANGES (Cinex International) Producer, Director, Screenplay, Gerard Damiano; 81 minutes; Rating X; April release. No other credits.

MY SECRET LIFE (Jack H. Harris Enterprises) Producer, Jack H. Harris; Director, Leland R. Thomas; Screenplay, John Hofsess; Narration, Robert Fathergill; Choreography, Rod Stewart; Photography, John McNichols; In DeLuxe Color; Rating X; 90 minutes; April release. CAST: Jack Woods, Leon Jervis, Patricia Murphy, Cheryl Smith, Rod Stewart, Adriana Collier, E. Edd Fenner, Phyllis Dugan, Jamie Redding, Judy Kleismeyer.

THE SCANDALOUS ADVENTURES OF BURAI-KAN (Toho) Producer, Ninjin Kurabu; Director, Masahiro Shinoda; Screenplay, Shuji Terayama; From play by Makuami Kawatake; Photography, Kozo Okazaki; Music, Masaru Sato; 100 minutes; April release. CAST: Tatsuya Nakadai (Naojiro), Suisen Ichikawa (His mother), Shima Iwashita (Michiose), Tetsuro Tamba (Soshun), Shoichi Ozawa (Ushimatsu), Masakane Yonekura (The Killer).

**Chuck Connors
in "The Deserter"**

**Jack Woods, Judy Kleismeyer
in "My Secret Life"**

Pamela Franklin, Sandor Eles
in "And Soon the Darkness"

Michael York, Alexandra Stewart
in "Zeppelin"

SAMURAI BANNERS (Toho) Producer, Toshiro Mifune; Director, Hiroshi Inagaki; Screenplay, Shinobu Hashimoto; Based on story by Yasushi Inouye; Photography, Kazuo Yamada; Music, Masaru Sato; 166 minutes; April release. CAST: Toshiro Mifune (Kansuke), Yoshiko Sakuma (Princess Yufu), Mayumi Ozora (Princess Okoto), Kinnosuke Nakamura (Shingen Takeda), Kankuro Nakamura (Katsuyori), Ganemon Nakamura (Nobukata), Katsuo Nakamura (Nobusato).

THE EMPEROR AND THE GENERAL (Toho) Producers, Sanezumi Fujimoto, Tomyuki Tanaka; Director, Kihachi Okamoto; Screenplay, Shinobu Hashimoto; Based on book by Soichi Oya; Photography, Hiroshi Murai; Music, Masaru Sato; 158 minutes; April release. CAST: Toshiro Mifune (Gen. Anami), So Yamamura (Yonai), Chishu Ryo (Suzuki), Seiji Miyaguchi (Togo), Takashi Shimura (Board Chief), Koshiro Matsumoto (Emperor), Toshiro Kurosawa (Major).

AND SOON THE DARKNESS (Levitt-Pickman) Producers, Albert Fennell, Brian Clemens; Director, Robert Fuest; Story and Screenplay, Brian Clemens, Terry Nation; Music, Laurie Johnson; 98 minutes; In Color; April release. CAST: Pamela Franklin (Jane), Michele Dotrice (Cathy), Sandor Eles (Paul), John Nettleton (Gendarme), Clare Kelly (Schoolmistress), Hana-Maria Pravda (Mme. Lassal), John Franklyn (Old Man), Claude Betrand (Lassal), Jean Carmet (Renier).

AN ELEPHANT CALLED SLOWLY (American Continental) Producers, Bill Travers, James Hill; Director, James Hill; Screenplay, Bill Travers, James Hill; Photography, Simon Trevor; Music, Bert Kaempfert, Howard Blake; Associate Producer, Monty Ruben; A Morning Star Production presented by The Walter Reade Organization in Movielab Color; 91 minutes; Rating G; April release. CAST: Bill Travers (Bill), Virginia McKenna (Ginny), George Adamson (Himself), Vinay Inambar (Mr. Mophagee), Joab Collins (Henry), Ali Twaha (Mutiso), Raffles Harman.

SNOW COUNTRY (Toho) Director, Shiro Toyoda; Screenplay, Toshio Yasumi; Photography, Jun Yasumoto; Music, Ikuma Dan; 120 minutes; April release. No other credits. CAST: Keiko Kishi (Komako), Ryo Ikebe (Shimamura), Kaoru Yachigusa (Yoko), Kisaya Morishige (Imura).

ZEPPELIN (Warner Bros.) Executive Producer, J. Ronald Getty; Producer, Owen Crump; Director, Etienne Perier; Screenplay, Arthur Rowe, Donald Churchill; Story, Owen Crump; Photography, Alan Hume; Music, Roy Budd; Costumes, Sue Yelland; Assistant Director, Kipp Gowans; In Panavision and Technicolor; Rating G; 101 minutes; May release. CAST: Michael York (Geoffrey), Elke Sommer (Erika), Peter Carsten (Maj. Tauntler), Marius Goring (Prof. Altschul), Anton Diffring (Col. Hirsch), Andrew Keir (Lt. Cmdr. von Gorian), Rupert Davies (Capt. Whitney), Alexandra Stewart (Stephanie Ross), William Marlow (Lt. Cmdr. Anderson), Alan Rothwell (Bradner), Richard Hurndall (Rear Admiral), John Gill (Meier), Michael Robbins (Scot's Sergeant), Ben Howard (Jamie), George Mickell (German Officer), Arnold Diamond (Maj. Proudfoot), Clive Morton (Lord Delford), Bryan Coleman (Col. Whippen), Gary Waldhorn (Harlich), Ronald Adam (Prime Minister).

THE CAT O' NINE TAILS (National General) Producer, Salvatore Argento; Direction and Screenplay, Dario Argento; Story, Dario Argento, Luigi Collo, Dardano Sacchetti; Art Director, Carlo Leva; Assistant Director, Roberto Pariante; Music, Ennio Morricone; Photography, Erico Menczer; In Techniscope and Technicolor; Rating GP; 112 minutes; May release. CAST: Karl Malden (Franco), James Franciscus (Carlo), Catherine Spaak (Anna), Cinzia De Carolis (Lori), Carlo Alighiero (Dr. Calabresi), Vittorio Congia (Cameraman), Pier Paolo Capponi (Police Superintendent), Corrado Olmi (Morsella), Tino Carraro (Terzi), Aldo Reggiani (Dr. Casoni), Horst Frank (Dr. Braun), Emilio Marchesini (Dr. Mombelli), Tom Felleghy (Dr. Esson), Rada Rassimov (Bianca Merusi), Werner Pochat (Manuel).

Virginia McKenna, Bill Travers
in "An Elephant Called Slowly"

James Franciscus, Karl Malden
in "The Cat o' Nine Tails"

VILLAIN (MGM) Producers, Alan Ladd, Jr., Jay Kanter; Director, Michael Tuchner; Screenplay, Dick Clement, Ian La Frenais; Adapted by Al Lettieri; From novel "The Burden of Proof" by James Barlow; Executive Producer, Elliott Kastner; Photography, Christopher Challis; Assistant Director, Kip Gowans; Music, Jonathan Hodge; In Color; Rating R; 90 minutes; May release. CAST: Richard Burton (Vic), Ian McShane (Wolfe), Nigel Davenport (Bob), Donald Sinden (Gerald), Fiona Lewis (Venetia), T. P. McKenna (Frank), Joss Ackland (Edgar), Cathleen Nesbitt (Mrs. Dakin), Elizabeth Knight (Patti), Colin Welland (Tom), Tony Selby (Duncan), John Hallam (Terry), Del Henney (Webb), Ben Howard (Henry), James Cossins (Brown), Anthony Sagar (Danny), Clive Francis (Vivian), Stephen Sheppard (Benny), Brook Williams (Kenneth), Wendy Hutchinson (Mrs. Lowis), Michael Robbins (Barzun), Sheila White (Veronica), Cheryl Hall (Judy), Shirley Cain (Mrs. Mathews), Lindy Miller (Gilly), Godfrey James (Car Lot Manager), Bonita Thomas (Stripper), Leslie Schofield (Detective). Photos not supplied.

THE NIGHT DIGGER (MGM) Producers, Alan D. Courtney, Norman S. Powell; Director, Alastair Reid; Screenplay, Roald Dahl; Based on novel "Nest in a Falling Tree" by Joy Crowley; Executive Producer, William O. Harbach; Music, Bernard Herrmann; Photography, Alex Thomson; Assistant Director, Michael Dryhurst; Costumes, Gabriella Falk; Rating R; 110 minutes; May release. CAST: Patricia Neal (Maura), Pamela Brown (Mother), Nicholas Clay (Billy), Jean Anderson (Mrs. McMurtrey), Graham Crowden (Bolton), Yootha Joyce (Mrs. Palafox), Peter Sallis (Rev. Palafox), Brigit Forsyth (Nurse), Sebastian Breaks (Dr. Robinson), Diana Patrick (Mary), Jenny McCracken (Farmwife), Bruce Myles (Clerk), Zoe Alexander (Stroke Patient), Christopher Reynalds (Young Billy), Elaine Ives Cameron (Gypsy), Sibylla Kay (Whore). Photos not supplied.

WHEN EIGHT BELLS TOLL (Cinerama) Producer, Elliott Kastner; Director, Etienne Perier; Screenplay, Alistair MacLean; Based on his novel; Photography, Arthur Ibbetson; Music, Wally Stott; Art Director, Jack Maxted; Costumes, Sue Yelland; Associate Producer, Denis Holt; Assistant Director, Anthony Waye; A Winkast Film in Panavision and EastmanColor; 94 minutes; Rating GP; May release. CAST: Anthony Hopkins (Philip), Robert Morley (Sir Arthur), Nathalie Delon (Charlotte), Jack Hawkins (Sir Anthony), Corin Redgrave (Hunslett), Derek Bond (Lord Charnley), Ferdy Mayne (Lavorski), Maurice Roeves (Pilot), Leon Collins (Tim), Wendy Allnutt (Sue), Peter Arne (Imrie), Oliver MacGreevy (Quinn), Jon Croft (Durran), Tom Chatto (Lord Kirkside), Charlie Stewart (Sgt.), Edward Burnham (Macullum), Del Henney (Guard).

DAUGHTERS OF DARKNESS (Gemini-Maron) Producers, Paul Collet, Alain C. Guilleaume; Director, Harry Kumel; Screenplay, Pierre Drouot, Harry Kumel; Photography, Edward Van Der Enden; Music, Francois De Roubiax; In Color; 87 minutes; Rating R; May release. CAST: Delphine Seyrig (Elisabeth), Daniele Ouimet (Valerie), John Karlen (Stefan), Andrea Rau (Ilona), Paul Esser (Porter), Georges Jamin (Man), Joris Collet (Butler), Fons Rademakers (Mother).

KURONEKO "Black Cat" (Toho) Direction and Screenplay, Kaneto Shindo; May release. No other credits. CAST: Kichiemon Nakamura (Son), Nobuko Otawa (Mother), Kiwaki Taichi (Wife).

THE COP (Audubon) Producer, Vera Belmont; Director, Yves Boisset; Screenplay, Claude Veillot, Yves Boisset; Photography, Jean-Marc Ripert; Music, Antoine Duhamel; In Color; 100 minutes; Rating R; May release. CAST: Michel Bouquet (Inspector), Francoise Fabian (Helene), Bernard Fresson (Barnero), John Garko (Dan), Michel Constantin (Viletti), Theo Sarapo (Lupo), Henri Garcin (Beausourire), Adolfo Celi (Commissioner).

DAWN OF JUDO (Shochiku) Direction and Screenplay, Kunio Watanabe; Photography, Hiroshi Nishimae; In Color; 105 minutes; May release. CAST: Muga Takewaki (Sanshiro), Koji Takahashi (Shogoto), Nana Ozaki (Saotome), Yuji Hori (Murai), Joji Takagi (Higaki).

LOVE ME—LOVE MY WIFE (Cimber) Produced, Directed, Written, Photographed, Edited by Enzo Battaglia; An Intercontinental Arts production in Ektachrome Color; 81 minutes; Rating X; June release. CAST: Pier Angeli (Elizabeth), Glenn Saxon (Stephen), Colette Descombe (Alexandra).

David Gumpilil, Lucien John, Jenny Agutter in "Walkabout"

WALKABOUT (20th Century-Fox) Executive Producer, Max L. Raab; Producer, Si Litvinoff; Direction and Photography, Nicolas Roeg; Screenplay, Edward Bond; From novel by James Vance Marshall; Music, John Barry; Associate Producer, Anthony J. Hope; Designer, Brian Eatwell; Assistant Director, Kevin Kavanagh; In DeLuxe Color; 95 minutes; Rating GP; June release. CAST: Jenny Agutter (Girl), Lucien John (Brother), David Gumpilil (Aborigine), John Meillon (Father), Peter Carver (No Hoper), John Illingsworth (Husband), Barry Donnelly (Australian Scientist), Noelene Brown (German Scientist), Carlo Manchini (Italian Scientist).

PETER RABBIT AND TALES OF BEATRIX POTTER (MGM) Executive Producer, John Brabourne; Producer, Richard Goodwin; Director, Reginald Mills; Adaptation, Richard Goodwin, Christine Edzard; Choreography, Frederick Ashton; Music, John Lanchbery; Sets and Costumes, Christine Edzard; An EMI Production; In Technicolor; 90 minutes; Rating G; June release. CAST: Erin Geraghty (Beatrix Potter), Joan Benham (Nurse), Wilfred Babbage (Butler), and members of The Royal Ballet. Photos not supplied.

FEVER (Variety) Produced, Directed, Written, and Photographed by Armando Bo; In EastmanColor; 80 minutes; Rating X; June release. CAST: Isabel Sarli, Armando Bo.

THE DIRTY OUTLAWS (Transvue) Producers, Ugo Guerra, Franco Rossetti; Director, Franco Rossetti; Screenplay, Vincenzo Cerami, Ugo Guerra, Franco Rossetti; Photography, Angelo Filippini; Music, Gianni Ferrio; Story, Ugo Guerra; Assistant Director, Roberto Bessi; In Techniscope and Technicolor; 89 minutes; Rating R; June release. CAST: Chip Corman (Steve), Rosemarie Dexter (Katy), Dana Ghia (Lucy), Franco Giornelli (Asher), Piero Lulli (Sam), Aldo Berti (Jonat), and Andrea Scotti, Giovanni Petrucci, Pino Polidori, Dino Strando, John Bartha, Giorgio Gruden, Antonio Cantafora, Sandro Serafini, Giuseppe Castellani, Claudio Trionfi, G. Luigi Crescenzi.

Anthony Hopkins, Robert Morley in "When Eight Bells Toll"

Wayde Preston, Montgomery Ford, Bud Spencer, Stanley Gordon, William Berger in "Today We Kill . . ."

Chip Corman, Dana Ghia, Franco Giornelli in "The Dirty Outlaws"

LANGUAGE OF LOVE (Paragon) Director, Torgny Wickman; Photography, Max Wilen; Music, Mats Olsson; A Swedish Films Production AB in Color; 80 minutes; Rating X; June release. CAST: In panel discussion are Dr. Cullhed, Dr. Bergstrom-Walen, Inge and Sten Hegeler.

TODAY WE KILL ... TOMORROW WE DIE! (Cinerama) Director, Tonino Cervi; Screenplay, Dario Argento; Photography, Sergio Doffizi; Music, Francesco Lawagnino; Presented by Herman Cohen in Eastman-Color; 95 minutes; Rating GP; June release. CAST: Montgomery Ford (Bill), Bud Spencer (O'Bannion), Tatsuya Nakadai (El Fego), William Berger (Colt), Wayde Preston (Jeff), Stanley Gordon (Bunny).

THE PEOPLE AND THEIR GUNS (Impact) Directed by Joris Ivens with the collaboration of Marceline Loridan and J. P. Sergent; Subtitled "The People's War in Laos"; 97 minutes; June release. A documentary on the conflict in Laos.

SCARS OF DRACULA (American Continental) Producer, Aida Young; Director, Roy Ward Baker; Screenplay, John Elder; Based on characters created by Bram Stoker; Photography, Moray Grant; Music, James Bernard; Art Director, Scott MacGregor; Assistant Director, Derek Whitehurst; A Hammer Production for Anglo Emi in Technicolor; 96 minutes; Rating R; June release. CAST: Christopher Lee (Dracula), Dennis Waterman (Simon), Jenny Hanley (Sarah), Christopher Matthews (Paul), Patrick Troughton (Klove), Michael Gwynn (Priest), Wendy Hamilton (Julie), Anouska Hempel (Tania), Delia Lindsay (Alice), Bob Todd (Burgomaster), Toke Townley (Wagonmaster), Michael Ripper (Landlord), David Lealand (1st Officer), Richard Durden (2nd Officer), Morris Bush (Farmer), Margot Boht (Landlord's wife), Clive Barrie (Fat Young Man).

RED LION (Toho) Director, Kihachi Okamoto; Screenplay, Kihachi Okamoto, Sakae Hirosawa; Photography, Takao Saito; A Mifune Production; 116 minutes; June release. CAST: Toshiro Mifune (Gonzo), Etsushi Takahishi (Hanzo), Shima Iwashita (Tomi).

MACHIBUSE (Toho) Director, Hiroshi Inagaki; Screenplay, Kyu Fujiki, Hideo Oguni; Photography, Kazuo Yamada; Music, Masaru Sato; A Mifune Production; 121 minutes; June release. CAST: Toshiro Mifune, Shintaro Katsu, Kinnosuhe Nakamura, Ruriko Saaoka, Yujiro Ishihara.

THE HORROR OF FRANKENSTEIN (American Continental) Producer-Director, Jimmy Sangster; Screenplay, Jimmy Sangster, Jeremy Burnham; Based on characters created by Mary Shelley; Photography, Moray Grant; Music, James Bernard; Art Director, Scott MacGregor; Assistant Director, Derek Whitehurst; A Hammer Production for Anglo Emi in Technicolor; 95 minutes; Rating R; June release. CAST: Ralph Bates (Victor), Kate O'-Mara (Alys), Graham James (Wilhelm), Veronica Carlson (Elizabeth), Bernard Archard (Father), Dennis Price (Grave-robber), Joan Rice (His wife), David Prowse (Monster).

BEYOND CONTROL (Mishkin) Producers, Peter Hellstern, Martin Hellstern; Director, Anthony Baker; Screenplay, Anthony Baker, Martin Roda-Becher, Charles Niessen, Ed Marcus, Joe Juliano; Photography, Igor Luther; Music, Charles Niessen; In Color; 89 minutes; June release. CAST: William Berger (Jimmy), Anthony Baker (Frank), Georgia Moll (Brigitte), Helga Anders (Monica), Grit Botcher (Christina), Willy Birgel (District Attorney).

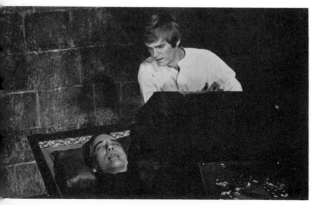

Christopher Lee, Christopher Matthews in "Scars of Dracula"

Dave Prowse, Joan Rice in "Horror of Frankenstein"

**Vanessa Redgrave, Michael Gothard
in "The Devils"**

**Oliver Reed, Georgina Hale
in "The Devils"**

THE REVENGE OF OKENOJO (Daei) Director, Kon Ichikawa; Screenplay, Daisuke Ito, Telnosuke Kinusaga, Natto Wada; Photography, Setsuo Kobayashi; Music, Yasushi Akutagawa; 113 minutes; June release. CAST: Kazuo Hasegawa (Ukonojo), Fujika Yamamoto (Ohatsu), Ayako Wakao (Lady Namiji), Ganjiri Nakamura (Lord Dobe), Raizo Ichikawa (Youngest thief).

BAND OF ASSASSINS (Toho) Director, Tadashi Sawashima; Screenplay, Kenro Matsuura; Photography, Kozuo Yamada; Music, Masau Sato; A Mifune Production; 122 minutes; June release. CAST: Toshiro Mifune, Isami Kondo, Keiju Kobayashi, Kinya Kitaoli, Rentaro Mikuni.

THE HUNTING PARTY (United Artists) Executive Producers, Jules Levy, Arthur Gardner; Producer, Lou Morheim; Director, Don Medford; Screenplay, William Norton, Gilbert Alexander, Lou Morheim; Story, Gilbert Alexander, Lou Morheim; Music, Riz Ortolani; Photography, Cecilio Paniagua; Assistant Director, Jose Maria Ochoa; In DeLuxe Color; 108 minutes; Rating R; July release. CAST: Oliver Reed (Frank), Candice Bergen (Melissa), Gene Hackman (Brandt), Simon Oakland (Matthew), Ronald Howard (Nelson), G. D. Spradlin (Sam), Bernard Kay (Buford), Eugenio Escudero Garcia (Mario), Mitchell Ryan (Doc), L. Q. Jones (Hog), William Watson (Loring), Rayford Barnes (Crimp), Dean Selmier (Collins), Ritchie Adams (Owney), Carlos Bravo, Bud Strait (Cowboys), Ralph Brown (Sheriff), Marian Collier (Teacher), Max Slaten (Telegrapher), Rafael Escudero Garcia (Mexican), Emilio Rodriques Guiar (Priest), Sara Atkinson (Red-head), Francisca Tu (Chinese), Lilibeth Solison (Blonde), Marisa Tovar (Mexican), Christine Larroude, Stephanie Pieritz (Other Girls).

THE DEVILS (Warner Bros.) Producers, Robert H. Solo, Ken Russell; Direction and Screenplay, Ken Russell, Based on play by John Whiting and book by Aldous Huxley; Photography, David Watkin; Choreography, Terry Gilbert; Associate Producer, Roy Baird; Music, Peter Maxwell Davies; Costumes, Shirley Russell; Assistant Director, Ted Morley; In Panavision and Technicolor; 109 minutes; Rating X; July release. CAST: Vanessa Redgrave (Sister Jeanne), Oliver Reed (Father Grandier), Dudley Sutton (Baron de Laubardemont), Max Adrian (Ibert), Gemma Jones (Madeleine), Murray Melvin (Mignon), Michael Gothard (Father Barre), Georgina Hale (Philippe), Brian Murphy (Adam), Christopher Logue (Richelieu), Graham Armitage (Louis XIII), John Woodvine (Trincant), Andrew Faulds (Rangier), Kenneth Colley (Legrand), Judith Paris (Sister Judith), Catherine Willmer (Sister Catherine), Iza Teller (Sister Iza).

THE RED TENT (Paramount) Producer, Franco Cristaldi; Director, Mickail K. Kalatozov; Screenplay, Ennio De Concini, Richard Adams; Photography, Leonid Kalashnikov; Music, Ennio Morricone; Associate Producer, Fernando Ghia; Costumes, Natalia Meshkova; Associate Director, Igor Petrov; Assistant Directors, Marina Lebesheva, Valerj Sirovski, Marina Volocic; In Technicolor; 121 minutes; Rating G; July release. CAST: Sean Connery (Amundsen), Claudia Cardinale (Valeria), Hardy Kruger (Lundborg), Peter Finch (Nobile), Massimo Girotti (Romagna), Luigi Vannucchi (Zappi), Mario Adorf (Biagi), Edward Marzevuc (Malmgren), Boris Kmelnizki (Viglieri), Juri Solomin (Troiani), Juri Vizbor (Behounek), Donatas Banionis (Mariano), Otar Koberidze (Cecioni), Grigori Gaj (Samoilovich), Nikita Mikhalkov (Chuknovsky), Nicolai Ivanov (Kolka).

**Gene Hackman, Candice Bergen
in "The Hunting Party"**

**Claudia Cardinale, Sean Connery
in "The Red Tent"**

"Black Peter"

Elliott Gould, Bibi Andersson, Max
von Sydow in "The Touch"

BLACK PETER (Billings) Producer, Czechoslovak State
Film Co.; Director, Milos Forman; Screenplay, Milos
Forman, Jaroslav Papousek, Ivan Passer; Photography,
Jan Nemecek; Music, Jiri Slitr; 85 minutes; July release.
CAST: Ladislav Jakim (Peter), Pavla Martinkova (Paula),
Pavel Sedlacek (Lada), Jan Ostroll (Peter's father),
Bozena Matuskova (Peter's mother), Vladimir Puchholt
(Cenda), Zdenek Kulhanek (Zdenek).

MURPHY'S WAR (Paramount) Producer, Michael Dee-
ley; Director, Peter Yates; Screenplay, Stirling Silliphant;
From novel by Max Catto; Photography, Douglas Slocombe; Music, John Barry; Designer, Disley Jones; Assistant Director, Bert Batt; In EastmanColor; 108 minutes;
July release. CAST: Peter O'Toole (Murphy), Sian Phillips (Hayden), Phillipe Noiret (Brezan), Horst Janson
(Lauchs), John Hallam (Ellis), Ingo Mogendorf (Voght).

THE HUNTED SAMURAI (Toho) Producers, Eiichi
Imado, Kunifumi Tokieda; Director, Keiichi Ozawa;
Screenplay, Seiji Hoshikawa; Photography, Minoru
Yokoyama; Music, Hajime Kabur; In Colorscope; 87
minutes; July release. CAST: Hideki Takahashi (Rop-
peita), Isao Natusyagi (Kyonosuke), Seiichiro Kameishi
(Tarao), Masako Izumi (Toki), Yochiro Aoki (Aochi),
Shoki Fukae (Nachi), Kishiro Kawami (Jisaku).

THE BRAZEN WOMEN OF BALZAC (Globe) Director, Josef Zachar; Screenplay, Kurt Nachtman; Photography, Kurt Junek; Music, Claudius Alzner; A Lisa Film in
Color; 80 minutes; July release. CAST: Joachim Hansen
(Fabian), Edwige Fenech (Felicita), Angelica Ott (Ara-
bella), Michaela May (Eugenie), Caterina Alt (Sophie),
Frances Fair (Annette), Ivan Nessbeth (Manuel), Sieg-
hardt Rupp (George), Walter Buschoff (Leuwenstam).

THE TOUCH (Cinerama) Produced, Directed, and Writ-
ten by Ingmar Bergman; Photography, Sven Nykvist; In
Color; 112 minutes; Rating R; July release. CAST: Bibi
Andersson (Karin), Elliott Gould (David), Max Von Sy-
dow (Dr. Andreas Vergerus), Sheila Reid (Sara), Barbro
Hiort of Ornas (Karin's mother), Staffan Hallerstam
(Anders), Maria Nolgard (Agnes).

THE NUN (Altura) Producer, Georges de Beauregard;
Director, Jacques Rivette; Screenplay, Jean Gruault,
Jacques Rivette; Based on novel "La Religieuse" by Denis
Diderot; Photography, Alain Levent; Music, Jean-Claude
Eloy; A Fleetwood Films production; 130 minutes; Rating
G; July release. CAST: Anna Karina (Suzanne), Liselotte
Pulver (Mme. de Chelles), Micheline Presle (Mme. de
Moni), Francine Barge (Soeur Ste. Christine), Francisco
Rabal (Dan Morel).

**THE HOUSE THAT SCREAMED (American Interna-
tional)** Producer, Arturo Gonzalez; Director, Narciso
Ibanez Serrador; Screenplay, Luis Verna Penafiel; Based
on story by Juan Tebar; Photography, Manuel Berenguer;
Music, Waldo de los Rios; Art Director, Ramiro Gomez;
Costumes, Victor Cortezo; Assistant Director, Mahnahen
Velasco; In EastmanColor; An Anabel Film; 99 minutes;
Rating GP; July release. CAST: Lilli Palmer (Mme. Four-
neau), Chistina Galbo (Theresa), John Moulder-Brown
(Luis), Mary Maude (Irenee), Candida Losada (Mlle.
Desprez), Tomas Blanco (M. Baldie), Pauline Challenor
(Catherine), Maribel Martin (Isabelle), Conchita Paredes
(Suzanne), Victor Israel (Brechard).

THE RED ANGEL (Daiei) Director, Yasuzo Masumura;
Screenplay, Ryozo Kasahara; Photography, Setsuo
Kobayashi; 95 minutes; July release. CAST: Ayako
Wakao (Nurse), Shinsuke Ashida (Doctor), Yusuke
Kawazu (Pvt. Orihara), Jotaro Senba (Pvt. Sakamoto).

Sian Phillips, Peter O'Toole
in "Murphy's War"

Anna Karina
in "The Nun"

**Hildegard Neil, Roger Moore
in "The Man Who Haunted Himself"**

**Sinead Cusack, Peter Sellers
in "Hoffman"**

THE MAN WHO HAUNTED HIMSELF (Levitt-Pickman) Producer, Michael Relph; Director, Basil Dearden; Screenplay, Basil Dearden, Michael Relph; Music, Michael J. Lewis; An Associated British Production for Anglo EMI; In Technicolor; 94 minutes; Rating GP, August release. CAST: Roger Moore (Pelham), Hildegard Neil (Eve), Alastair Mackenzie (Michael), Hugh Mackenzie (James), Kevork Malikyan (Luigi), Thorley Walters (Bellamy), Anton Rodgers (Alexander), Olga Georges-Picot (Julie), Freddie Jones (Psychiatrist), John Welsh (Freeman), Edward Chapman (Barton), Laurence Hardy (Mason).

HOFFMAN (Levitt-Pickman) Producer, Ben Arbeid; Director, Alvin Rakoff; Screenplay, Ernest Gebler; Based on his novel; Music, Ron Grainer; An Associated British Production for Anglo EMI; In Technicolor; 111 minutes; Rating GP; August release. CAST: Peter Sellers (Hoffman), Sinead Cusack (Janet), Jeremy Bulloch (Tom), Ruth Dunning (Mrs. Mitchell), David Lodge (Foreman), Ron Taylor (Guitarist), and Kay Hall, Karen Murtagh, Cindy Burrows, Elizabeth Bayley.

CHRISTA (American International) Title changed to "Swedish Fly Girls"; Produced, Directed, and Written by Jack O'Connell; Photography, Henning Kristiansen; Music, Manfred Mann; In Color; 100 minutes; Rating R; August release. CAST: Birte Tove (Christa), Clinton Greyn (Derek), Baard Ove (Torben), Daniel Gelin (Andre), Gastone Rosilli (Michael), Cyrus Elias (Umberto).

BLACK JESUS (Plaza) Producer, Photographer, Carlo Lizzani; Director, Valerio Zurlini; Screenplay, Valerio Zurlini, Franco Brusati; 93 minutes; Rating GP; August release. CAST: Woody Strode (Maurice Lalubi), Jean Servais (Commandant), Franco Citti (Thief).

ZATOICHI'S CANE SWORD (Daiei) Director, Kimiyoshi Yasuda; Screenplay, Ryozo Kasahari; Photography, Senkichiro Takeida; 90 minutes; August release. CAST: Shintaro Katsu, Shino Fujimura, Yeshihiro Aoyama, Makoto Fujita, Eijiro Tono.

YOG—MONSTER FROM SPACE (American International) Director, Ishiro Honda; Screenplay, El Ogawa; Photography, Taaichi Kankura; Music, Akira Ifukube; A Toho Production; 84 minutes; Rating GP; August release. CAST: Akira Kubo (Taro), Atsuko Takahashi (Ayako), Yoshio Tsuchiya (Kyoichi), Kenji Sahara (Makoto), Noritake Saito (Rico), Yukiko Kobayashi (Saki).

THERMIDOR (Altura) Formerly "Ca Ira"; Producer, Moris Ergas; Director, Tinto Brass; Translation of original text by Ursule Molinaro and English adaptation by Clem Perry; 97 minutes; August release. A documentary on modern revolution with the voices of Ben Gazzara, Irene Worth, Al Freeman, Jr., Michael Tolan, Edith Piaf.

SAMURAI ASSASSIN (Toho) Director, Kihachi Okamoto; Screenplay, Shinobu Hashimoto; Story, Jiromasa Gunji; Photography, Hiroshi Murai; Music, Masaru Sato; A Mifune Production; 122 minutes; August release. CAST: Toshiro Mifune (Tsuruchiyo), Keiju Kobayashi (Einosuke), Yunosuke Ito (Kenmotsu), Koshiro Matsumoto (Naosuke Li), Michiyo Aratama (Oki-ku/Kikuhime).

NEXT (Maron-Gemini) Producers, Sergio Martino, Antonio Crescenz; Director, Luciano Martino; Screenplay, Eduardo M. Borchero, Ernesto Gastaldi, Vittorio Caronia; Photography, Emilio Foriscot; Music, Nora Orlandi; 81 minutes; Rating R; August release. CAST: Alberto De Mendoza (Neil), Edwige Fenech (Julie), Cristina Airoldi (Carol), George Hilton (George), Ivan Rassimov (Jean).

DEEP END (Paramount) Producer, Helmut Jedele; Director, Jerzy Skolimowski; Screenplay, Jerzy Skolimowski, J. Gruza, B. Sulik; Photography, Charly Steinberger; Music, Cat Stevens and the Can; In Color; 87 minutes; Rating R; August release. CAST: Jane Asher (Susan), John Moulder-Brown (Mike), Diana Dors (Lady client), Karl Michael Vogler (Swimming instructor), Christopher Sandford (Fiance), Louise Martini (Prostitute), Erica Beer (Baths cashier).

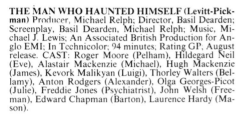

**Birte Tove, Clinton Greyn
in "Swedish Fly Girls"**

**John Moulder Brown, Jane Asher
in "Deep End"**

Rosemary Dexter, Tony Anthony, Luciana Paluzzi
in "Cometogether"

Paulo Cesar Pereio
in "O Bravo Guerreiro"

COMETOGETHER (Allied Artists) Producers, Tony
Anthony, Saul Swimmer; Director, Saul Swimmer;
Screenplay, Saul Swimmer, Tony Anthony; Photography,
Tonino Delli Colli; Assistant Director, Giorgio Gentili;
Music, Stelvio Cipriani; ABKCO presents a William Cash
Production in Color; 90 Minutes; Rating R; September
release. CAST: Tony Anthony (Tony), Luciana Paluzzi
(Lisa), Rosemary Dexter (Ann).

THE ANONYMOUS VENETIAN (Allied Artists) Pro-
ducer, Ultra Film/Turi Vasile; Director, Enrico Maria
Salerno; Screenplay, Enrico Maria Salerno, Giuseppe
Berto; Photography, Marcello Gatti; Music, Stelvio Cip-
riani; In EastmanColor; Presented by Emanuel L. Wolf;
91 minutes; Rating GP; September release. CAST: Tony
Musante (Enrico), Florinda Bolkan (Valeria), Toti Cal
Monte (House Owner), Alessandro Grinfan (Factory
Manager), Brizio Montinaro (Waiter), Giuseppe Bella
(South Technician).

UNE SIMPLE HISTOIRE (New Yorker) Producer,
Marcel Hanoun; In collaboration with R.T.F.; Direction,
Screenplay, Marcel Hanoun; Music, Vivaldi, Cimarosa; 60 minutes; September release. CAST:
Micheline Bezancon (Mother).

THE HOUR AND TURN OF AUGUSTO MATRAGA
(New Yorker) Produced, Directed, and Written by
Roberto Santos; Based on novel by Joao Guimaraes Rosa;
Photography, Helio Silva; Music, Geraldo Vandre; 110
minutes; September release. CAST: Leonardo Vilar
(Augusto), Maria Ribeiro (His wife), Jofre Soares (Bandit
Chief), Mauricio Do Valle (Priest).

O BRAVO GUERREIRO (New Yorker) Producer-
Director, Gustavo Dahl; Screenplay, Gustavo Dahl,
Roberto Marinho de Azevedo Neto; Photography, Al-
phonso Beato; Assistant Director, Antonio Caimon; 80
minutes; September release. CAST: Paulo Cesar Pereio
(Miguel), Mario Lago (Augusto), Italo Rossi (Frota),
Maria Lucia Dahl (Clara), Cezar Ladeiro (Virgilio), Paulo
Gracindo (Pericles).

THE DECEASED (New Yorker) Producers, Jofre Ro-
drigues, Aluizio Leite Garcia; Director, Leon Hirszman;
Screenplay, Leon Hirszman, Eduardo Coutinho, Nelson
Rodrigues; Photography, Jose Araujo Medeiros; Music,
Nelson Gnatalli; 100 minutes; September release. CAST:
Fernanda Montenegro (Wife), Ivan Candido (Husband),
Paulo Gracindo (Lover).

THE PLANTATION BOY (New Yorker) Producers,
MAPA Filmes/Glauber Rocha; Direction and Screen-
play, Walter Lima, Jr.; Adapted from novel by Jose Lins
de Rego; Photography, Reinhaldo Barros; Music, Pedro
Santos; 90 minutes; September release. CAST: Savio
Rolim (Carlinho), Rodolfo Arena (Grandfather), Anecy
Rocha (Aunt), Geraldo Del Rey (Uncle), Maria Luisa
Dahl (Maria Luisa).

OTHON Producer, Klaus Hellwig; Direction and Screen-
play, Jean-Marie Straub, Daniele Huillet; Photography,
Ugo Piccone; 84 minutes; November release. CAST:
Adriano Apra (Othon), Anne Brumagge (Plautine),
Ennio Lauricella (Galba), Olimpia Carlisi (Camille), An-
thony Pensabene (Vinius), Jean-Claude Biette (Martian),
Jubarithe Semaran (Lacus).

"Matraga"

"Othon"

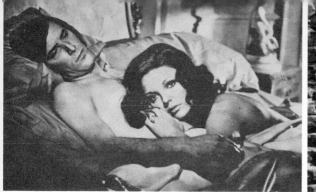

Tom Bell, Joan Collins
in "Quest for Love"

Tony Musante, Florinda Bolkan
in "The Anonymous Venetian"

REVENGE (Rank) Producer, George H. Brown; Director, Sidney Hayers; Screenplay, John Kruse, Photography, Ken Hodges; Assistant Director, Stuart Freeman; Costumes, Courtenay Elliott; Executive Producer, Peter Rogers; 89 minutes; September release. CAST: Joan Collins (Carol), James Booth (Jim), Ray Barrett (Harry), Sinead Cusack (Rose), Tom Marshall (Lee), Kenneth Griffith (Seely), Zuleika Robson (Jill), Angus Mackay (Priest), Ronald Clarke (Brewery Driver's Mate), Patrick McAlinney (George), Artro Morris (Jacko), Donald Morley (Inspector), Martin Carroll (Undertaker), Richard Holden (Pub Customer), Geoffrey Hughes (Brewery Driver), Basil Lord (Sales Representative), Barry Andrews (Sgt.).

QUEST FOR LOVE (Rank) Producer, Peter Eton; Director, Ralph Thomas; Screenplay, Terence Feely; From short story "Random Quest" by John Wyndham; Assistant Director, Bert Batt; Costumes, Emma Porteous; Executive Producer, Peter Rogers; 91 minutes; September release. CAST: Joan Collins (Ottilie), Tom Bell (Colin), Denholm Elliott (Tom), Laurence Naismith (Sir Henry), Lyn Ashley (Jennifer), Juliet Harmer (Geraldine), Neil McCallum (Jimmy).

THE BEAR AND THE DOLL (Paramount) Producer, Mag Bodard; Director, Michel Deville; Screenplay, Nina Companeez, Michel Deville; Photography, Claude Lecompte; In Color; 90 minutes; Rating GP; September release. CAST: Brigitte Bardot (Felicia), Jean-Pierre Cassel (Gaspard), Daniel Ceccaldi (Ivan), Xavier Gelin (Reginald).

A YOUNG COUPLE (Trans World) Director, Rene Gainville; Screenplay, Jean-Louis Curtis; An Entervolve Film produced by Les Filmes de L'Epee and Terra Films in Color; 84 minutes; Rating GP; September release. CAST: Anna Gael (Veronique), Alain Libolt (Gilles), Anny Duperey (Ariane), Jean-Francois Calve (Charles), Christian Kerville (Alex), Corinne Lapolitaine (Janine), Francois Gabriel (Jean).

ADIOS SABATA (United Artists) Producer, Alberto Grimaldi; Director, Frank Kramer; Story and Screenplay, Renato Izzo, Gianfranco Parolini; Photography, Sandro Mancori; Music, Bruno Nicolai; Associate Producer, Roberto Cocco, Assistant Director, Ignazio Dolce; In Technicolor; 106 minutes; Rating GP; September release. CAST: Yul Brynner (Sabata), Dean Reed (Ballantine), Pedro Sanchez (Escudo), Gerard Herter (Skimmel), Sal Borgese (September), Franco Fantasia (Ocano), Joseph Persaud (Gitano), Gianni Rizzo (Folgen), Salvatore Billa (Manuel), Massimo Carocci (Juan), Antonio Gradoli (Major).

LUST FOR A VAMPIRE (American Continental) Producer, Michael Style; Director, Jimmy Sangster; Screenplay, Tudor Gates; Based on characters created by J. Sheridan Le Fanu; A Hammer Production in Color; 95 minutes; Rating R. September release. CAST: Ralph Bates (Giles), Barbara Jefford (Countess), Suzanna Leigh (Janet), Michael Johnson (Richard), Yutte Stensgaard (Mircalla/Carmilla), Mike Raven (Count).

INN OF EVIL (Toho) Director, Masaki Kobayashi; Screenplay, Tomoe Ryu; Story, Shugoroo Yamamoto; Photography, Kozo Okazaki; Art Director, Hiroshi Mizutani; Music, Toru Takemitsu; In Black and White; 120 minutes; September release. CAST: Tatsuya Nakadai (Sadahichi), Komaki Kurihara (Omitsu), Ganuemon Nakamura (Ikuzo), Kei Yamamoto (Tomijiro), Kei Satoh (Yohie), Wakako Sakai (Okiwa).

SWAN LAKE (Celebrity Concert Corp.) Directors, Konstantin Sergeyev, Apollinari Dudko; Screenplay, Konstantin Sergeyev, Apollinari Dudko, Isaak Glickman; Choreography Konstantin Sergeyev based on Petipa-Ivanov original; Music, P. I. Tchaikovsky; Played by Leningrad Philharmonic; Photography, Anatoly Nazarov; A Lenfilm-Sovexportfilm production in EastmanColor; 90 minutes plus intermission; September release. CAST: Yelena Yevteyeva (Odette/Odile), John Markovsky (Siegfried), Makhmud Esambayev (Rotbart), Valeri Panov (Jester), and Kirov Ballet.

"Plantation Boy"

Micheline Bezancon
in "Une Simple Histoire"

217

Yona Magalhaes, Lydio Sylva
in "Black God, White Devil"

Orson Welles, Tuesday Weld
in "A Safe Place"

THE BIG CITY (New Yorker) Producers, Luiz Carlos Barreto, Zelita Vlana, MAPA Filmes; Director, Carlos Diegues; Screenplay, Carlos Diegues, Leopoldo Serran; Photography, Fernando Duarte; 80 minutes; September release. CAST: Anecy Rocha (Luzia), Antonio Pilanga (Calunga), Leonardo Vilar (Jasao), Joel Barcelos (Ignacio).

BLACK GOD, WHITE DEVIL (New Yorker) Producers, Glauber Rocha, Jarbas Barbosa, Luiz Augusta Mendez; Direction, Story, and Screenplay, Glauber Rocha; Photography, Waldemar Lima; Music, Villa Lobos; 120 minutes; September release. CAST: Gerardo Del Rey (Manoel), Yona Magalhaes (Rosa), Lydio Sylvia (Sebastian), Othon Bestos (Corisco), Mauricio Do Valle (Antonio), Sonia Dos Homildes (Dada).

SWORDS OF DEATH (Toho) Director, Tomu Uchida; Screenplay, Daisuke Ito; Photography, Tokuzo Kuroda; Music, Taichiro Kosugi; 76 minutes; September release. CAST: Kinnosuke Nakamura (Musashi), Rentaro Mikuni (Baiken), Hideko Okiyama (Wife).

SECRET RITES (AVCO Embassy) Produced, Directed, and Written by Ramiro Arango; In DeLuxe Color; Presented by Joseph E. Levine; 93 minutes; October release. A Documentary depicting bizarre customs throughout the world.

A TOWN CALLED HELL (Scotia International) Producer, S. Benjamin Fisz; Director, Robert Parrish; Screenplay, Richard Aubrey; In Technicolor and Franscope; A Benmar-Zurbano Production; 95 minutes; Rating R; October release. CAST: Robert Shaw (Priest), Stella Stevens (Alvira), Martin Landau (Colonel), Telly Savalas (Don Carlos), Michael Craig (Paco), Dudley Sutton (Spectre), Al Lettieri (La Bomba), Aldo Sambrell (Celebra), Fernando Rey (Blind Farmer).

A SAFE PLACE (Columbia) Executive Producer, Bert Schneider; Direction and Screenplay, Henry Jaglom; Photography, Dick Kratina; Assistant Director, Steve Kesten; A BBS Production in Color; 94 minutes; Rating GP; October release. CAST: Tuesday Weld (Susan/Noah), Orson Welles (Magician), Jack Nicholson (Mitch), Philip Proctor (Fred), Gwen Welles (Bari), Dov Lawrence (Larry), Fanny Birkenmaier (Maid), Rhonda Alfaro (Girl in rowboat), Sylvia Zapp (Susan at 5), Richard Finnochio, Barbara Flood, Roger Garrett, Jordon Hahn, Francesca Hilton, Julie Robinson, Jennifer Walker (Friends).

WR—MYSTERIES OF THE ORGANISM (Cinema V) Direction and Screenplay, Dusan Makavejev; Photography, Pega Popovic, Aleksandar Petkovic; 80 minutes; October release. CAST: Milena Dravic (Milena), Jagoda Kaloper (Jagoda), Ivica Vidovic (Vladimir), Zoran Radmilovic (Radmilovic), Tuli Kupferberg (Guerilla Poet), Jackie Curtis (Transvestite), Michael Gelovani (Stalin).

SMIC, SMAC, SMOC (GSF) Direction, Screenplay, Photography, Claude Lelouch; Assistant Director, Claude Pinoteau; Music, Francis Lai; 90 minutes; October release. CAST: Catherine Allegret (Catherine), Amidou (Midou), Jean Collomb (Jeannot), Charles Gerard (Charlot), Francis Lai (Blindman).

SCREAM OF THE DEMON LOVER (New World) Producer-Director, J. L. Merino; Story and Screenplay, E. Colombo; Photography, Emanuela Di Cola; Music, Luigi Malatesta; In Telecolor; 75 minutes; Rating R; October release. CAST: Jeffrey Chase (Baron), Jennifer Hartley (Ivana), Ronald Grey (Inspector), Agostina Belli, Mariano Videl Molina, Christiana Galloni, Antonio Gimenez Escribano, Enzo Fisichella.

Martin Landau, Fernando Rey, Robert Shaw
in "A Town Called Hell"

Catherine Allegret, Amidou
in "Smic, Smac, Smoc"

Robert Strauss, Diana Kjaer
in "Dagmar's Hot Pants"

Thommy Berggren
in "Joe Hill"

IN THE NAME OF THE FATHER (Vides) Producer, Franco Cristaldi; Direction, Screenplay, Marco Bellochio; Photography, Franco di Giacomo; Music, Nicola Piovani; Costumes, Enrico Job; In EastmanColor; 115 minutes; October release. CAST: Yves Benayton (Angelo), Renato Scarpa (Vice Rector), Laura Betti (Franco's mother), Aldo Sassi (Franco), Lou Castel (Salvatore).

DAGMAR'S HOT PANTS (Trans American) Producer-Director, Vernon P. Becker; Screenplay, Vernon P. Becker, Louis M. Heyward; Photography, Tony Hemric; Designer, Gustav Wiklund; Music, Les Baxter; Song, Jimmy Haskell, Guy Fosberg; In Movielab Color; 94 minutes; October release. CAST: Diana Kjaer (Dagmar), Robert Strauss (Businessman), Tommy Blom (Brother), Ole Soltoft (Lover), Anne Grete (Friend), Anne-Lie Alexandersson (Successor), Tor Isedal (Gangster).

SACCO AND VANZETTI (UMC) Producers, Harry Colombo, George Papi; Director, Giuliano Montaldo; Screenplay, Favrizio Onofri, Giuliano Montaldo; Photography, Silvano Ippolitti; 120 minutes; Rating GP; October release. CAST: Gian Maria Volonte (Vanzetti), Riccardo Cucciolla (Sacco), Milo O'Shea (Moore), Cyril Cusack (Katzman), Rosanna Fratello (Committeewoman), Geoffrey Keen (Judge), William Prince (Thompson), Claude Mann (Newspaperman).

MEDEA (New Line) Producer, Franco Rossellini; Direction and Screenplay, Pier Paolo Pasolini; From play by Euripides; Photography, Ennio Guarnieri; A European International-Janus Film; 100 minutes; October release. CAST: Maria Callas (Medea), Giuseppi Gentile (Jason), Laurent Terzieff (Centaur), Margereth Clementi (Glauce).

JOE HILL (Paramount) Produced, Directed, and Written by Bo Widerberg; Photography, Petter Davidsson, Jorgen Persson; Music, Stefan Grossman; A Sagittarius Production in Color, 114 minutes, Rating GP; October release. CAST: Thommy Berggren (Joe Hill), Ania Schmidt (Lucia), Kelvin Malave (The Fox), Everl Anderson (Blackie), Cathy Smith (Cathy), Hasse Persson (Paul), Wendy Geier (Elizabeth), Franco Molinari (Tenor).

THE DEBUT (Maron-Gemini) Producers, Ivan Klenikov, Odinokov, G. Beglov; Director, Gleb Panfilov; Screenplay, E. Gavrilovich, Gleb Panfilov; Photography, D. Dolinin; Black and White; 95 minutes; October release. CAST: Inna Churikova (Pasha), V. Telichkina (Valia), T. Stekanova (Katia), L. Kuravlev (Arkadi), M. Kononev (Pavlik).

VIVA LA MUERTE (Raab) Producer, Jacques Poitreneaud; Direction and Screenplay, Fernando Arrabal; Photography, Jean-Marc Ripert; Music, Jean-Yves Bosseur; 90 minutes; October release. CAST. Anouk Ferjac (Aunt), Nuria Espert (Mother), Ivan Henriques (Father), Mahdi Chaouch (Boy), Jazia Klibi (Girl).

GOYOKIN (Toho) Producers, Fuji Telecasting Co. and Tokyo Eiga; Director, Hideo Gosha; Screenplay, Hideo Gosha, Kei Tasaka; 124 minutes; October release. No other credits. CAST: Tatsuya Nakadel (Magobei), Tetsuro Tamba (Taito), Kinnosuka Nakamura (Sanmon), Ruriko Asaoka (Oriha).

MAID IN SWEDEN (Cannon) Executive Producers, Dennis Friedland, Christopher C. Dewey; Producer, Ami Artzi; Director, Floch Johnson; Screenplay, Ronnie Friedland, George Norris; Photography, Hasse Welin, Roland Sterner; Music, Peter L. Kauff, Bob Nash; Songs, Charles Silverman; In DeLuxe Color; 90 minutes; Rating X; November release. CAST: Kristina Lindberg (Inga), Monika Ekman (Greta), Krister Ekman (Casten), Leif Naslun (Bjorn), Per Axel Arosenius (Father), Itela Frodi (Mother), Tina Hedstrom (Helen), Henrik Meyer (Ole), Vivianne Ojengen (Brita), Jim Engelau (Leonard).

"WR—Mysteries of the Organism"

Krister Ekman, Monica Ekman, Kristina Lindberg
in "Maid in Sweden"

219

Viveca Lindfors, Boris Karloff, Jean-Pierre Aumont
in "Cauldron of Blood"

Yvonne Mitchell, Sharon Gurney
in "Crucible of Horror"

CAULDRON OF BLOOD (Cannon) Producer, Robert D. Weinbach; Director, Edward Mann; Screenplay, John Melson, Edward Mann; Photography, Francisco Sempere; Music, Ray Ellis; In EastmanColor; 101 minutes; Rating GP; November release. CAST: Jean-Pierre Aumont (Marchand), Boris Karloff (Badulescu), Viveca Lindfors (Tania), Rosenda Monteros (Valerie), Milo Queseda (Shanghai), Dianik Zurakowska (Elga), Ruben Rojo (Pablo).

CRUCIBLE OF HORROR (Cannon) Executive Producer, Dennis Friedland; Producer, Gabrielle Beaumont; Director, Viktors Ritelis; Screenplay, Olaf Pooley; Assistant Directors, Nick Granby, Richard Maclaine; Music, John Hotchkis; In EastmanColor; 91 minutes; Rating GP; November release. CAST: Michael Gough (Eastwood), Yvonne Mitchell (Edith), Sharon Gurney (Jane), Simon Gough (Rupert), Olaf Pooley (Reid), David Butler (Gregson), Nicholas Jones (Benjy), Mary Hignett (Servant), Howard Goorney (Gas Attendant).

CUBA: BATTLE OF THE 10,000,000 (New Yorker) Direction and Text, Chris Marker; Photography, Santiago Alvarez, "Noticierios" Icaic; Music, Leo Brouver; Narration, Georges Kiejman, Edouard Luntz; 55 minutes; A Documentary.

ONE NIGHT AT DINNER (International) Director, Giuseppe Patroni Griffi; Screenplay, Dario Argento, Giuseppe Patroni Griffi; Based on latter's play; Photography, Tonio Delli Colli; Music, Ennio Morricone; A Euro-International Co-Production in Color; 110 minutes; Rating R; November release. CAST: Jean-Louis Trintignant (Michel), Tony Musante (Max), Florinda Bolkan (Nina), Annie Girardot (Giovanna), Lino Capolicchio (Ric).

TWO HUNDRED MOTELS (United Artists) Producers, Jerry Good, Herb Cohen; Direction and Screenplay, Frank Zappa, Tony Palmer; Music, Frank Zappa; Designer, Cal Schenkel; Art Director, Leo Austin; Assistant Director, David Alexander; In Technicolor; 98 minutes; November release. CAST: The Mothers of Invention (Themselves), Theodore Bikel (Rance), Ringo Starr (Larry the Dwarf), Keith Moon (Hot Nun), Jimmy Carl Black (Lonesome Cowboy Burt), Martin Lickert (Jeff), Janet Ferguson, Lucy Offerall (Groupies), Pamela Miller (Interviewer), and Themselves: Don Preston, Motorhead Sherwood, Mark Volman, Howard Kaylan, Ian Underwood, Aynsley, George Duke, Jim Pons, Frank Zappa.

MADDALENA (Rand & Co.) Producers, Joseph Fryd, Alfred Piccolo; Director, Jergy Kawalerowicz; Screenplay, Sergio Bazina, Jergy Kawalerowicz; Photography, Gabor Pogainy; Music, Ennio Morricone; In Color; 105 minutes; Rating R; November release. CAST: Lisa Gaxtoni (Maddalena), Eric Woofe (Priest), Ivo Garani (Husband).

THE DIRTY HEROES (NMD) Producer, Edmundo Amati; Director, Alberto DeMartino; Screenplay and Story, Dino Verdo, Vincenzo Flamini, Alberto Verucci, Franco Silvestri, Alberto DeMartino; Photography, Gianni Bergamini; Art Director, Nedo Azzini; Music, Ennio Morricone; Assistant Director, Giorgio Ubaldi; In Technicolor; 105 minutes; Rating G; November release. CAST: Frederick Stafford (Sesamo), Daniela Bianchi (Kristina), Curt Jergens (General Von Keist), Adolfo Celi (Rollman), Helmut Schneider (Gen. Hassler), Michael Constantine (Petrowsky), Faida Nicols (Marta).

THE MARCO MEN (NMF) Producers, Sam X. Abarbanel, Angel Ibarra; Director, Julio Coll; Screenplay, Howard Berk, Santiago Moncado; In Technicscope and EastmanColor; A Pan Latina Films-P.E.A. Films Co-production; 95 minutes; Rating M; November release. CAST: Tom Tryon (Harry), Laura Guerrieri (Sonia), Jose Bodalo (Marcos), Ana Castor (Sonia), and Mirko Ellis, Jesus Puente, Richard Deacon.

Fidel Castro
in "Cuba . . ."

Jean-Pierre Aumont, Rosenda Monteros
in "Cauldron of Blood"

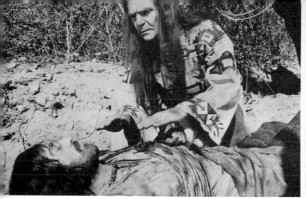

**Richard Harris, Henry Wilcoxon
in "Man in the Wilderness"**

**Zalman King, Charlotte Rampling
in "The Ski Bum"**

MAN IN THE WILDERNESS (Warner Bros.) Producer, Sanford Howard; Director, Richard C. Sarafian; Screenplay, Jack DeWitt; Photography, Gerry Fisher; Music, Johnny Harris; Designer, Dennis Lynton Clark; Art Director, Gumersindo Andres; Assistant Director, Juan C. L. Rodero; In Technicolor; 105 minutes; Rating GP; November release. CAST: Richard Harris (Zachary), John Huston (Capt. Henry), John Bindon (Coulter), Ben Carruthers (Longbow), Prunella Ransome (Grace), Henry Wilcoxon (Indian Chief), Percy Herbert (Fogarty), Dennis Waterman (Lowrie).

RAGA (Apple) Producer-Director, Howard Worth; Executive Producer, Gary Haber; Screenplay, Associate Producer, Nancy Bacal; Photography, Jimmy Allen; Additional Music, Colin Walcott; In EastmanColor; 96 minutes; November release. A documentary on Indian musician-teacher-composer Ravi Shankar.

ZATOICHI MEETS YOJIMBO (Bijou) Director, Kihachi Okamoto; Screenplay, Tetsuo Yoshida; Photography, Kazuo Miyagawa; A Daieie presentation of a Katsu Production in Color; 116 minutes; November release. CAST: Toshiro Mifune (Yojimbo), Shintaro Katsu (Zatoichi), Ayako Wakao (Courtesan), Kanjuro Arashi (Stonecutter), Osamu Takizawa (Elder).

BLACK BEAUTY (Paramount) Producers, Peter L. Andrews, Malcolm B. Heyworth; Director, James Hill; Screenplay, Wolf Mankowitz; Based on novel by Anna Sewell; Photography, Chris Menges; Music, Lionel Bart, John Cameron; In Color; Rating G; 106 minutes; November release. CAST: Mark Lester (Joe), Walter Slezak (Hackenschmidt), Peter Lee Lawrence (Gervaise), Ursula Glas (Maria), Patrick Mower (Sam), John Nettleton (Sir William), Maria Rohm (Anne), Eddie Golden (Evans), Clive Geraghty (Roger), Johnny Hoey (Muldoon), Margaret Lacey (Anna).

EL TOPO (ABK) Producer, Roberto Viskin; Direction and Screenplay, Alexandro Jodorowsky; Photography, Raphael Corkidi; Music, Mr. Jodorowsky; 123 minutes; November release. CAST: Alexandro Jodorowsky (El Topo), Mara Lorenzio (Mara), Paula Romo (Woman in black), Jacqueline Luis (small woman), David Silva (Colonel), Hector Martinez (First Master), Juan Jose Gurrola (Second Master), Victor Fosado (Third Master), Agustin Isunza (Fourth Master), Brontis Jodorowsky (Brontis as a child), Robert John (Brontis as a man).

CALCUTTA (New Yorker) Produced, Directed, Written, and Narrated by Louis Malle; November release. No other credits. A documentary on India's largest city.

THE SKI BUM (AVCO Embassy) Executive Producer, Joseph E. Levine; Producer, David R. Dawdy; Director, Bruce Clark; Screenplay, Marc Siegler, Bruce Clark; Suggested by novel of same name by Romain Gary; Photography, Vilmos Zsigmond; Music, Joseph Byrd; Associate Producer, Marc Siegler; In Widescreen and Technicolor; 94 minutes; Rating R; December release. CAST: Zalman King (Johnny), Charlotte Rampling (Samantha), Joseph Mell (Burt), Dimitra Arless (Liz), Anna Karen (Golda), Tedd King (Maxwell), Dwight Marfield (Dr. Graham), Freddie James (Brad), Lori Shelle (Lisa).

EVEN DWARFS STARTED SMALL (New Line) Producer, Francisco Ariza; Directed and Written by Werner Herzog; Photography, Thomas Mauch; 96 minutes; December release. CAST: Helmut Doring (Hombre), Gerd Gickel (Pepe), Paul Glauer (Azucar), Gisela Hertwig (Pobrecita), Gerhard Marz (Territory), Hertel Minkner (Chicklets).

THE DECAMERON (United Artists) Producer, Alberto Grimaldi; Direction and Screenplay, Pier Paolo Pasolini; Photography, Tonino Delli Colli; Based on Boccaccio's tales; 101 minutes; Rating X; December release. CAST: Franco Citti (Clappelleto), Ninetto Davoli (Andreuccio), Angela Luce (Peronella), Pier Paolo Pasolini (Giotto), Silvana Mangano.

**Dennis Waterman, Richard Harris
in "Man in the Wilderness"**

**Charlotte Rampling, Zalman King
in "The Ski Bum"**

221

Dawn Addams

Alan Alda

Lola Albright

Alan Arkin

Anne Bancroft

BIOGRAPHICAL DATA

(Name, real name, place and date of birth, and school attended)

ABBOTT, JOHN: London, June 5, 1905.

ADAMS, EDIE: (Elizabeth Edith Enke) Kingston, Pa., Apr. 16, 1931. Juilliard School of Music, Columbia.

ADAMS, JULIE: (Betty May) Waterloo, Iowa, Oct. 17, 1928. Little Rock Jr. College.

ADDAMS, DAWN: Felixstowe, Suffolk, Eng., Sept. 21, 1930. Royal Academy.

ADRIAN, IRIS: (Iris Adrian Hostetter) Los Angeles, May 29, 1913.

AGAR, JOHN: Chicago, Jan. 31, 1921.

AHERNE, BRIAN: Worcestershire, Eng., May 2, 1902. Malvern College, U. of London.

AHN, PHILIP: Los Angeles, Mar. 29, 1911. U. of Calif.

ALBERGHETTI, ANNA MARIA: Pesaro, Italy, May 15, 1936.

ALBERT, EDDIE: (Eddie Albert Heimberger) Rock Island, Ill., Apr. 22, 1908. U. of Minn.

ALBRIGHT, LOLA: Akron, Ohio, July 20, 1925.

ALDA, ALAN: NYC, Jan. 28, 1936, Fordham.

ALDA, ROBERT: (Alphonso D'Abruzzo) New York City, Feb. 26, 1914. NYU.

ALEJANDRO, MIGUEL: NYC, 1958.

ALLBRITTON, LOUISE: Oklahoma City, July 3, 1920. U. of Oklahoma.

ALLEN, STEVE: New York City, Dec. 26, 1921.

ALLEN, WOODY: Brooklyn, Dec. 1, 1935.

ALLENTUCK, KATHERINE: NYC, Oct. 16, 1954; Calhoun.

ALLYSON, JUNE: (Ella Geisman) Westchester, N.Y., Oct. 7, 1923.

AMECHE, DON: (Dominic Amichi) Kenosha, Wisc., May 31, 1908.

AMES, ED: Boston, July 9, 1929.

AMES, LEON: (Leon Wycoff) Portland, Ind., Jan. 20, 1903.

ANDERSON, JUDITH: Adelaide, Australia, Feb. 10, 1898.

ANDERSON, MICHAEL, JR.: London, Eng., 1943.

ANDES, KEITH: Ocean City, N.J., July 12, 1920. Temple U., Oxford.

ANDRESS, URSULA: Switz. 1936.

ANDREWS, DANA: Collins, Miss., Jan. 1, 1912. Sam Houston College.

ANDREWS, EDWARD: Griffin, Ga., Oct. 9, 1914. U. VA.

ANDREWS, HARRY: Tonbridge, Kent, Eng., Nov. 10, 1911.

ANDREWS, JULIE: (Julia Elizabeth Wells) Surrey, Eng. Oct. 1, 1935.

ANGEL, HEATHER: Oxford, Eng., Feb. 9, 1909. Wycombe Abbey School.

ANN-MARGRET: (Olsson) Valsjobyn, Sweden, Apr. 28, 1941. Northwestern U.

ANSARA, MICHAEL: Lowell, Mass., Apr. 15, 1922. Pasadena Playhouse.

ANTHONY, TONY: Clarksburg, W. Va., Oct 16, 1937. Carnegie Tech.

ARCHER, JOHN: (Ralph Bowman) Osceola, Neb., May 8, 1915. U. of S. Calif.

ARDEN, EVE: (Eunice Quedens) Mill Valley, Calif., Apr. 30, 1912.

ARKIN, ALAN: NYC, Mar. 26, 1934. LACC.

ARLEN, RICHARD: Charlottesville, Va., Sept. 1, 1900. St. Thomas College.

ARNAZ, DESI: Santiago, Cuba, Mar. 2, 1917, Colegio de Dolores.

ARNESS, JAMES: (Aurness) Minneapolis, Minn., May 26, 1923. Beloit College.

ARTHUR, JEAN: NYC, Oct. 17, 1908.

ARTHUR, ROBERT: (Robert Arthaud) Aberdeen, Wash., June 18. U. of Wash.

ASTAIRE, FRED: (Fred Austerlitz) Omaha, Neb., May 10, 1899.

ASTOR, MARY: (Lucile V. Langhanke) Quincy, Ill., May 3, 1906. Kenwood-Loring School.

ATTENBOROUGH, RICHARD: Cambridge, Eng., Aug. 29, 1923. RADA.

AULIN, EWA: Stockholm, Sweden, Feb. 14, 1950.

AUMONT, JEAN PIERRE: Paris, Jan. 5, 1913. French Nat'l School of Drama.

AUTRY, GENE: Tioga, Texas, Sept. 29, 1907.

AVALON, FRANKIE: (Francis Thomas Avallone) Philadelphia, Sept. 18, 1940.

AYLMER, FELIX: Corsham, Eng., Feb. 21, 1889. Oxford.

AYRES, LEW: Minneapolis, Minn., Dec. 28, 1908.

BACALL, LAUREN: (Betty Perske) NYC, Sept. 16, 1924. AADA.

BACKUS, JIM: Cleveland, Ohio, Feb. 25, 1913. AADA.

BADDELEY, HERMIONE: Shropshire, Eng., Nov. 13, 1908. Margaret Morris School.

BAILEY, PEARL: Newport News, Va., March 29, 1918.

BAIN, BARBARA: Chicago, Sept. 13, 1934. U. Ill.

BAKER, CARROLL: Johnstown, Pa., May 28, 1931. St. Petersburg Jr. College.

BAKER, DIANE: Hollywood, Feb. 25, USC.

BAKER, STANLEY: Glamorgan, Wales, Feb. 28, 1928.

BALIN, INA: Brooklyn, Nov. 12, 1937. NYU.

BALL, LUCILLE: Jamestown, N.Y., Aug. 6, 1911. Chatauqua Musical Inst.

BALSAM, MARTIN: NYC, Nov. 4, 1919. Actors Studio.

BANCROFT, ANNE: (Anna Maria Italiano) Bronx, N.Y., Sept. 17, 1931. AADA.

BANNEN, IAN: Airdrie, Scot., June 29, 1928.

BARDOT, BRIGITTE: Paris, 1934.

BARKER, LEX: (Alexander Crichlow Barker) Rye, N.Y., May 8, 1919.

BARRIE, WENDY: London, May 8, 1919.

BARRON, KEITH: Mexborough, Eng., Aug. 8, 1936. Sheffield Playhouse.

BARRY, DONALD: (Donald Barry de Acosta) Houston, Tex. Texas School of Mines.

BARRY, GENE: (Eugene Klass) NYC, June 14, 1921.

BARRYMORE, JOHN BLYTH: Beverly Hills, Calif., June 4, 1932. St. John's Military Academy.

BARTHOLOMEW, FREDDIE: London, Mar. 28, 1924.

BASEHART, RICHARD: Zanesville, Ohio, Aug. 31, 1914.

BATES, ALAN: Allestree, Derbyshire, Eng., Feb. 17, 1934. RADA.

BAXTER, ALAN: East Cleveland, Ohio, Nov. 19, 1911. Williams U.

BAXTER, ANNE: Michigan City, Ind., May 7, 1923, Ervine School of Drama.

BEAL, JOHN: (J. Alexander Bliedung) Joplin, Mo., Aug. 13, 1909. Pa. U.

Jean-Paul Belmondo   Jacqueline Bisset   Ralph Bellamy   Claire Bloom   Rossano Brazzi

BEATTY, ROBERT: Hamilton, Ont., Can., Oct. 19, 1909. U. of Toronto.

BEATTY, WARREN: Richmond, Virginia, March 30, 1937.

BEAUMONT, HUGH: Lawrence, Kan., Feb. 16, 1909. U. of Chattanooga, USC.

BEERY, NOAH, JR.: NYC, Aug. 10, 1916. Harvard Military Academy.

BELAFONTE, HARRY: NYC, Mar. 1, 1927.

BELASCO, LEON: Odessa, Russia, Oct. 11, 1902.

BEL GEDDES, BARBARA: NYC, Oct. 31, 1922.

BELLAMY, RALPH: Chicago, June 17, 1905.

BELMONDO, JEAN PAUL: Paris, 1933.

BENNETT, BRUCE: (Herman Brix) Tacoma, Wash., U. of Wash.

BENNETT, JOAN: Palisades, N.J., Feb. 27, 1910. St. Margaret's School.

BENNY, JACK: (Jack Kubelsky) Waukegan, Ill., Feb. 14, 1894.

BERGEN, CANDICE: Los Angeles, 1946.

BERGEN, EDGAR: Chicago, Feb. 16, 1903. Northwestern U.

BERGEN, POLLY: Knoxville, Tenn., July 14, 1930. Compton Jr. College.

BERGERAC, JACQUES: Biarritz, France, May 26, 1927. Paris U. of Law.

BERGMAN, INGRID: Stockholm, Sweden, Aug. 29, 1917. Royal Dramatic Theatre School.

BERLE, MILTON: (Milton Berlinger) NYC, July 12, 1908. Professional Children's School.

BERLINGER, WARREN: Brooklyn, Aug. 31, 1937. Columbia University.

BEST, JAMES: Corydon, Ind., July 26, 1926.

BETTGER, LYLE: Philadelphia, Feb. 13, 1915. AADA.

BETZ, CARL: Pittsburgh, Mar. 9. Duquesne, Carnegie Tech.

BEYMER, RICHARD: Avoca, Iowa, Feb. 21, 1939.

BIKEL, THEODORE: Vienna, May 2, 1924. RADA.

BISHOP, JOEY: (Joseph Abraham Gottlieb) Bronx, N.Y., Feb. 3, 1918.

BISHOP, JULIE: (formerly Jacqueline Wells) Denver, Colo., Aug. 30, 1917. Westlake School.

BISSET, JACQUELINE: Waybridge, Eng., Sept. 13, 1944.

BIXBY, BILL: San Francisco, Jan. 22, 1934. U. Cal.

BLACK, KAREN: (Ziegler) Park Ridge, Ill., 1943; Northwestern.

BLACKMER, SIDNEY: Salisbury, N.C., July 13, 1898. U. of N.C.

BLAINE, VIVIAN: (Vivian Stapleton) Newark, N.J., Nov. 21, 1924.

BLAIR, BETSY: (Betsy Boger) NYC, Dec. 11.

BLAIR, JANET: (Martha Jane Lafferty) Blair, Pa., Apr. 23, 1921.

BLAKE, AMANDA: (Beverly Louise Neill) Buffalo, N.Y., Feb. 20.

BLAKE, ROBERT: Nutley, N.J., 1933.

BLONDELL, JOAN: NYC, Aug. 30, 1909.

BLOOM, CLAIRE: London, Feb. 15, 1931. Badminton School.

BLUE, BEN: Montreal, Can., Sept. 12, 1901.

BLUE, MONTE: Indianapolis, Jan. 11, 1890.

BLYTH, ANN: Mt. Kisco, N.Y., Aug. 16, 1928. New Wayburn Dramatic School.

BOGARDE, DIRK: London, Mar. 28, 1921. Glasgow & Univ. College.

BOLGER, RAY: Dorchester, Mass., Jan. 10, 1906.

BOND, DEREK: Glasgow, Scot., Jan. 26, 1920. Askes School.

BONDI, BEULAH: Chicago, May 3, 1892.

BOONE, PAT: Jacksonville, Fla., June 1, 1934. Columbia U.

BOONE, RICHARD: Los Angeles. Stanford U.

BOOTH, SHIRLEY: NYC, Aug. 30, 1907.

BORGNINE, ERNEST: Hamden, Conn., Jan. 24, 1918. Randall School of Dramatic Art.

BOWMAN, LEE: Cincinnati, Dec. 28, 1914. AADA.

BOYD, STEPHEN: (William Millar) Belfast, Ire., 1928.

BOYER, CHARLES: Figeac, France, Aug. 28, 1899. Sorbonne U.

BRACKEN, EDDIE: NYC, Feb. 7, 1920. Professional Children's School.

BRADY, SCOTT: (Jerry Tierney) Brooklyn, Sept. 13, 1924. Bliss-Hayden Dramatic School.

BRAND, NEVILLE: Kewanee, Ill., Aug. 13, 1921.

BRANDO, JOCELYN: San Francisco, Nov. 18, 1919. Lake Forest College. AADA.

BRANDO, MARLON: Omaha, Neb., Apr. 3, 1924. New School of Social Research.

BRASSELLE, KEEFE: Elyria, Ohio, Feb. 7.

BRAZZI, ROSSANO: Bologna, Italy, 1916. U. of Florence.

BRENT, GEORGE: Dublin, Ire., Mar. 15, 1904. Dublin U.

BRENT, ROMNEY: (Romulo Larralde) Saltillo, Mex., Jan. 26, 1902.

BRIALY, JEAN-CLAUDE: Aumale, Algeria, 1933. Strasbourg Dramatic Cons.

BRIAN, DAVID: NYC, Aug. 5, 1914. CCNY.

BRIDGES, BEAU: Los Angeles, Dec. 9, 1941. UCLA.

BRIDGES, LLOYD: San Leandro, Calif., Jan. 15, 1913.

BRITT, MAY: (Maybritt Wilkins) Sweden, March 22, 1936.

BRODIE, STEVE: (Johnny Stevens) Eldorado, Kan., Nov. 25, 1919.

BROMFIELD, JOHN: (Farron Bromfield) South Bend, Ind., June 11, 1922. St. Mary's College.

BRONSON, CHARLES: (Buchinsky) Scooptown, Pa., Nov. 3, 1922.

BROOKS, GERALDINE: (Geraldine Stroock) NYC, Oct. 29, 1925. AADA.

BROWN, JAMES: Desdemona, Tex., Mar. 22, 1920. Baylor U.

BROWN, JIM: Manhasset, L.I., N.Y., Feb. 17, 1936. Syracuse U.

BROWN, JOE E.: Helgate, Ohio, July 28, 1892.

BROWN, TOM: NYC, Jan. 6, 1913. Professional Children's School.

BROWNE, CORAL: Melbourne, Aust., July 23, 1913.

BRUCE, VIRGINIA: Minneapolis, Sept. 29, 1910.

BRYNNER, YUL: Sakhalin Island, Japan, June 15, 1915.

BUCHHOLZ, HORST: Berlin, Ger., Dec. 4, 1933. Ludwig Dramatic School.

BUETEL, JACK: Dallas, Tex., Sept. 5, 1917.

BUJOLD, GENEVIEVE: Montreal, Can., 1944.

BURKE, PAUL: New Orleans, July 21, 1926. Pasadena Playhouse.

BURNETT, CAROL: San Antonio, Tex., Apr. 26, 1933. UCLA.

BURNS, GEORGE: (Nathan Birnbaum) NYC, Jan. 20, 1896.

BURR, RAYMOND: New Westminster, B.C., Can., May 21, 1917. Stanford, U. of Cal., Columbia.

BURTON, RICHARD: (Richard Jenkins) Pontrhydyfen, S. Wales, Nov. 10, 1925. Oxford.

BUTTONS, RED: (Aaron Chwatt) NYC, Feb. 5, 1919.

BUZZI, RUTH: Wequetequock, R.I., July 24, 1936. Pasadena Playhouse.

Claudia Cardinale

David Carradine

Carol Channing

Jackie Cooper

Julie Christie

BYGRAVES, MAX: London, Oct. 16, 1922. St. Joseph's School.

BYRNES, EDD: NYC, July 30, 1933. Haaren High.

CABOT, SUSAN: Boston, July 6, 1927.

CAESAR, SID: Yonkers, N.Y., Sept. 8, 1922.

CAGNEY, JAMES: NYC, July 1, 1904. Columbia.

CAGNEY, JEANNE: NYC, Mar. 25, 1919. Hunter.

CAINE, MICHAEL: (Maurice Michelwhite) London, Mar. 14, 1933.

CALHOUN, RORY: (Francis Timothy Durgin) Los Angeles, Aug. 8, 1923.

CALLAN, MICHAEL: (Martin Calinieff) Philadelphia, Nov. 22, 1935.

CALVERT, PHYLLIS: London, Feb. 18, 1917. Margaret Morris School.

CALVET, CORINNE: (Corinne Dibos) Paris, Apr. 30. U. of Paris.

CAMBRIDGE, GODFREY: NYC, Feb. 26, 1933. CCNY.

CAMERON, ROD: (Rod Cox) Calgary, Alberta, Can., Dec. 7, 1912.

CAMPBELL, GLEN: Apr. 22, 1935

CANALE, GIANNA MARIA: Reggio Calabria, Italy, Sept. 12.

CANNON, DYAN: (Samille Diane Friesen) Jan. 4, 1929, Tacoma, Wash.

CANOVA, JUDY: Jacksonville, Fla., Nov. 20, 1916.

CAPUCINE: (Germaine Lefebvre) Toulon, France, Jan. 6, 1935.

CARDINALE, CLAUDIA: Tunis, NAfrica, Apr. 15, 1939; College Paul Cambon.

CAREY, HARRY, JR.: Saugus, Calif., May 16, Black Fox Military Academy.

CAREY, MACDONALD: Sioux City, Iowa, Mar. 15, 1913. U. of Wisc., U. of Iowa.

CAREY, PHILIP: Hackensack, N.J., July 15, 1925. U. of Miami.

CARMICHAEL, HOAGY: Bloomington, Ind., Nov. 22, 1899. Ind. U.

CARMICHAEL, IAN: Hull, Eng., June 18, 1920. Scarborough College.

CARNE, JUDY: (Joyce Botterill) Northampton, Eng., 1939. Bush-Davis Theatre School.

CARNEY, ART: Mt. Vernon, N.Y., Nov. 4, 1918.

CARON, LESLIE: Paris, July 1, 1931. Nat'l Conservatory, Paris.

CARR, VIKKI: (Florence Cardona) July 19, 1942. San Fermardo, Col.

CARRADINE, DAVID: Hollywood, Dec. 8, 1940. San Francisco State.

CARRADINE, JOHN: NYC, Feb. 5, 1906.

CARREL, DANY: Tourane, Indochina, Sept. 20, 1936. Marseilles Cons.

CARROLL, DIAHANN: (Johnson) NYC, July 17, 1935. NYU.

CARROLL, JOHN: (Julian LaFaye) New Orleans.

CARROLL, MADELEINE: West Bromwich, Eng., Feb. 26, 1906. Birmingham U.

CARROLL, PAT: Shreveport, La., May 5, 1927. Catholic U.

CARSON, JOHNNY: Corning, Iowa, Oct. 23, 1925. U. of Neb.

CARSTEN, PETER: (Ransenthaler) Weissenberg, Bavaria, Apr. 30, 1929; Munich Akademie for Actors.

CASS, PEGGY: (Mary Margaret) Boston, May 21, 1925.

CASSAVETES, JOHN: NYC, Dec. 9, 1929. Colgate College, Academy of Dramatic Arts.

CASSIDY, DAVID: NYC, Apr. 12, 1950.

CASTLE, PEGGIE: Appalachia, Va., Dec. 22, 1927. Mills College.

CAULFIELD, JOAN: Orange, N.J., June 1. Columbia U.

CERVI, GINO: Bologna, Italy. May 3, 1901.

CHAKIRIS, GEORGE: Norwood, O., Sept. 16, 1933.

CHAMBERLAIN, RICHARD: Beverly Hills, Cal., March 31, 1935. Pomona.

CHAMPION, GOWER: Geneva, Ill., June 22, 1921.

CHAMPION, MARGE: Los Angeles, Sept. 2, 1926.

CHANDLER, LANE: (Lane Oakes) Culbertson, Mont., June 4, 1899. Ill. U.

CHANEY, LON, JR.: (Creighton Chaney) Oklahoma City, 1915.

CHANNING, CAROL: Seattle, Jan. 31, 1921. Bennington.

CHAPLIN, CHARLES: London, Apr. 16, 1889.

CHAPLIN, GERALDINE: Santa Monica, Cal. July 31, 1944. Royal Ballet.

CHAPLIN, SYDNEY: Los Angeles, Mar. 31, 1926. Lawrenceville.

CHARISSE, CYD: (Tula Ellice Finklea) Amarillo, Tex., Mar. 3, 1923. Hollywood Professional School.

CHASE, ILKA: NYC, Apr. 8, 1905.

CHER: (Cheryl La Piere) 1946.

CHIARI, WALTER: Veronea, Italy, 1930.

CHRISTIAN, LINDA: (Blanca Rosa Welter) Tampico, Mex., Nov. 13, 1923.

CHRISTIE, JULIE: Chukua, Assam, India, Apr. 14, 1941.

CHRISTOPHER, JORDAN: Youngstown, O., Oct. 23, 1940. Kent State.

CHURCHILL, SARAH: London, Oct. 7, 1916.

CILENTO, DIANE: Queensland, Australia, Oct. 5, 1933. AADA.

CLARK, DANE: NYC, Feb. 18, 1915. Cornell and Johns Hopkins U.

CLARK, DICK: Mt. Vernon, N.Y., Nov. 30, 1929, Syracuse University.

CLARK, PETULA: England, 1932.

CLARK, MAE: Philadelphia, Aug. 16, 1910.

CLEMENTS, STANLEY: Long Island, N.Y., July 16, 1926.

CLOONEY, ROSEMARY: Maysville Ky., May 23, 1928.

COBB, LEE J.: NYC, Dec. 8, 1911. CCNY.

COBURN, JAMES: Laurel, Neb., Aug. 31, 1928. LACC.

COCA, IMOGENE: Philadelphia, Nov. 18, 1908.

COLBERT, CLAUDETTE: (Claudette Chauchoin) Paris, Sept. 13, 1907. Art Students League.

COLE, GEORGE: London, Apr. 22, 1925.

COLLINS, JOAN: London, May 23, 1933. Francis Holland School.

COMER, ANJANETTE: Dawson, Tex., Aug. 7, 1942. Baylor, Tex. U.

CONANT, OLIVER: NYC, Nov. 15, 1955; Dalton.

CONNERY, SEAN: Edinburgh, Scot. Aug. 25, 1930.

CONNORS, CHUCK: (Kevin Joseph Connors) Brooklyn, Apr. 10, 1924. Seton Hall College.

CONTE, RICHARD: (Nicholas Conte) NYC, Mar. 24, 1914. Neighborhood Playhouse.

COOGAN, JACKIE: Los Angeles, Oct. 26, 1914. Villanova College.

COOK, ELISHA, JR.: San Francisco, Dec. 26, 1907. St. Albans.

COOPER, BEN,: Hartford, Conn., Sept. 30. Columbia U.

COOPER, JACKIE: Los Angeles, Sept. 15, 1921.

COOPER, MELVILLE: Birmingham, Eng., Oct. 15, 1896. King Edward's School.

COOTE, ROBERT: London, Feb. 4, 1909. Hurstpierpont College.

CORCORAN, DONNA: Quincy, Mass., Sept. 29.

CORD, ALEX: (Viespi) Floral Park, L.I., Aug. 3, 1931. NYU, Actors Studio.

CORDAY, MARA: (Marilyn Watts) Santa Monica Calif., Jan. 3, 1932.

COREY, JEFF: NYC, Aug. 10, 1914. Fagin School.

CORRI, ADRIENNE: Glasgow, Scot., Nov. 13, 1933. RADA.

    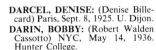

Noel Coward   Arlene Dahl   Claude Dauphin   Gloria DeHaven   Michael Douglas

CORTESA, VALENTINA: Milan, Italy, Jan. 1, 1925.

COSBY, BILL: Philadelphia, 1937. Temple U.

COTTEN, JOSEPH: Petersburg, VA., May 13, 1905.

COURTENAY, TOM: Hull, Eng., 1937. RADA.

CORLAN, ANTHONY: Cork City, Ire., May 9, 1947; Birmingham School of Dramatic Arts.

COURTLAND, JEROME: Knoxville, Tenn., Dec. 27, 1926.

COWARD, NOEL: Teddington-on-the-Thames, Eng., Dec. 16, 1899.

COX, WALLY: (Wallace Cox) Detroit, Dec. 6, 1924. CCNY.

CRABBE, BUSTER (LARRY): (Clarence Linden) Oakland, Calif., U. of S. Cal.

CRAIG, JAMES: (James H. Meador) Nashville, Tenn., Feb. 4, 1912. Rice Inst.

CRAIG, MICHAEL: India in 1929.

CRAIN, JEANNE: Barstow, Cal., May 25, 1925.

CRAWFORD, BRODERICK: Philadelphia, Dec. 9, 1911.

CRAWFORD, JOAN: (Billie Cassin) San Antonio, Tex., Mar. 23, 1908.

CRENNA, RICHARD: Los Angeles, Nov. 30, 1927. USC.

CRISTAL, LINDA: (Victoria Moya) Buenos Aires, 1935.

CROSBY, BING: (Harry Lillith Crosby) Tacoma, Wash., May 2, 1904. Gonzaga College.

CROWLEY, PAT: Olyphant, Pa., Sept. 17, 1933.

CULP, ROBERT: Berkeley, Calif., Aug. 16, 1930. U. of Wash.

CUMMINGS, CONSTANCE: Seattle, Wash., May 15, 1910.

CUMMINGS, ROBERT: Joplin, Mo., June 9, 1910. Carnegie Tech.

CUMMINS, PEGGY: Prestatyn, N. Wales, Dec. 18, 1926. Alexandra School.

CURTIS, TONY: (Bernard Schwartz) NYC, June 3, 1925.

CUSHING, PETER: Kenley, Surrey, Eng., May 26, 1913.

CUTTS, PATRICIA: London, July 20, 1927. RADA.

DAHL, ARLENE: Minneapolis, Aug. 11, 1927. U. Minn.

DALTON, TIMOTHY: Wales, 1945; RADA.

DAMONE, VIC: (Vito Farinola) Brooklyn, June 12, 1928.

DANIELS, WILLIAM: Bklyn, Mar. 31, 1927. Northwestern.

DANTINE, HELMUT: Vienna, Oct. 7, 1918. U. Calif.

DANTON, RAY: NYC, Sept. 19, 1931. Carnegie Tech.

DARBY, KIM: (Deborah Zerby) North Hollywood, Cal., July 8, 1948.

DARCEL, DENISE: (Denise Billecard) Paris, Sept. 8, 1925. U. Dijon.

DARIN, BOBBY: (Robert Walden Cassotto) NYC, May 14, 1936. Hunter College.

DARREN, JAMES: Philadelphia, June 8, 1936. Stella Adler School.

DARRIEUX, DANIELLE: Bordeaux, France, May 1, 1917. Lycee LaTour.

DA SILVA, HOWARD: Cleveland, Ohio, May 4, 1909. Carnegie Tech.

DAUPHIN, CLAUDE: Corbeil, France, Aug. 19, 1903. Beaux Arts School.

DAVIDSON, JOHN: Pittsburgh, Dec. 13, 1941. Denison U.

DAVIES, RUPERT: Liverpool, Eng., 1916.

DAVIS, BETTE: Lowell, Mass., Apr. 5, 1908. John Murray Anderson Dramatic School.

DAVIS, OSSIE: Cogdell, Ga., Dec. 18, 1917. Howard U.

DAVIS, SAMMY, JR.: NYC, Dec. 8, 1925.

DAY, DENNIS: (Eugene Dennis McNulty) NYC, May 21, 1917. Manhattan College.

DAY, DORIS: (Doris Kappelhoff) Cincinnati, Apr. 3, 1924.

DAY, LARAINE: (Johnson) Roosevelt, Utah, Oct. 13, 1920.

DAYAN, ASSEF: Israel, 1945. U. Jerusalem.

DEAN, JIMMY: Plainview, Tex., Aug. 10, 1928.

DE CARLO, YVONNE: (Peggy Yvonne Middleton) Vancouver, B.C., Can., Sept. 1, 1924. Vancouver School of Drama.

DE CORDOVA, ARTURO: Merida, Yucatan, May 8, 1908. Cavin Inst.

DEE, FRANCES: Los Angeles, Nov. 26, 1907. Chicago U.

DEE, JOEY: (Joseph Di Nicola) Passaic, N.J., June 11, 1940. Patterson State College.

DEE, SANDRA: (Alexandra Zuck) Bayonne, N.J., Apr. 23, 1942.

DE FORE, DON: Cedar Rapids, Iowa, Aug. 25, 1917. U. Iowa.

DE HAVEN, GLORIA: Los Angeles, July 23, 1925.

DE HAVILLAND, OLIVIA: Tokyo, Japan, July 1, 1916. Notre Dame Convent School.

DEL RIO, DOLORES: (Dolores Ansunsolo) Durango, Mex., Aug. 3, 1905. St. Joseph's Convent.

DENISON, MICHAEL: Doncaster, York, Eng., Nov. 1, 1915. Oxford.

DENNIS, SANDY: Hastings, Neb., Apr. 27, 1937. Actors Studio.

DEREK, JOHN: Hollywood, Aug. 12, 1926.

DE SICA, VITTORIO: Sora, Caserta, Italy, July 7, 1902.

DEVINE, ANDY: Flagstaff, Ariz., Oct. 7, 1905. Ariz. State College.

DE WILDE, BRANDON: Brooklyn, Apr. 9, 1942.

DE WOLFE, BILLY: (William Andrew Jones) Wollaston, Mass., Feb. 18.

DEXTER, ANTHONY: (Walter Reinhold Alfred Fleischmann) Talmadge, Neb., Jan. 19, 1919. U. Iowa.

DICKINSON, ANGIE: Kulm, N. Dak., Sept. 30, 1932. Glendale College.

DIETRICH, MARLENE: (Maria Magdalene von Losch) Berlin, Ger., Dec. 27, 1904. Berlin Music Academy.

DIFFRING, ANTON: Loblenz, Ger. Berlin Dramatic Art School.

DILLER, PHYLLIS: Lima, O., July 17, 1917. Bluffton College.

DILLMAN, BRADFORD: San Francisco, Apr. 14, 1930. Yale.

DOMERGUE, FAITH: New Orleans, June 16, 1925.

DONAHUE, TROY: (Merle Johnson) NYC, Jan. 27, 1937. Columbia U.

DONNELL, JEFF: (Jean Donnell) South Windham, Me., July 10, 1921. Yale Drama School.

DONNELLY, RUTH: Trenton, N.J., May 17, 1896.

DORS, DIANA: Swindon, Wilshire, Eng., Oct. 23, 1931. London Academy of Music.

DOUGLAS, KIRK: Amsterdam, N.Y., Dec. 9, 1916. St. Lawrence U.

DOUGLAS, MELVYN: (Melvyn Hesselberg) Macon, Ga., Apr. 5, 1901.

DOUGLAS, MICHAEL: Hollywood, Sept. 25, 1944. U. Cal.

DRAKE, BETSY: Paris, Sept. 11, 1923.

DRAKE, CHARLES: (Charles Ruppert) NYC, Oct. 2, 1914. Nichols College.

DREW, ELLEN: (formerly Terry Ray) Kansas City, Mo., Nov. 23, 1915.

DRIVAS, ROBERT: Chicago, Nov. 21, 1938. U. Chi.

DRU, JOANNE: (Joanne LaCock) Logan, W. Va., Jan. 31, 1923. John Robert Powers School.

DUFF, HOWARD: Bremerton, Wash., Nov. 24, 1917.

DUKE, PATTY: NYC, Dec. 14, 1946.

DULLEA, KEIR: Cleveland, N.J., May 30, 1936. Neighborhood Playhouse, SF State Col.

DUNAWAY, FAYE: Tallahassee, Fla., Jan, 14, 1941. Fla. U.

DUNCAN, SANDY: Henderson, Tex., Feb. 20, 1946; Len Morris Col.

DUNN, MICHAEL: Shattuck, Okla., Oct. 20, 1934. U. Mich.

225

| Samantha Eggar | Peter Falk | Mia Farrow | Robert Forster | Greer Garson |

DUNNE, IRENE: Louisville, Ky., Dec. 20, 1904. Chicago College of Music.

DUNNOCK, MILDRED: Baltimore, Jan. 25, 1906. Johns Hopkins and Columbia U.

DURANTE, JIMMY: NYC, Feb. 10, 1893.

DVORAK, ANN: (Ann McKim) NYC, Aug. 2, 1912.

EASTON, ROBERT: Milwaukee, Nov. 23, 1930. U. of Texas.

EASTWOOD, CLINT: San Francisco, May 31, 1931. LACC.

EATON, SHIRLEY: London, 1937. Aida Foster School.

EDEN, BARBARA: (Moorhead) Tucson, Ariz., 1934.

EDWARDS, VINCE: NYC, July 9, 1928. AADA.

EGAN, RICHARD: San Francisco, July 29, 1923, Stanford U.

EGGAR, SAMANTHA: London, 1940.

EKBERG, ANITA: Malmo, Sweden, Sept. 29, 1931.

ELLIOTT, DENHOLM: London, May 31, 1922. Malvern College.

ELSOM, ISOBEL: Cambridge, Eng., Mar. 16, 1894.

ELY, RON: (Ronald Pierce) Hereford, Tex. June 21, 1938.

EMERSON, FAYE: Elizabeth, La., July 8, 1917. San Diego State College.

ERDMAN, RICHARD: Enid, Okla., June 1, 1925.

ERICKSON, LEIF: Alameda, Calif., Oct. 27, 1914. U. of Calif.

ERICSON, JOHN: Dusseldorf, Ger., Sept. 25, 1926. AADA.

ESMOND, CARL: Vienna, June 14, 1906. U. of Vienna.

EVANS, DALE: (Francis Smith) Uvalde, Texas, Oct. 31, 1912.

EVANS, EDITH: London, Feb. 8, 1888.

EVANS, GENE: Holbrook, Ariz., July 11, 1922.

EVANS, MAURICE: Dorchester, Eng., June 3, 1901.

EVERETT, CHAD: (Ray Cramton) South Bend, Ind., June 11, 1936.

EWELL, TOM: (Yewell Tompkins) Owensboro, Ky., Apr. 29, 1909. U. of Wisc.

FABIAN: (Fabian Forte) Philadelphia, Feb. 6, 1940.

FABRAY, NANETTE: (Ruby Nanette Fabares) San Diego, Oct. 27, 1920.

FAIRBANKS, DOUGLAS JR.: NYC, Dec. 9, 1909, Collegiate School.

FALK, PETER: NYC, Sept. 16, 1927, New School.

FARENTINO, JAMES: Brooklyn, 1938.

FARR, FELICIA: Westchester, N.Y., Oct. 4, 1932. Penn State College.

FARRELL, CHARLES: Onset Bay, Mass., Aug. 9, 1901. Boston U.

FARROW, MIA: Los Angeles, 1945.

FAYE, ALICE: (Ann Lepert) NYC, May 5, 1915.

FELDON, BARBARA: (Hall) Pittsburgh, Mar. 12, 1941; Carnegie Tech.

FELLOWS, EDITH: Boston, May 20, 1923.

FERRER, JOSE: Santurce, P.R., Jan. 8, 1912. Princeton U.

FERRER, MEL: Elberon, N.J., Aug. 25, 1917. Princeton U.

FERRIS, BARBARA: London 1943.

FIELD, BETTY: Boston, Feb. 8, 1913. AADA.

FIELD, SALLY: Pasadena, Cal., Nov. 6, 1946.

FIGUEROA, RUBEN: NYC 1958.

FINCH, PETER: London, Sept. 28, 1916.

FINNEY, ALBERT: Salford, Lancashire, Eng., May 9, 1936. RADA.

FISHER, EDDIE: Philadelphia, Aug. 10, 1928.

FITZGERALD, GERALDINE: Dublin, Ire., Nov. 24, 1914. Dublin Art School.

FLEMING, RHONDA: (Marilyn Louis) Los Angeles, Aug. 10, 1922.

FLEMYNG, ROBERT: Liverpool, Eng., Jan. 3, 1912. Haileybury College.

FLYNN, JOE: Youngstown, O., Nov. 8, 1924; Notre Dame.

FOCH, NINA: Leyden, Holland, Apr. 20, 1924.

FONDA, HENRY: Grand Island, Neb., May 16, 1905. Minn. U.

FONDA, JANE: NYC, Dec. 21, 1937. Vassar.

FONDA, PETER: NYC, Feb. 23, 1939. U. of Omaha.

FONTAINE, JOAN: Tokyo, Japan, Oct. 22, 1917.

FORD, GLENN: (Gwyllyn Samuel Newton Ford) Quebec, Can., May 1, 1917.

FORD, PAUL: Baltimore, Nov. 2, 1901. Dartmouth.

FOREST, MARK: (Lou Degni) Brooklyn, Jan. 1933.

FORREST, STEVE: Huntsville, Tex., Sept. 29. UCLA.

FORSTER, ROBERT: (Foster, Jr.) Rochester, N.Y., July 13, 1941. Rochester U.

FORSYTHE, JOHN: Penn's Grove, N.J., Jan. 29, 1918.

FOX, JAMES: London, 1939.

FRANCIS, CONNIE: (Constance Franconero) Newark, N.J., Dec. 12, 1938.

FRANCIOSA, ANTHONY: NYC, Oct. 25, 1928.

FRANCIS, ANNE: Ossining, N.Y., Sept. 16.

FRANCIS, ARLENE: (Arlene Kazanjian) Boston, Oct. 20, 1908. Finch School.

FRANCISCUS, JAMES: Clayton, Mo., Jan. 31; Yale.

FRANCKS, DON: Vancouver, Can., Feb. 28, 1932.

FRANZ, ARTHUR: Perth Amboy, N.J., Feb. 29, 1920. Blue Ridge College.

FRANZ, EDUARD: Milwaukee, Wisc., Oct. 31, 1902.

FREEMAN, AL, JR.: San Antonio, Texas, 1934. CCLA.

FREEMAN, MONA: Baltimore, June 9, 1926.

FURNEAUX, YVONNE: Lille, France, 1928. Oxford U.

GABEL, MARTIN: Philadelphia, June 19, 1912. AADA.

GABIN, JEAN: Villette, France, May 17, 1904.

GABOR, EVA: Budapest, Hungary, Feb. 11, 1925.

GABOR, ZSA ZSA: (Sari Gabor) Budapest, Hungary, Feb. 6, 1923.

GAM, RITA: Pittsburgh, Apr. 2, 1928.

GARBO, GRETA: (Greta Gustafson) Stockholm, Sweden, Sept. 18, 1906.

GARDINER, REGINALD: Wimbledon, Eng., Feb. 1903. RADA.

GARDNER, AVA: Smithfield, N.C., Dec. 24, 1922. Atlantic Christian College.

GARNER, JAMES: (James Baumgarner) Norman, Okla., Apr. 7, 1928. Berghof School.

GARNER, PEGGY ANN: Canton, Ohio, Feb. 3, 1932.

GARRETT, BETTY: St. Joseph, Mo., May 23, 1919. Annie Wright Seminary.

GARRISON, SEAN: NYC, Oct. 19, 1937.

GARSON, GREER: Ireland, Sept. 29, 1908.

GASSMAN, VITTORIO: Genoa, Italy, Sept. 1, 1922. Rome Academy of Dramatic Art.

GAVIN, JOHN: Los Angeles, Apr. 8. Stanford U.

GAYNOR, JANET: Philadelphia, Oct. 6, 1906.

GAYNOR, MITZI: (Francesca Mitzi Von Gerber) Chicago, Sept. 4, 1930.

GAZZARA, BEN: NYC, Aug. 28, 1930.

GENN, LEO: London, Aug. 9, 1905. Cambridge.

John Gielgud Gloria Grahame George Grizzard Barbara Harris David Hemmings

GIELGUD, JOHN: London, Apr. 14, 1904. RADA.

GILLMORE, MARGOLO: London, May 31, 1897. AADA.

GILMORE, VIRGINIA: (Sherman Poole) Del Monte, Calif., July 26, 1919. U. of Calif.

GINGOLD, HERMIONE: London, Dec. 9, 1897.

GISH, LILLIAN: Springfield, Ohio, Oct. 14, 1896.

GLEASON, JACKIE: Brooklyn, Feb. 26, 1916.

GODDARD, PAULETTE: (Levy) Great Neck, N.Y., June 3, 1911.

GORDON, RUTH: Wollaston, Mass., Oct. 30, 1896. AADA.

GORING, MARIUS: Newport, Isle of Wight; 1912; Cambridge; Old Vic.

GOULD, ELLIOTT: (Goldstein); Bklyn, Aug. 29, 1938. Columbia U.

GOULET, ROBERT: Lawrence, Mass., Nov. 26, 1933. Edmonton School.

GRABLE, BETTY: St. Louis, Mo., Dec. 18, 1916. Hollywood Professional School.

GRAHAME, GLORIA: (Gloria Grahame Hallward) Los Angeles, Nov. 28, 1929.

GRANGER, FARLEY: San Jose, Calif., July 1, 1925.

GRANGER, STEWART: (James Stewart) London, May 6, 1913. Webber-Douglas School of Acting.

GRANT, CARY: (Archibald Alexander Leach) Bristol, Eng., Jan. 18, 1904.

GRANT, KATHRYN: (Olive Grandstaff) Houston, Tex., Nov. 25, 1933. UCLA.

GRAVES, PETER: (Aurness) Minneapolis, Mar. 18, 1926. U. of Minn.

GRAY, COLEEN: (Doris Jensen) Staplehurst, Neb., Oct 23, 1922. Hamline U.

GRAYSON, KATHRYN: (Zelma Hedrick) Winston-Salem, N.C., Feb. 9, 1923.

GREENE, LORNE: Ottawa, Can., Feb. 12, 1915.

GREENE, RICHARD: Plymouth, Eng., Aug. 25, 1918. Cardinal Vaughn School.

GREENWOOD, JOAN: London, 1919. RADA.

GREER, JANE: Washington, D.C., Sept. 9, 1924.

GREY, VIRGINIA: Los Angeles, Mar. 22, 1923.

GRIFFITH, ANDY: Mt. Airy, N.C., June 1, 1926. U.N.C.

GRIFFITH, HUGH: Marian Glas, Anglesey, N. Wales, May 30, 1912.

GRIMES, GARY: San Francisco, June 2, 1955.

GRIZZARD, GEORGE: Roanoke Rapids, N.C., Apr. 1, 1928, U.N.C.

GUARDINO, HARRY: Brooklyn, Dec. 23, 1925.

GUINNESS, ALEC: London, Apr. 2, 1914. Pembroke Lodge School.

HACKETT, BUDDY: (Leonard Hacker) Brooklyn, Aug. 31, 1924.

HACKMAN, GENE: San Bernardino, Jan. 30, 1931.

HALE, BARBARA: DeKalb, Ill., Apr. 18, 1922. Chicago Academy of Fine Arts.

HAMILTON, GEORGE: Memphis, Tenn., Aug. 12, 1939. Hackley School.

HAMILTON, MARGARET: Cleveland, Ohio, Dec. 9, 1902. Hathaway-Brown School.

HAMILTON, NEIL: Lynn, Mass., Sept. 9, 1899.

HARDING, ANN: (Dorothy Walton Gatley) Fort Sam Houston, Texas, Aug. 17, 1904.

HARRIS, BARBARA: (Sandra Markowitz) Evanston, Ill., 1937.

HARRIS, JULIE: Grosse Pointe, Mich., Dec. 2, 1925. Yale Drama School.

HARRIS, RICHARD: Limerick, Ire., Oct. 1, 1930. London Acad.

HARRIS, ROSEMARY: Ashby, Eng., Sept. 19, 1930. RADA

HARRISON, NOEL: London, Jan. 29, 1936.

HARRISON, REX: Huyton, Cheshire, Eng., Mar. 5, 1908.

HARTMAN, ELIZABETH: Youngstown, O., Dec. 23, 1941. Carnegie Tech.

HARVEY, LAURENCE: (Laruska Skikne) Yonishkis, Lithuania, Oct. 1, 1928. Meyerton College.

HAVER, JUNE: Rock Island, Ill., June 10, 1926.

HAVOC, JUNE: (June Hovick) Seattle, Wash., Nov. 8, 1916.

HAWKINS, JACK: London, Sept. 14, 1910. Trinity School.

HAYDEN, LINDA: Stanmore, Eng., Aida Foster School.

HAYDEN, STERLING: (John Hamilton) Montclair, N.J., March 26, 1916.

HAYES, HELEN: (Helen Brown) Washington, D.C., Oct. 10, 1900. Sacred Heart Convent.

HAYES, MARGARET: (Maggie) Baltimore, Dec. 5, 1925.

HAYWARD, SUSAN: (Edythe Marrener) Brooklyn, June 30, 1919.

HAYWORTH, RITA: (Margarita Cansino) NYC, Oct. 17, 1919.

HECKART, EILEEN: Columbus, Ohio, Mar. 29, 1919. Ohio State U.

HEDISON, DAVID: Providence, R.I., May 20, 1929. Brown U.

HEMMINGS, DAVID: Guilford, Eng.; Nov. 18, 1938.

HENDERSON, MARCIA: Andover, Mass., July 22, 1932. AADA.

HENDRIX, WANDA: Jacksonville, Fla., Nov. 3, 1928.

HENREID, PAUL: Trieste, Jan. 10, 1908.

HENRY, BUCK: (Zuckerman) NYC, 1931; Dartmouth.

HEPBURN, AUDREY: Brussels, Belgium, May 4, 1929.

HEPBURN, KATHARINE: Hartford, Conn., Nov. 8, 1909. Bryn Mawr

HESTON, CHARLTON: Evanston, Ill., Oct. 4, 1924. Northwestern U.

HEYWOOD, ANNE: (Violet Pretty) Birmingham, Eng., Dec. 11, 1933.

HICKMAN, DARRYL: Hollywood, Calif., July 28, 1933. Loyola U.

HICKMAN, DWAYNE: Los Angeles, May 18, 1934. Loyola.

HILL, STEVEN: Seattle, Wash., Feb. 24, 1922. U. Wash.

HILLER, WENDY: Bramhall, Cheshire, Eng., Aug. 15, 1912. Winceby House School.

HOFFMAN, DUSTIN: Los Angeles, Aug. 8, 1937. Pasadena Playhouse.

HOLBROOK, HAL: (Harold) Cleveland, O., Feb. 17, 1925.

HOLDEN, WILLIAM: O'Fallon, Ill., Apr. 17, 1918. Pasadena Jr. Coll.

HOLLIMAN, EARL: Tennasas Swamp, Delhi, La., Sept. 11. UCLA.

HOLLOWAY, STANLEY: London, Oct. 1, 1890.

HOLM, CELESTE: NYC, Apr. 29, 1919.

HOMEIER, SKIP: (George Vincent Homeier) Chicago, Oct. 5, 1930. UCLA.

HOMOLKA, OSCAR: Vienna, Aug. 12, 1898. Vienna Dramatic Academy.

HOOKS, ROBERT: Washington, D.C., Apr. 18, 1937. Temple.

HOPE, BOB: London, May 26, 1904.

HOPKINS, MIRIAM: Bainbridge, Ga., Oct. 18, 1902. Syracuse U.

HOPPER, DENNIS: Dodge City, Kan., May 17, 1936.

HORNE, LENA: Brooklyn, June 30, 1917.

HORTON, ROBERT: Los Angeles, July 29, 1924. UCLA.

HOUGHTON, KATHARINE: Hartford, Conn., Mar. 10, 1945. Sarah Lawrence.

HOUSER, JERRY: Los Angeles, July 14, 1952; Valley Jr. Col.

HOWARD, RONALD: Norwood, Eng., Apr. 7, 1918. Jesus College.

| Page Johnson | Jennifer Jones | Aron Kincaid | Sally Kellerman | Hardy Kruger |

HOWARD, TREVOR: Kent Eng., Sept. 29, 1916. RADA.

HOWES, SALLY ANN: London, July 20, 1934.

HUDSON, ROCK: (Roy Fitzgerald) Winnetka, Ill., Nov. 17, 1925.

HUNNICUTT, ARTHUR: Gravelly, Ark., Feb. 17, 1911. Ark. State.

HUNT, MARSHA: Chicago, Oct. 17, 1917.

HUNTER, IAN: Cape Town, S.A., June 13, 1900. St. Andrew's College.

HUNTER, KIM: (Janet Cole) Detroit, Nov. 12, 1922.

HUNTER, TAB: (Arthur Kelm) NYC, July 11, 1931.

HUSSEY, RUTH: Providence, R.I., Oct. 30, 1917. U. of Mich.

HUSTON, JOHN: Nevada, Mo., Aug. 5, 1906.

HUTTON, BETTY: (Betty Thornberg) Battle Creek, Mich., Feb. 26, 1921.

HUTTON, LAUREN: (Mary): Charleston, S.C., Nov. 17, 1943. Newcomb Col.

HUTTON, ROBERT: (Robert Winne) Kingston, N.Y., June 11, 1920. Blair Academy.

HYDE-WHITE, WILFRID: Gloucestershire, Eng., May 12, 1903. RADA.

HYER, MARTHA: Fort Worth, Tex., Aug. 10, 1930. Northwestern U.

IRELAND, JOHN: Vancouver, B.C., Can., Jan. 30, 1915.

IVES, BURL: Hunt Township, Ill., June 14, 1909. Charleston Ill. Teachers College.

JACKSON, ANNE: Alleghany, Pa., Sept. 3, 1926. Neighborhood Playhouse.

JACKSON, GLENDA: Birkenhead, Eng.; RADA.

JAECKEL, RICHARD: Long Beach, N.Y., Oct. 10, 1926.

JAFFE, SAM: NYC, Mar. 8, 1898.

JAGGER, DEAN: Lima, Ohio, Nov. 7, 1903. Wabash College.

JANSSEN, DAVID: (David Meyer) Naponee, Neb., Mar. 27, 1930.

JARMAN, CLAUDE, JR.: Nashville, Tenn., Sept. 27, 1934.

JASON, RICK: NYC, May 21, 1926. AADA.

JEAN, GLORIA: (Gloria Jean Schoonover) Buffalo, N.Y., Apr. 14, 1928.

JEFFREYS, ANNE: Goldsboro, N.C., Jan. 26, 1923. Anderson College.

JERGENS, ADELE: Brooklyn, Nov. 26, 1922.

JESSEL, GEORGE: NYC, Apr. 3, 1898.

JOHNS, GLYNIS: Durban, S. Africa, Oct. 5, 1923.

JOHNSON, CELIA: Richmond, Surrey, Eng., Dec. 18, 1908. RADA.

JOHNSON, PAGE: Welch, W. Va., Aug. 25, 1930. Ithaca.

JOHNSON, RAFER: Hillsboro, Tex., Aug. 18, 1935. UCLA.

JOHNSON, RICHARD: Essex, Eng., 1927. RADA.

JOHNSON, VAN: Newport, R.I., Aug. 28, 1916.

JONES, CAROLYN: Amarillo, Tex., Apr. 28, 1933.

JONES, DEAN: Morgan County, Ala., Jan. 25, 1936. Ashburn College.

JONES, JACK: Bel-Air, Calif., Jan. 14, 1938.

JONES, JAMES EARL: Arkabutla, Miss., Jan. 17, 1931. U. Mich.

JONES, JENNIFER: (Phyllis Isley) Tulsa, Okla., Mar. 2, 1919. AADA.

JONES, SHIRLEY: Smithton, Pa., March 31, 1934.

JONES, TOM: (Thomas Jones Woodward) Pontypridd, Wales, June 7, 1940.

JOURDAN, LOUIS: Marseilles, France, June 18, 1921.

JURADO, KATY: (Maria Christina Jurado Garcia) Guadalajara, Mex., 1927.

KASZNAR, KURT: Vienna, Aug. 12, 1913. Gymnasium, Vienna.

KAUFMANN, CHRISTINE: Lansdorf, Graz, Austria, Jan. 11, 1945.

KAYE, DANNY: (David Daniel Kominski) Brooklyn, Jan. 18, 1913.

KAYE, STUBBY: NYC, Nov. 11, 1918.

KEACH, STACY: Savannah, Ga., June 2, 1941; UCal., Yale.

KEDROVA, LILA: Greece, 1918.

KEEL, HOWARD: (Harold Keel) Gillespie, Ill., Apr. 13, 1919.

KEITH, BRIAN: Bayonne, N.J., Nov. 14, 1921.

KEITH, IAN: Boston, Feb. 27, 1899. AADA.

KEITH, ROBERT: Fowler, Ind., Feb. 10, 1898.

KELLERMAN, SALLY: Long Beach, Cal., June 2, 1938; Actors Studio West.

KELLY, GENE: Pittsburgh, Aug. 23, 1912. U. of Pittsburgh.

KELLY, GRACE: Philadelphia, Nov. 12, 1929. AADA.

KELLY, JACK: Astoria, N.Y., Sept. 16, 1927. UCLA.

KELLY, NANCY: Lowell, Mass., Mar. 25, 1921. Bentley School.

KENNEDY, ARTHUR: Worcester, Mass., Feb. 17, 1914. Carnegie Tech.

KENNEDY, GEORGE: NYC, Feb. 18, 1925.

KERR, DEBORAH: Helensburgh, Scot., Sept. 30, 1921. Smale Ballet School.

KERR, JOHN: NYC, Nov. 15, 1931. Harvard and Columbia.

KIDDER, MARGOT: Yellow Knife, Can., Oct. 17, 1948; UBC.

KILEY, RICHARD: Chicago, Mar. 31, 1922. Loyola.

KINCAID, ARON: (Norman Neale Williams III) Los Angeles, June 15, 1943. UCLA.

KITT, EARTHA: North, S.C., Jan. 26, 1928.

KNIGHT, ESMOND: East Sheen, Eng., May 4, 1906.

KNIGHT, SHIRLEY: Goessel, Kan., July 5. Wichita U.

KNOWLES, PATRIC: (Reginald Lawrence Knowles) Horsforth, Eng., Nov. 11, 1911.

KNOX, ALEXANDER: Strathroy, Ont., Can., Jan. 16, 1907. Western Ontario U.

KNOX, ELYSE: Hartford, Conn., Dec. 14, 1917. Traphagen School.

KOHNER, SUSAN: Los Angeles, Nov. 11, 1936. U. of Calif.

KORVIN, CHARLES: (Geza Korvin Karpathi) Czechoslovakia, Nov. 21. Sorbonne.

KOSLECK, MARTIN: Barkotzen, Ger., Mar. 24, 1914. Max Reinhardt School.

KREUGER, KURT: St. Moritz, Switz., July 23, 1917. U. of London.

KRUGER, HARDY: Berlin, Ger., Apr. 12, 1928.

KRUGER, OTTO: Toledo, Ohio, Sept. 6, 1885. Michigan and Columbia U.

KWAN, NANCY: Hong Kong, May 19, 1939. Royal Ballet.

LAKE, VERONICA: (Constance Ockleman) Brooklyn, Nov. 14, 1919. McGill U.

LAMARR, HEDY: (Hedwig Kiesler) Vienna, Sept. 11, 1915.

LAMAS, FERNANDO: Buenos Aires, Jan. 9, 1920.

LAMB, GIL: Minneapolis, June 14, 1906. U. of Minn.

LAMOUR, DOROTHY: Dec. 10, 1914. Spence's School.

LANCASTER, BURT: NYC, Nov. 2, 1913. NYU.

LANCHESTER, ELSA: (Elsa Sullivan) London, Oct. 28, 1902.

LANE, ABBE: Brooklyn, Dec. 14, 1935.

LANGAN, GLENN: Denver, Colo., July 8, 1917.

LANGE, HOPE: Redding Ridge, Conn., Nov. 28, 1933. Reed College.

| Carol Lawrence | John Phillip Law | Virna Lisi | James MacArthur | Mercedes McCambridge |

LANGTON, PAUL: Salt Lake City, Apr. 17, 1913. Travers School of Theatre.

LANSBURY, ANGELA: London, Oct. 16, 1925. London Academy of Music.

LASSER, LOUISE: NYC. Brandeis U.

LAURIE, PIPER: (Rosetta Jacobs) Detroit, Jan. 22, 1932.

LAW, JOHN PHILLIP: Hollywood, Sept. 7, 1937. Neighborhood Playhouse., UHawaii.

LAWFORD, PETER: London, Sept. 7, 1923.

LAWRENCE, BARBARA: Carnegie, Okla., Feb. 24, 1930. UCLA.

LAWRENCE, CAROL: (Laraia) Melrose Park, Ill., Sept. 5, 1935.

LEACHMAN, CLORIS: Des Moines, Iowa, June 30, 1930.

LEDERER, FRANCIS: Karlin, Prague, Czechoslovakia, Nov. 6, 1906.

LEE, CHRISTOPHER: London, May 27, 1922. Wellington College.

LEE, MICHELE: (Dusiak) Los Angeles, June 24, 1942. LACC.

LEIGH, JANET: (Jeanette Helen Morrison) Merced, Calif., July 6, 1927. College of Pacific.

LEIGHTON, MARGARET: Barnt Green, Worcestershire, Eng., Feb. 26, 1922. Church of England College.

LEMBECK, HARVEY: Brooklyn, Apr. 15, 1923. U. of Ala.

LEMMON, JACK: Boston, Feb. 8, 1925. Harvard.

LENZ, RICK: Springfield, Ill., Nov. 21, 1939. U. Mich.

LESLIE, BETHEL: NYC, Aug. 3, 1929. Breaney School.

LESLIE, JOAN: (Joan Brodell) Detroit, Jan. 26, 1925. St. Benedict's.

LEVENE, SAM: NYC, 1907.

LEWIS, JERRY: Newark, N.J., Mar. 16, 1926.

LILLIE, BEATRICE: Toronto, Can., May 29, 1898.

LINCOLN, ABBEY: (Anna Marie Woolridge) Chicago.

LINDFORS, VIVECA: Uppsala, Sweden, Dec. 29, 1920. Stockholm Royal Dramatic School.

LISI, VIRNA: Rome, 1938.

LIVESEY, ROGER: Barry, Wales, June 25, 1906. Westminster School.

LOCKE, SONDRA: Shelbyville, Tenn., 1947.

LOCKHART, JUNE: NYC, June 25, 1925. Westlake School.

LOCKWOOD, MARGARET: Karachi, Pakistan, Sept. 15, 1916. RADA.

LOLLOBRIGIDA, GINA: Subiaco, Italy, 1928. Rome Academy of Fine Arts.

LOM, HERBERT: Prague, Czechoslovakia, 1917. Prague U.

LONDON, JULIE: (Julie Peck) Santa Rosa, Calif., Sept. 26, 1926.

LONG, RICHARD: Chicago, Dec. 17, 1927.

LOPEZ, PERRY: NYC, July 22, 1931. NYU.

LORD, JACK: (John Joseph Ryan) NYC, Dec. 30, 1930. NYU.

LOREN, SOPHIA: (Sofia Scicolone) Rome, Italy, Sept. 20, 1934.

LOUISE, TINA: (Blacker) Feb. 11, 1934.

LOY, MYRNA: (Myrna Williams) Helena, Mont., Aug. 2, 1905. Westlake School.

LUND, JOHN: Rochester, N.Y., Feb. 6, 1913.

LUNDIGAN, WILLIAM: Syracuse, N.Y., June 12, 1914. Syracuse U.

LUPINO, IDA: London, Feb. 4, 1918. RADA.

LYNDE, PAUL: Mt. Vernon, Ohio, June 13, 1926. Northwestern U.

LYNLEY, CAROL: NYC, Feb. 13, 1942.

LYNN, JEFFREY: Auburn, Mass., 1910. Bates College.

LYON, SUE: Davenport, Iowa, July 10, 1946.

LYONS, ROBERT F.: Albany, N.Y.; AADA.

MacARTHUR, JAMES: Los Angeles, Dec. 8, 1937. Harvard.

MacGINNIS, NIALL: Dublin, Ire., Mar. 29, 1913. Dublin U.

MacLAINE, SHIRLEY: (Beatty) Richmond, Va., Apr. 24, 1934.

MacMAHON, ALINE: McKeesport, Pa., May 3, 1899. Barnard College.

MacMURRAY, FRED: Kankakee, Ill., Aug. 30, 1908. Carroll College.

MacRAE, GORDON: East Orange, N.J., Mar. 12, 1921.

MADISON, GUY: (Robert Moseley) Bakersfield, Calif., Jan. 19, 1922. Bakersfield Jr. College.

MAGNANI, ANNA: Alexandria, Egypt, Mar. 7, 1908. Rome Academy of Dramatic Art.

MAHARIS, GEORGE: Astoria, L.I., N.Y., Sept. 1, 1928. Actors Studio.

MAHONEY, JOCK: (Jacques O'-Mahoney) Chicago, Feb. 7, 1919. U. of Iowa.

MALDEN, KARL: (Malden Sekulovich) Gary, Ind., Mar. 22, 1914.

MALONE, DOROTHY: Chicago, Jan. 30, 1925. S. Methodist U.

MARAIS, JEAN: Cherbourg, France, Dec. 11, 1913. St. Germain.

MARCH, FREDRIC: (Frederick McIntyre Bickel) Racine, Wisc., Aug. 31, 1897. U. of Wisc.

MARGO: (Maria Marguerita Guadalupe Boldao y Castilla) Mexico City, May 10, 1918.

MARGOLIN, JANET: NYC, July 25, 1943. Walden School.

MARLOWE, HUGH: (Hugh Hipple) Philadelphia, Jan. 30, 1914.

MARSHALL, BRENDA: (Ardis Anderson Gaines) Isle of Negros, P.I., Sept. 29, 1915. Texas State College.

MARSHALL, E. G.: Owatonna, Minn., June 18, 1910. U. of Minn.

MARTIN, DEAN: (Dino Crocetti) Steubenville, Ohio, June 17, 1917.

MARTIN, MARY: Weatherford, Tex., Dec. 1, 1914. Ward-Belmont School.

MARTIN, TONY: (Alfred Norris) Oakland, Cal., Dec. 25, 1913. St. Mary's College.

MARVIN, LEE: NYC, Feb. 19, 1924.

MARX, GROUCHO: (Julius Marx) NYC, Oct. 2, 1895.

MASON, JAMES: Huddersfield, Yorkshire, Eng., May 15, 1909. Cambridge.

MASON, PAMELA: (Pamela Kellino) Westgate, Eng., Mar. 10, 1918.

MASSEN, OSA: Copenhagen, Den., Jan. 13, 1916.

MASSEY, DANIEL: London, Oct. 10, 1933. Eaton and King's Colleges.

MASSEY, RAYMOND: Toronto, Can., Aug. 30, 1896. Oxford.

MASTROIANNI, MARCELLO: Fontana Liri, Italy, 1924.

MATTHAU, WALTER: (Matuschanskayasky) NYC, Oct. 1, 1923.

MATURE, VICTOR: Louisville, Ky., Jan. 29, 1916.

MAY, ELAINE: (Berlin) Philadelphia, Apr. 21, 1932.

MAYEHOFF, EDDIE: Baltimore, July 7, Yale.

McCALLUM, DAVID: Scotland, Sept. 19, 1933. Chapman Coll.

McCAMBRIDGE, MERCEDES: Joliet, Ill., March 17, 1918, Mundelein College.

McCARTHY, KEVIN: Seattle, Wash., Feb. 15, 1914. Minn. U.

McCLORY, SEAN: Dublin, Ire., March 8, 1924. U. of Galway.

McCLURE, DOUG: Glendale, Calif., May 11, 1938. UCLA.

McCREA, JOEL: Los Angeles, Nov. 5, 1905. Pomona College.

McDERMOTT, HUGH: Edinburgh, Scot., Mar. 20, 1908.

McDOWALL, RODDY: London, Sept. 17, 1928. St. Joseph's.

McDOWELL, MALCOLM: (Taylor) Leeds, Eng., June 1943.

Harry Morgan

Anna Magnani

Don Murray

Isa Miranda

Jack Nicholson

McGAVIN, DARREN: Spokane, Wash., May 7, 1922. College of Pacific.

McGIVER, JOHN: NYC, Nov. 5, 1915. Fordham, Columbia U.

McGUIRE, DOROTHY: Omaha, Neb., June 14, 1919. Wellesley.

McKAY, GARDNER: NYC, June 10, 1932. Cornell.

McKENNA, VIRGINIA: London, June 7, 1931.

McKUEN, ROD: Oakland, Cal., Apr. 29, 1933.

McNAIR, BARBARA: Chicago, March 4, 1939. UCLA.

McNALLY, STEPHEN: (Horace McNally) NYC, July 29, Fordham U.

McNAMARA, MAGGIE: NYC, June 18. St. Catherine.

McQUEEN, BUTTERFLY: Tampa, Fla., Jan. 8, 1911. UCLA.

McQUEEN, STEVE: Slater, Mo., Mar. 24, 1932.

MEADOWS, AUDREY: Wuchang, China, 1924. St. Margaret's.

MEADOWS, JAYNE: (formerly, Jayne Cotter) Wuchang, China, Sept. 27, 1923. St. Margaret's.

MEDFORD, KAY: (Maggie O'Regin) NYC, Sept. 14, 1920.

MEDWIN, MICHAEL: London, 1925. Instut Fischer.

MEEKER, RALPH: (Ralph Rathgeber) Minneapolis, Nov. 21, 1920. Northwestern U.

MELL, MARISA: Vienna, Austria, 1942.

MERCOURI, MELINA: Athens, Greece, Oct. 18, 1915.

MEREDITH, BURGESS: Cleveland, Ohio, Nov. 16, 1909. Amherst.

MEREDITH, LEE: (Judi Lee Sauls) Oct. 1947. AADA.

MERKEL, UNA: Covington, Ky., Dec. 10, 1903.

MERMAN, ETHEL: (Ethel Zimmerman) Astoria, N.Y., Jan. 16, 1909.

MERRILL, DINA: (Nedinia Hutton) NYC, Dec. 9, 1925. Geo. Wash. U.

MERRILL, GARY: Hartford, Conn., Aug. 2, 1915. Bowdoin, Trinity.

MIFUNE, TOSHIRO: Tsingtao, China, Apr.1, 1920.

MILES, SARAH: Eng., Dec. 31, 1943.

MILES, VERA: Boise City, Okla., Aug. 23, 1929.

MILLAND, RAY: (Reginald Truscott-Jones) Neath, Wales, Jan. 3, 1908. King's College.

MILLER, ANN: (Lucille Ann Collier) Chireno, Tex., Apr. 12, 1919. Lawler Professional School.

MILLER, MARVIN: St. Louis, July 18, 1913. Washington U.

MILLS, HAYLEY: London, Apr. 18, 1946. Elmhurst School.

MILLS, JOHN: Suffolk, Eng., Feb. 22, 1908.

MIMIEUX, YVETTE: Los Angeles, Jan. 8, 1941. Hollywood High.

MINEO, SAL: NYC, Jan. 10, 1939. Lodge School.

MINNELLI, LIZA: Los Angeles, Mar. 12, 1945.

MIRANDA, ISA: (Ines Sampietro) Milan, Italy, July 5, 1917.

MITCHELL, CAMERON: Dalastown, Pa., Nov. 1918. N.Y. Theatre School.

MITCHELL, JAMES: Sacramento, Calif., Feb. 29, 1920. LACC.

MITCHUM, ROBERT: Bridgeport, Conn., Aug. 6, 1917.

MONTALBAN, RICARDO: Mexico City, Nov. 25, 1920.

MONTAND, YVES: (Yves Montand Livi) Mansummano, Tuscany, Oct. 13, 1921.

MONTGOMERY, BELINDA: Winnipeg, Can., July 23, 1950.

MONTGOMERY, ELIZABETH: Los Angeles, Apr. 15, 1933. AADA.

MONTGOMERY, GEORGE: (George Letz) Brady, Mont., Aug. 29, 1916. U. of Mont.

MONTGOMERY, ROBERT: (Henry, Jr.) Beacon, N.Y., May 21, 1904.

MOORE, CONSTANCE: Sioux City, Iowa, Jan. 18, 1922.

MOORE, DICK: Los Angeles, Sept. 12, 1925.

MOORE, KIERON: County Cork, Ire., 1925. St. Mary's College.

MOORE, MARY TYLER: Brooklyn, Dec. 29, 1937.

MOORE, ROGER: London, Oct. 14, 1927. RADA.

MOORE, TERRY: (Helen Koford) Los Angeles, Jan. 7, 1929.

MOOREHEAD, AGNES: Clinton, Mass., Dec. 6, 1906. AADA.

MORE, KENNETH: Gerrards Cross, Eng., Sept. 20, 1914. Victoria College.

MOREAU, JEANNE: France, Jan. 3, 1928.

MORENO, RITA: (Rosita Alverio) Humacao, P.R., Dec. 11, 1931.

MORGAN, DENNIS: (Stanley Morner) Prentice, Wisc., Dec. 10, 1920. Carroll College.

MORGAN, HARRY (HENRY): (Harry Bratsburg) Detroit, Apr. 10, 1915. U. of Chicago.

MORGAN, MICHELE: (Simone Roussel) Paris, Feb. 29, 1920. Paris Dramatic School.

MORISON, PATRICIA: NYC, 1919.

MORLEY, ROBERT: Wiltshire, Eng., May 26, 1908. RADA.

MORRIS, GREG: Cleveland, O., 1934. Ohio State.

MORRIS, HOWARD: NYC, Sept. 4, 1919. NYU.

MORROW, VIC: Bronx, N.Y., Feb. 14, 1932. Fla. Southern College.

MORSE, ROBERT: Newton, Mass., May 18, 1931.

MOSTEL, ZERO: Brooklyn, Feb. 28, 1915. CCNY.

MURPHY, GEORGE: New Haven, Conn., July 4, 1904. Yale.

MURRAY, DON: Hollywood, July 31, 1929. AADA.

MURRAY, KEN: (Don Court) NYC, July 14, 1903.

NADER, GEORGE: Pasadena, Calif., Oct. 19, 1921. Occidental College.

NAPIER, ALAN: Birmingham, Eng., Jan. 7, 1903. Birmingham University.

NATWICK, MILDRED: Baltimore, June 19, 1908. Bryn Mawr.

NEAL, PATRICIA: Packard, Ky., Jan. 20, 1926. Northwestern U.

NEFF, HILDEGARDE: (Hildegard Knef) Ulm, Ger., Dec. 28, 1925. Berlin Art Academy.

NELSON, BARRY: (Robert Nielsen) Oakland, Cal., 1925.

NELSON, DAVID: NYC, Oct. 24, 1936. USC.

NELSON, GENE: (Gene Berg) Seattle, Wash., Mar. 24, 1920.

NELSON, HARRIET HILLIARD: (Peggy Lou Snyder) Des Moines, Iowa, July 18.

NELSON, LORI: (Dixie Kay Nelson) Santa Fe, N.M., Aug. 15, 1933.

NELSON, OZZIE: (Oswald) Jersey City, N.J., Mar. 20, 1907. Rutgers U.

NELSON, RICK: (Eric Hilliard Nelson) Teaneck, N.J., May 8, 1940.

NESBITT, CATHLEEN: Cheshire, Eng., Nov. 24, 1889. Victoria College.

NEWLEY, ANTHONY: Hackney, London, Sept. 21, 1931.

NEWMAN, PAUL: Cleveland, Ohio, Jan. 26, 1925. Yale.

NEWMAR, JULIE: (Newmeyer) Los Angeles; Aug. 16, 1935.

NICHOLS, MIKE: (Michael Igor Peschkowsky) Berlin, Nov. 1931. U. Chicago.

NICHOLSON, JACK: Neptune, N.J., Apr. 22, 1937.

NICOL, ALEX: Ossining, N.Y., Jan. 20, 1919. Actors Studio.

Heather North

Carroll O'Connor

Barbara Parkins

Harve Presnell

Suzanne Pleshette

NIELSEN, LESLIE: Regina, Saskatchewan, Can., Feb. 11, 1926. Neighborhood Playhouse.

NIVEN, DAVID: Kirriemuir, Scot., Mar. 1, 1910. Sandhurst College.

NOLAN, LLOYD: San Francisco, Aug. 11, 1902. Stanford U.

NORRIS, CHRISTOPHER: NYC, Oct. 7, 1953; Lincoln Square Acad.

NORTH, HEATHER: Pasadena, Cal., Dec. 13, 1950; Actors Workshop.

NORTH, SHEREE: (Dawn Bethel) Los Angeles, Jan. 17, 1933. Hollywood High.

NOVAK, KIM: (Marilyn Novak) Chicago, Feb. 18, 1933. LACC.

NUGENT, ELLIOTT: Dover, Ohio, Sept. 20, 1900. Ohio State U.

NUYEN, FRANCE: (Vannga) Marseilles, France, July 31, 1939. Beaux Arts School.

OBERON, MERLE: (Estelle Merle O'Brien Thompson) Tasmania, Feb. 19, 1911.

O'BRIAN, HUGH: (Hugh J. Krampe) Rochester, N.Y., Apr. 19, 1928. Cincinnati U.

O'BRIEN, EDMOND: NYC, Sept. 10, 1915. Fordham, Neighborhood Playhouse.

O'BRIEN, MARGARET: (Angela Maxine O'Brien) Los Angeles, Jan. 15, 1937.

O'BRIEN, PAT: Milwaukee, Nov. 11, 1899. Marquette U.

O'CONNELL, ARTHUR: NYC, Mar. 29, 1908. St. John's.

O'CONNOR, CARROLL: Bronx, N.Y., 1925; Dublin National Univ.

O'CONNOR, DONALD: Chicago, Aug. 28, 1925.

O'HARA, MAUREEN: (Maureen FitzSimons) Dublin, Ire., Aug. 17, 1921. Abbey School.

O'HERLIHY, DAN: Wexford, Ire., May 1, 1919. National U.

OLIVIER, LAURENCE: Dorking, Eng., May 22, 1907. St. Edward's, Oxford.

O'NEAL, PATRICK: Ocala, Fla., Sept. 26, 1927. U. of Fla.

O'NEAL, RYAN: Los Angeles, Apr. 20, 1941.

O'NEILL, JENNIFER: Rio de Janeiro, Feb. 20, 1949; Neighborhood Playhouse.

O'SHEA, MICHAEL: NYC, Mar. 17, 1906.

O'SULLIVAN, MAUREEN: Byle, Ire., May 17, 1911. Sacred Heart Convent.

O'TOOLE, PETER: Connemara, Ireland, Aug. 2, 1932. RADA.

OWEN, REGINALD: Wheathampstead, Eng., Aug. 5, 1887. Tree's Academy.

PAGE, GERALDINE: Kirksville, Mo., Nov. 22, 1924. Goodman School.

PAGET, DEBRA: (Debralee Griffin) Denver, Aug. 19, 1933.

PAIGE, JANIS: (Donna Mae Jaden) Tacoma, Wash., Sept 16, 1922.

PALANCE, JACK: Lattimer, Pa., Feb. 18, 1920. U. N.C.

PALMER, BETSY: East Chicago, Ind., Nov. 1, 1929. DePaul U.

PALMER, GREGG: (Palmer Lee) San Francisco, Jan. 25, 1927. U. Utah.

PALMER, LILLI: Posen, Austria, May 24, 1914. Ilka Gruning School.

PALMER, MARIA: Vienna, Sept. 5, 1924. College de Bouffement.

PAPAS, IRENE: Chiliomodion, Greece, 1929.

PARKER, ELEANOR: Cedarville, Ohio, June 26, 1922. Pasadena Playhouse.

PARKER, FESS: Fort Worth, Tex., Aug. 16, 1927. USC.

PARKER, JEAN: (Mae Green) Deer Lodge, Mont., Aug. 11, 1918.

PARKER, SUZY: (Cecelia Parker) San Antonio, Tex. Oct. 28, 1933.

PARKER, WILLARD: (Worster Van Eps) NYC, Feb. 5, 1912.

PARKINS, BARBARA: Vancouver, Can., May 22, 1945.

PARSONS, ESTELLE: Lynn Mass. Nov. 20, 1927. Boston U.

PARSONS, LOUELLA: Freeport, Ill., Aug. 6, 1893. Dixon College.

PATRICK, NIGEL: London, May 2, 1913.

PATTERSON, LEE: Vancouver, Can., 1929. Ontario College of Art.

PAVAN, MARISA: (Marisa Pierangeli) Cagliari, Sardinia, June 19, 1932. Torquado Tasso College.

PEACH, MARY: Durban, S. Africa, 1934.

PEARSON, BEATRICE: Denison, Tex., July 27, 1920.

PECK, GREGORY: La Jolla, Calif., Apr. 5, 1916. U. of Calif.

PEPPARD, GEORGE: Detroit, Oct. 1, 1933. Carnegie Tech.

PERKINS, ANTHONY: NYC, Apr. 14, 1932. Rollins College.

PERREAU, GIGI: (Ghislaine) Los Angeles, Feb. 6, 1941.

PETERS, JEAN: (Elizabeth) Canton, Ohio, Oct. 15, 1926. Ohio State U.

PETTET, JOANNA: London, Nov. 16, 1944; Neighborhood Playhouse.

PICERNI, PAUL: NYC, Dec. 1, 1922. Loyola U.

PICKENS, SLIM: (Louis Bert Lindley, Jr.) Kingsberg, Calif., June 29, 1919.

PICKFORD, MARY: (Gladys Mary Smith) Toronto, Can., Apr. 8, 1893.

PIDGEON, WALTER: East St. John, N.B., Can., Sept. 23, 1898.

PINE, PHILLIP: Hanford, Calif., July 16, 1925. Actors' Lab.

PLEASENCE, DONALD: Workshop, Eng., Oct. 5, 1919. Sheffield School.

PLESHETTE, SUZANNE: NYC, Jan. 31, 1937. Syracuse U.

PLUMMER, CHRISTOPHER: Toronto, Can., Dec. 13, 1927.

PODESTA, ROSANA: Tripoli, June 20, 1934.

POITIER, SIDNEY: Miami, Fla., Feb. 20, 1924.

POLLARD, MICHAEL J.: Pacific, N.J., May 30, 1939.

POWELL, ELEANOR: Springfield, Mass., Nov. 21, 1913.

POWELL, JANE: (Suzanne Burce) Portland, Ore., Apr. 1, 1929.

POWELL, WILLIAM: Pittsburgh, July 29, 1892. AADA.

POWERS, MALA: (Mary Ellen) San Francisco, Dec. 29, 1921. UCLA.

PRENTISS, PAULA: (Paula Ragusa) San Antonio, Tex., Mar. 4, 1939. Northwestern U.

PRESLE, MICHELINE: (Micheline Chassagne) Paris, Aug. 22, 1922. Rouleau Drama School.

PRESLEY, ELVIS: Tupelo, Miss., Jan. 8, 1935.

PRESNELL, HARVE: Modesto, Calif., Sept. 14, 1933. USC.

PRESTON, ROBERT: (Robert Preston Meservey) Newton Highlands, Mass., June 8, 1913. Pasadena Playhouse.

PRICE, DENNIS: Twyford, Eng. 1915. Oxford.

PRICE, VINCENT: St. Louis, May 27, 1911. Yale.

PRINCE, WILLIAM: Nicholas, N.Y., Jan. 26, 1913. Cornell U.

PROVINE, DOROTHY: Deadwood, S.D., Jan. 20, 1937. U. of Wash.

PROWSE, JULIET: Bombay, India, Sept. 25, 1936.

PURCELL, LEE: Cherry Point, N.C., 1947; Stephens.

PURCELL, NOEL: Dublin, Ire., Dec. 23, 1900. Irish Christian Brothers.

PURDOM, EDMUND: Welwyn Garden City, Eng., Dec. 19. St. Ignatius College.

231

Janice Rule

Kurt Russell

Jane Russell

Michael Sarrazin

Jennifer Salt

QUAYLE, ANTHONY: Lancashire, Eng., 1913. Old Vic School.

QUINN, ANTHONY: Chihuahua, Mex., Apr. 21, 1915.

RAFFERTY, FRANCES: Sioux City, Iowa, June 26, 1922. UCLA.

RAFT, GEORGE: NYC, 1903.

RAINES, ELLA: (Ella Wallace Rains Olds) Snoqualmie Falls, Wash., Aug. 6, 1921. U. of Washington.

RANDALL, TONY: Tulsa, Okla., Feb. 26, 1920. Northwestern U.

RANDELL, RON: Sydney, Australia, Oct. 8, 1920. St. Mary's College.

RAY, ALDO: (Aldo DeRe) Pen Argyl, Pa. Sept. 25, 1926. UCLA.

RAYE, MARTHA: (Margie Yvonne Reed) Butte, Mont., Aug. 27, 1916.

RAYMOND, GENE: (Raymond Guion) NYC, Aug. 13, 1908.

REAGAN, RONALD: Tampico, Ill., Feb. 6, 1911. Eureka College.

REASON, REX: Berlin, Ger., Nov. 30, 1928. Pasadena Playhouse.

REDFORD, ROBERT: Santa Monica, Calif., Aug. 18, 1937. AADA.

REDGRAVE COLIN: London, July 16, 1939.

REDGRAVE, LYNN: London, Mar. 8, 1943.

REDGRAVE, MICHAEL: Bristol, Eng., Mar. 20, 1908. Cambridge.

REDGRAVE, VANESSA: London, Jan. 30, 1937.

REDMAN, JOYCE: County Mayo, Ire., 1919. RADA.

REED, DONNA: (Donna Mullenger) Denison, Iowa, Jan. 27, 1921. LACC.

REED, OLIVER: Wimbledon, Eng., 1938.

REEVES, STEVE: Glasgow, Mont., Jan. 21, 1926.

REID, ELLIOTT: NYC, Jan. 16, 1920.

REINER, CARL: NYC, Mar. 20, 1922. Georgetown.

REMICK, LEE: Quincy, Mass., Dec. 14, 1935. Barnard College.

RETTIG, TOMMY: Jackson Heights, N.Y., Dec. 10, 1941.

REYNOLDS, BURT: West Palm Beach, Fla.,Feb. 11, 1936. Fla. State U.

REYNOLDS, DEBBIE: (Mary Frances Reynolds) El Paso, Tex., Apr. 1, 1932.

REYNOLDS, MARJORIE: Buhl, Idaho, Aug. 12, 1921.

RHOADES, BARBARA: Poughkeepsie, N.Y., 1947.

RICH, IRENE: Buffalo, N.Y., Oct. 13, 1897. St. Margaret's School.

RICHARDS, JEFF: (Richard Mansfield Taylor) Portland, Ore., Nov. 1. USC.

RICHARDSON, RALPH: Cheltenham, Eng., Dec. 19, 1902.

RICKLES, DON: NYC, May 8, 1926. AADA.

RIGG, DIANA: Doncaster, Eng., July 20, 1938. RADA.

ROBARDS, JASON: Chicago, July 26, 1922. AADA.

ROBERTSON, CLIFF: La Jolla, Calif., Sept. 9, 1925. Antioch College.

ROBINSON, EDWARD G.: (Emanuel Goldenberg) Bucharest, Rum., Dec. 12, 1893. Columbia U.

ROBSON, FLORA: South Shields, Eng., Mar. 28, 1902. RADA.

ROCHESTER: (Eddie Anderson) Oakland, Calif., Sept. 18, 1905.

ROGERS, CHARLES "BUDDY": Olathe, Kan., Aug. 13, 1904. U. of Kan.

ROGERS, GINGER: (Virginia Katherine McMath) Independence, Mo., July 16, 1911.

ROGERS, ROY: (Leonard Slye) Cincinnati, Nov. 5, 1912.

ROLAND, GILBERT: (Luis Antonio Damaso De Alonso) Juarez, Mex., Dec. 11, 1905.

ROMAN, RUTH: Boston, Dec. 23. Bishop Lee Dramatic School.

ROMERO, CESAR: NYC, Feb. 15, 1907. Collegiate School.

ROONEY, MICKEY: (Joe Yule, Jr.) Brooklyn, Sept. 23, 1920.

ROSS, KATHARINE: Hollywood, Jan. 29, 1943.

ROTH, LILLIAN: Boston, Dec. 13, 1910.

ROUNDTREE, RICHARD: New Rochelle, N.Y., 1942.

ROWLANDS, GENA: Cambria, Wisc., June 19, 1936.

RULE, JANICE: Cincinnati, Aug. 15, 1931.

RUSH, BARBARA: Denver, Colo., Jan. 4. U. of Calif.

RUSSELL, JANE: Bemidji, Minn., June 21, 1921. Max Reinhardt School.

RUSSELL, JOHN: Los Angeles, Jan. 3, 1921. U. of Calif.

RUSSELL, KURT: Springfield, Mass., March 17, 1951.

RUSSELL, ROSALIND: Waterbury, Conn., June 4, 1911. AADA.

RUTHERFORD, ANN: Toronto, Can., 1924.

RYAN, ROBERT: Chicago, Nov. 11, 1913. Dartmouth.

SAINT, EVA MARIE: Newark, N.J., July 4, 1924. Bowling Green State U.

ST. JACQUES, RAYMOND: (James Arthur Johnson) Conn.

ST. JOHN, BETTA: Hawthorne, Calif., Nov. 26, 1929.

ST. JOHN, JILL: (Jill Oppenheim) Los Angeles, Aug. 19, 1940.

SALT, JENNIFER: Los Angeles, Sept. 4, 1944. Sarah Lawrence Col.

SANDERS, GEORGE: St. Petersburg, Russia, July 3, 1906. Brighton College.

SANDS, TOMMY: Chicago, Aug. 27, 1937.

SAN JUAN, OLGA: NYC, Mar. 16, 1927.

SARGENT, RICHARD: (Richard Cox) Carmel, Cal., 1933. Stanford U.

SARRAZIN, MICHAEL: Quebec City, Can., May 22, 1940.

SAVALAS, TELLY: (Aristotle) Garden City, N.Y., 1924. Columbia.

SAXON, JOHN: (Carmen Orrico) Brooklyn, Aug. 5, 1935.

SCHELL, MARIA: Vienna, Jan. 15, 1926.

SCHELL, MAXIMILIAN: Vienna, Dec. 8, 1930.

SCHNEIDER, ROMY: Vienna, Sept. 23, 1938.

SCOFIELD, PAUL: Hurstpierpont, Eng., Jan. 21, 1922. London Mask Theatre School.

SCOTT, GEORGE C.: Wise, Va., Oct. 18, 1927. U. of Mo.

SCOTT, GORDON: (Gordon M. Werschkul) Portland, Ore., Aug. 3, 1927. Oregon U.

SCOTT, MARTHA: Jamesport, Mo., Sept. 22, 1914. U. of Mich.

SCOTT, RANDOLPH: Orange County, Va., Jan. 23, 1903. U. of N.C.

SEARS, HEATHER: London, 1935.

SEBERG, JEAN: Marshalltown, Iowa, Nov. 13, 1938. Iowa U.

SECOMBE, HARRY: Swansea, Wales, Sept. 8, 1921.

SELLERS, PETER: Southsea, Eng., Sept. 8, 1925. Aloysius College.

SELWART, TONIO: Wartenberg, Ger., June 9, 1906. Munich U.

SEYLER, ATHENE: (Athene Hannen) London, May 31, 1889.

SEYMOUR, ANNE: NYC, Sept. 11, 1909. American Laboratory Theatre.

SHARIF, OMAR: (Michel Shalboub) Alexandria, Egypt, Apr. 10, 1933.

SHATNER, WILLIAM: Montreal, Can., Mar. 22, 1931. McGill U.

SHAW, ROBERT: Orkney Isles, Scot., 1928.

SHAW, SEBASTIAN: Holt, Eng., May 29, 1905. Gresham School.

SHAWLEE, JOAN: Forest Hills, N.Y., Mar. 5, 1929.

SHAWN, DICK: (Richard Schulefand) Buffalo, N.Y., Dec. 1. U. of Miami.

SHEARER, MOIRA: Dunfermline, Scot., Jan. 17, 1926. London Theatre School.

Woody Strode

Carrie Snodgress

Robert Stack

Marlo Thomas

Chaim Topol

SHEARER, NORMA: Montreal, Can., Aug. 10, 1904.

SHEEN, MARTIN: (Ramon Estevez) Dayton, O., Aug. 3, 1940.

SHEFFIELD, JOHN: Pasadena, Calif., Apr. 11, 1931. UCLA.

SHEPHERD, CYBILL: Memphis, Tenn., 1950. Hunter, NYU.

SHORE, DINAH: (Frances Rose Shore) Winchester, Tenn., Mar. 1, 1917. Vanderbilt U.

SHOWALTER, MAX: (Formerly Casey Adams) Caldwell, Kan., June 2, 1917. Pasadena Playhouse.

SIDNEY, SYLVIA: NYC, Aug. 8, 1910. Theatre Guild School.

SIGNORET, SIMONE: (Simone Kaminker) Wiesbaden, Ger., Mar. 25, 1921. Solange Sicard School.

SILVERS, PHIL: (Philip Silversmith) Brooklyn, May 11, 1912.

SIM, ALASTAIR: Edinburgh, Scot., 1900.

SIMMONS, JEAN: London, Jan. 31, 1929. Aida Foster School.

SIMON, SIMONE: Marseilles, France, Apr. 23, 1914.

SINATRA, FRANK: Hoboken, N.J., Dec. 12, 1915.

SKELTON, RED: (Richard Skelton) Vincennes, Ind., July 18, 1913.

SLEZAK, WALTER: Vienna, Austria, May 3, 1902.

SMITH, ALEXIS: Penticton, Can., June 8, 1921. LACC.

SMITH, JOHN: (Robert E. Van Orden) Los Angeles, Mar. 6, 1931. UCLA.

SMITH, KATE: (Kathryn Elizabeth) Greenville, Va., May 1, 1909.

SMITH, KENT: NYC, Mar. 19, 1907. Harvard U.

SMITH, ROGER: South Gate, Calif., Dec. 18, 1932. U. Of Ariz.

SNODGRESS, CARRIE: Chicago, Oct. 27, 1946. UNI.

SOMMER, ELKE: Berlin, Nov. 5, 1941.

SONNY: (Salvatore Bono) 1935.

SORDI, ALBERTO: Rome, Italy, 1925.

SOTHERN, ANN: (Harriet Lake) Valley City, N.D., Jan. 22, 1909. Washington U.

STACK, ROBERT: Los Angeles, Jan. 13, 1919. USC.

STAMP, TERENCE: London, 1940.

STANG, ARNOLD: Chelsea, Mass., Sept. 28, 1925.

STANLEY, KIM: (Patricia Reid) Tularosa, N.M., Feb. 11, 1921. U. of Tex.

STANWYCK, BARBARA: (Ruby Stevens) Brooklyn, July 16, 1907.

STAPLETON, MAUREEN: Troy, N.Y., June 21, 1925.

STEEL, ANTHONY: London, May 21, 1920. Cambridge.

STEELE, TOMMY: London, Dec. 17, 1936.

STEIGER, ROD: Westhampton, N.Y., Apr. 14, 1925.

STERLING, JAN: (Jane Sterling Adriance) NYC, Apr. 3, 1923. Fay Compton School.

STERLING, ROBERT: (Robert Sterling Hart) Newcastle, Pa., Nov. 13, 1917. U. of Pittsburgh.

STEVENS, CONNIE: (Concetta Ann Ingolia) Brooklyn, Aug. 8, 1938. Hollywood Professional School.

STEVENS, KAYE: (Catherine) Pittsburgh, July 21, 1933.

STEVENS, MARK: (Richard) Cleveland, Ohio, Dec. 13, 1922.

STEVENS, STELLA: (Estelle Eggleston) Hot Coffee, Miss., 1936.

STEWART, ALEXANDRA: Montreal, Can., June 10. Louvre.

STEWART, ELAINE: Montclair, N.J., May 31, 1929.

STEWART, JAMES: Indiana, Pa., May 20, 1908. Princeton.

STEWART, MARTHA: (Martha Haworth) Bardwell, Ky., Oct. 7, 1922.

STOCKWELL, DEAN: Hollywood, March 5.

STORM, GALE: (Josephine Cottle) Bloomington, Tex., Apr. 5, 1922.

STRASBERG, SUSAN: NYC, May 22, 1938.

STRAUSS, ROBERT: NYC, Nov. 8, 1913.

STREISAND, BARBRA: Brooklyn, Apr. 24, 1942.

STRODE, WOODY: Los Angeles, 1914.

STRUDWICK, SHEPPERD: Hillsboro, N.C., Sept. 22, 1907. U. of N.C.

SULLIVAN, BARRY: (Patrick Barry) NYC, Aug. 29, 1912. NYU.

SULLY, FRANK: (Frank Sullivan) St. Louis, 1910. St. Teresa's College.

SUTHERLAND, DONALD: St. John, New Brunswick, July 17, 1934. U Toronto.

SWANSON, GLORIA: (Josephine May Swenson) Chicago, Mar. 27, 1898. Chicago Art Inst.

SWINBURNE, NORA: Bath, Eng., July 24, 1902. RADA.

SYLVESTER, WILLIAM: Oakland, Calif., Jan. 31, 1922. RADA.

SYMS, SYLVIA: London, 1934. Convent School.

TALBOT, LYLE: (Lysle Hollywood) Pittsburgh, Feb. 8, 1904.

TALBOT, NITA: NYC, Aug. 8, 1930. Irvine Studio School.

TAMBLYN, RUSS: Los Angeles, Dec. 30.

TANDY, JESSICA: London, June 7, 1909. Dame Owens' School.

TAYLOR, DON: Freeport, Pa., Dec. 13, 1920. Penn State U.

TAYLOR, ELIZABETH: London, Feb. 27, 1932. Byron House School.

TAYLOR, KENT: (Louis Weiss) Nashua, Iowa, May 11, 1907.

TAYLOR, ROD: (Robert) Sydney, Aust., Jan. 11, 1930.

TAYLOR-YOUNG, LEIGH: Wash., D.C., Jan. 25, 1945. Northwestern.

TEAL, RAY: Grand Rapids, Mich., Jan. 12, 1902. Pasadena Playhouse.

TEMPLE, SHIRLEY: Santa Monica, Calif., Apr. 23, 1928.

TERRY-THOMAS: (Thomas Terry Hoar Stevens) Finchley, London, July 14, 1911. Ardingly College.

TERZIEFF, LAURENT: Paris, 1935.

THATCHER, TORIN: Bombay, India, Jan. 15, 1905. RADA.

THAXTER, PHYLLIS: Portland, Me., Nov. 20, 1921. St. Genevieve School.

THOMAS, DANNY: (Amos Jacobs) Deerfield, Mich., Jan. 6, 1914.

THOMAS, MARLO: (Margaret) Detroit, Nov. 21, 1943. USC.

THOMAS, RICHARD: NYC, June 13, 1951. Columbia.

THOMPSON, MARSHALL: Peoria, Ill., Nov. 27, 1925. Occidental College.

THORNDIKE, SYBIL: Gainsborough, Eng., Oct. 24, 1882. Guild Hall School of Music.

TIERNEY, GENE: Brooklyn, Nov. 20, 1920. Miss Farmer's School.

TIERNEY, LAWRENCE: Brooklyn, Mar. 15, 1919. Manhattan College.

TIFFIN, PAMELA: (Wonso) Oklahoma City, Oct. 13, 1942.

TODD, RICHARD: Dublin, Ire., June 11, 1919. Shrewsbury School.

TOPOL: (Chaim Topol) Tel-Aviv, Israel, Sept. 9, 1935.

TORN, RIP: Temple, Tex., Feb. 6, 1931. U. Tex.

TOTTER, AUDREY: Joliet, Ill., Dec. 20.

TRAVERS, BILL: Newcastle-on-Tyne, Eng., Jan. 3, 1922.

TRAVIS, RICHARD: (William Justice) Carlsbad, N.M., Apr. 17, 1913.

TREMAYNE, LES: London, Apr. 16, 1913. Northwestern, Columbia, UCLA.

TRINTIGNANT, JEAN-LOUIS: Pont-St. Esprit, France, Dec. 11, 1930. Dullin-Balachova Drama School.

TRUEX, ERNEST: Kansas City, Mo., Sept. 19, 1890.

TRYON, TOM: Hartford, Conn., Jan. 14, 1926. Yale.

TSOPEI, CORINNA: Athens, Greece, June 21, 1944.

TUCKER, FORREST: Plainfield, Ind., Feb. 12, 1919. George Washington U.

Brenda Vaccaro **Jon Voight** **Teresa Wright** **Gig Young** **Susannah York**

TURNER, LANA: (Julia Jean Mildred Frances Turner) Wallace, Idaho, Feb. 8, 1920.

TUSHINGHAM, RITA: Liverpool, Eng., 1942.

TWIGGY: (Lesley Hornby) London, Sept. 19, 1949.

TYLER, BEVERLY: (Beverly Jean Saul) Scranton, Pa., July 5, 1928.

URE, MARY: Glasgow, Scot., 1934. Central School of Drama.

USTINOV, PETER: London, Apr. 16, 1921. Westminster School.

VACCARO, BRENDA: Brooklyn, Nov. 18, 1939. Neighborhood Playhouse.

VALLEE, RUDY: (Hubert) Island Pond, Vt., July 28, 1901. Yale.

VALLI, ALIDA: Pola, Italy, May 31, 1921. Rome Academy of Drama.

VAN CLEEF, LEE: Somerville, N.J., 1925.

VAN DOREN, MAMIE: (Joan Lucile Olander) Rowena, S.D., Feb. 6, 1933.

VAN DYKE, DICK: West Plains, Mo., Dec. 13, 1925.

VAN FLEET, JO: Oakland, Cal., 1922.

VAN ROOTEN, LUIS: Mexico City, Nov. 29, 1906. U. of Pa.

VAUGHN, ROBERT: NYC, Nov. 22, 1932. USC.

VENUTA, BENAY: San Francisco, Jan. 27, 1911.

VERA-ELLEN (ROHE): Cincinnati, Feb. 16, 1926.

VERDON, GWEN: Culver City, Calif., Jan. 13, 1925.

VIOLET, ULTRA: (Isabelle Collin-Dufresne) Grenoble, France.

VITALE, MILLY: Rome, Italy, July 16, 1938. Lycee Chateaubriand.

VOIGHT, JON: Yonkers, N.Y., Dec. 29, 1938. Catholic U.

VYE, MURVYN: Quincy, Mass., July 15, 1913. Yale.

WAGNER, ROBERT: Detroit, Feb. 10, 1930.

WALKER, CLINT: Hartford, Ill., May 30, 1927. USC.

WALKER, NANCY: (Ann Myrtle Swoyer) Philadelphia, May 10, 1921.

WALLACH, ELI: Brooklyn, Dec. 7, 1915. CCNY, U. of Tex.

WALLIS, SHANI: London, Apr. 5, 1941.

WALSTON, RAY: New Orleans, Nov. 22, 1918. Cleveland Playhouse.

WANAMAKER, SAM: Chicago, 1919. Drake.

WARD, BURT: (Gervis) Los Angeles, July 6, 1945.

WARDEN, JACK: Newark, N.J., Sept. 18, 1920.

WARREN, LESLEY ANN: NYC, Aug, 16, 1946.

WASHBOURNE, MONA: Birmingham, Eng., Nov. 27, 1903.

WATERS, ETHEL: Chester, Pa., Oct. 31, 1900.

WATLING, JACK: London, Jan. 13, 1923. Italia Conti School.

WAYNE, DAVID: (Wayne McKeehan) Travers City, Mich., Jan. 30, 1916. Western Michigan State U.

WAYNE, JOHN: (Marion Michael Morrison) Winterset, Iowa, May 26, 1907. USC.

WEAVER, DENNIS: Joplin, Mo., June 4, 1925. U. Okla.

WEAVER, MARJORIE: Crossville, Tenn., Mar. 2, 1913. Indiana U.

WEBB, ALAN: York, Eng., July 2, 1906. Dartmouth.

WEBB, JACK: Santa Monica, Calif, Apr. 2, 1920.

WELCH, RAQUEL: (Tejada) Chicago, Sept. 5, 1942.

WELD, TUESDAY: (Susan) NYC, Aug. 27, 1943. Hollywood Professional School.

WELDON, JOAN: San Francisco, Aug. 5, 1933. San Francisco Conservatory.

WELLES, ORSON: Kenosha, Wisc., May 6, 1915. Todd School.

WERNER, OSKAR: Vienna, Nov. 13, 1922.

WEST, MAE: Brooklyn, Aug. 17, 1892.

WHITE, CAROL: London, Apr. 1, 1944.

WHITE, JESSE: Buffalo, N.Y., Jan. 3, 1919.

WHITE, WILFRID HYDE: Gloucestershire, Eng., May 12, 1903. RADA.

WHITMAN, STUART: San Francisco, Feb. 1, 1929. CCLA.

WIDMARK, RICHARD: Sunrise, Minn., Dec. 26, 1914. Lake Forest U.

WILCOX-HORNE, COLIN: Highlands N.C., Feb. 4, 1937. U Tenn.

WILCOXON, HENRY: British West Indies, Sept. 8, 1905.

WILDE, CORNEL: NYC, Oct. 13, 1915. CCNY, Columbia.

WILDING, MICHAEL: Westcliff, Eng., July 23, 1912. Christ's Hospital.

WILLIAMS, EMLYN: Mostyn, Wales, Nov. 26, 1905. Oxford.

WILLIAMS, ESTHER: Los Angeles, Aug. 8, 1923.

WILLIAMS, GRANT: NYC, Aug. 18, 1930. Queens College.

WILLIAMS, JOHN: Chalfont, Eng., Apr. 15, 1903. Lancing College.

WILSON, FLIP: (Clerow Wilson) Jersey City, N.J., Dec. 8, 1933.

WILSON, MARIE: Anaheim, Calif., Dec. 30, 1917. Cumnock School.

WILSON, NANCY: Chillicothe, O., Feb. 20, 1937.

WILSON, SCOTT: Atlanta, Ga., 1942.

WINDSOR, MARIE: (Emily Marie Bertelson) Marysvale, Utah, Dec. 11, 1924. Brigham Young U.

WINN, KITTY: Wash., D.C., 1944. Boston U.

WINTERS, JONATHAN: Dayton Ohio, Nov. 11, 1925. Kenyon College.

WINTERS, ROLAND: Boston, Nov. 22, 1904.

WINTERS, SHELLEY: (Shirley Schrift) St. Louis, Aug. 18, 1922. Wayne U.

WINWOOD, ESTELLE: Kent, Eng., Jan. 24, 1883. Lyric Stage Academy.

WITHERS, GOOGIE: Karachi, India, Mar. 12, 1917. Italia Conti School.

WOOD, NATALIE: (Natasha Gurdin) San Francisco, July 20, 1938.

WOOD, PEGGY: Brooklyn, Feb. 9, 1894.

WOODWARD, JOANNE: Thomasville, Ga., Feb. 27, 1931. Neighborhood Playhouse.

WOOLAND, NORMAN: Dusseldorf, Ger., Mar. 16, 1910. Edward VI School.

WRAY, FAY: Alberta, Can., Sept. 10, 1907.

WRIGHT, TERESA: NYC, Oct. 27, 1918.

WYATT, JANE: Campgaw, N.J., Aug. 10, 1912. Barnard College.

WYMAN, JANE: (Sarah Jane Fulks) St. Joseph, Mo., Jan. 4, 1914.

WYMORE, PATRICE: Miltonvale, Kan., Dec. 17, 1927.

WYNN, KEENAN: NYC, July 27, 1916. St. John's.

WYNN, MAY: (Donna Lee Hickey) NYC, Jan. 8, 1930.

YORK, DICK: (Richard Allen York) Fort Wayne, Ind., Sept. 4, 1928. De Paul U.

YORK, MICHAEL: Fulmer, Eng., Mar. 27, 1942. Oxford.

YORK, SUSANNAH: London, 1942.

YOUNG, ALAN: (Angus) North Shield, Eng., Nov. 19, 1919.

YOUNG, GIG: (Byron Barr) St. Cloud, Minn., Nov. 4, 1913. Pasadena Playhouse.

YOUNG, LORETTA: (Gretchen) Salt Lake City, Jan. 6, 1913. Immaculate Heart College.

YOUNG, ROBERT: Chicago, Feb. 22, 1907.

ZETTERLING, MAI: Sweden, May 27, 1925. Ordtuery Theatre School.

ZIMBALIST, EFREM, JR.: NYC, Nov. 30, 1923. Yale.

234

OBITUARIES

ANDERSON, GILBERT M. (BRONCO BILLY), 88, first star of westerns, died Jan. 20, 1971 after a long illness in Hollywood. Born Max Aronson in Little Rock, Ark., he changed his name when he went into vaudeville. Made screen debut in 1903 in "The Great Train Robbery," the first reel film with a plot that he adapted from a vaudeville skit, and that was filmed in New Jersey. Moved to Calif. in 1907 and subsequently appeared in 375 "Bronco Billy" western films, most of which he wrote, directed, and acted in. Sold his interest in the company and bought the Longacre Theatre in NYC in an attempt to break into legitimate theatre. Was not successful and returned to Hollywood to find William S. Hart had won all his fans. Left the film business in 1920 and lived frugally in Calif. Except for those with singing cowboys, he still liked western movies. In 1958 he was awarded a special "Oscar" for his pioneering work in films. His widow and daughter survive.

ANGELI, PIER, 39, Italian-born actress, was found dead in her Beverly Hills, Calif., apartment on Sept. 10, 1971. The cause of death appeared to be an overdose of barbiturates. She had been under a doctor's care for stomach disorder. Film career began in 1950 and she appeared in "Tomorrow Is Too Late," "Teresa," "Somebody Up There Likes Me," "The Story of Three Loves," "The Silver Chalice," "The Light Touch," "The Angry Silence," and her last "Love Me, Love My Wife." Surviving are her mother, twin sister, actress Maria Pavan, her second husband, Italian composer-conductor Armando Trovajoli, and two sons. Burial was in Paris.

ANGOLD, EDIT, 76, German-born stage, radio, and screen character actress, died Oct. 4, 1971 after a long illness in Hollywood. Career began in Germany with Max Reinhardt, using the name of Edit Goldstandt. Among her films were "Tomorrow the World," "Murder without Tears," "White Tower," re-make of "Blue Angel," "So Ends Our Night," "Above Suspicion," and her last "The Ambushers." Her sister survives.

ARMSTRONG, LOUIS "Satchmo", 71, world-famous jazz trumpeter and raspy-voiced singer, died in his sleep from a heart attack on July 6, 1971 in his Queens, NY home. He had recently been hospitalized for heart and kidney ailments. Unofficially, he was known as "America's ambassador of goodwill to the world." He toured for the State Department and became the world's most loved black man and exponent of jazz, the music form he pioneered. Appeared in clubs, with bands, on Broadway, and in such films as "Pennies from Heaven," "Artists and Models," "Going Places," "Cabin in the Sky," "Jam Session," "Atlantic City," "Pillow to Post," "New Orleans," "Here Comes the Groom," "The Strip," "Glory Alley," "Glenn Miller Story," "High Society," and "Jazz on a Summer's Day." Surviving are his third wife, and an adopted son.

BAIRD, LEAH, 80, pioneer film star, and former Broadway actress, died of anemia in Hollywood on Oct. 3, 1971 after a long illness. For the past 17 years she had been under contract to Warner Bros. Survived by her husband, producer Arthur Beck.

BAKER, ELSIE, 78, stage and film actress, died of a heart attack in her Hollywood home on Aug. 16, 1971. Her career encompassed all facets of show business from vaudeville to tv. For the last 20 years had appeared in films and on tv. A son and daughter survive.

BALABAN, BARNEY, 83, film pioneer who became chairman of Paramount Pictures, died suddenly on Mar. 7, 1971 in his Byrma, Conn. home. His widow, a daughter, and son survive.

BIBERMAN, HERBERT, 71, director, died June 30, 1971 of bone cancer in his NYC home. Credits include "One Way Ticket," "Meet Nero Wolfe," "Salt of the Earth," "Master Race," "Abilene Town," "New Orleans," and his last "The Slaves." Surviving are his widow, actress Gale Sondergaard, a son, and daughter.

BLAGOI, GEORGE, 73, Russian-born actor, died in Hollywood on June 23, 1971. Had appeared in films for 45 years. His widow, actress Tina Blagoi, survives.

PIER ANGELI

LOUIS ARMSTRONG

SPRING BYINGTON (1940) 235

BRONSON, BETTY, 64, early film star, died Oct. 19, 1971 in Pasadena, Calif., after a brief illness. Became star at 17 in the 1924 silent film version of "Peter Pan." Born in New Jersey, she appeared in several films before she married Ludwig Lauerhass and retired to North Carolina. In 1961 she resumed her career as a character actress in both movies and television. Her most recent films were "Pocketful of Miracles," "Naked Kiss," "Blackbeard's Ghost," "Evel Knievel." Besides her husband, she leaves a son and 2 grandchildren.

BYINGTON, SPRING, 77, stage, film, and television actress, died Sept. 7, 1971 after a short illness in her Hollywood Hills home. Born in Colorado, she began her career at 14 with a stock company, subsequently appearing in over 30 plays and 75 movies, and in 1954 became America's favorite mother-in-law in "December Bride" on tv. Among her films are "Little Women," "Way Down East," "Ah, Wilderness!," "Mutiny on the Bounty," "The Jones Family," "The Devil and Miss Jones," "Dragonwyck," "My Brother Talks to Horses," "Roxie Hart," "Heaven Can Wait," "Angels in the Outfield," "Meet Me on Broadway," "In the Good Old Summertime," and "Don't Eat the Daisies." Surviving are two daughters.

CALVERT, CATHERINE, 80, former film and stage actress, died after a stroke on Jan. 18, 1971 in Uniondale, L.I. As the widow of playwright Paul Armstrong, she retired at 35 and married millionaire George Carruthers. A son survives.

CARMINATI, TULLIO, 77, Italian film and stage singer-actor, died in Rome after a stroke on Feb. 26, 1971. After Broadway success, he became a matinee idol following his 1934 film "One Night of Love" with Grace Moore. Other roles were in "Beauty and the Devil," "Roman Holiday," "Saint Joan," and "Great Lady."

COMINGORE, DOROTHY, stage and film actress, age unreported, died Dec. 30, 1971 in her home in Stonington, Conn. after a long illness. A native of Los Angeles, she appeared in "Mr. Smith Goes to Washington," in many comedies with The Three Stooges, "Citizen Kane," "Any Number Can Play," "The Hairy Ape," and "The Big Night." Surviving are her husband, John Crowe, a son, and a daughter.

CONKLIN, CHESTER, 83, pioneer comedian in Keystone Kops series, died in his Van Nuys, Calif. home on Oct. 11, 1971. Iowa-born, he joined a circus before turning to movies in 1913. He appeared in hundreds of Mack Sennett shorts, and many other two-reelers. With talkies, his career faded to occasional bit parts. Survived by his fourth wife.

COOPER, DAME GLADYS, 82, British stage and film actress, died in her sleep Nov. 17, 1971 in her London home after having been ill with pneumonia for 10 weeks. Career began at 17 on stage to which she always returned between films. Among her many screen roles were "Rebecca," "Kitty Foyle," "That Hamilton Woman," "Now Voyager," "Song of Bernadette," "White Cliffs of Dover," "Mrs. Parkington," "Love Letters," "Green Dolphin Street," "The Pirate," "Madame Bovary," and "My Fair Lady." Was a popular character in the tv series "The Rogues." In 1967 was made Dame of the British Empire. She was divorced twice before marrying the late actor Philip Merivale. Two daughters survive.

DALE, CHARLIE, 90, deadpan partner of Smith and Dale team, died in a Teaneck, N.J. nursing home on Nov. 16, 1971. The team originated in 1898 and lasted for 70 years, in vaudeville, and films. Joe Smith survives, as do a sister and brother.

DALL, JOHN, 50, stage and screen actor, died Jan. 15, 1971 of a heart attack in his Hollywood home. Was nominated for an Academy Award for his performance in "The Corn Is Green," and also appeared in "Rope," "Another Part of the Forest," "Spartacus," "Something in the Wind," and "The Man Who Cheated Himself." A brother survives.

DANIELS, BEBE, 70, star of silent films and early talkies, died Mar. 16, 1971 in London of a cerebral hemorrhage, following several strokes. Born in Dallas, Tex., began career at 7 in one-reelers, and in 1915 joined Harold Lloyd in his "Lonesome Luke" series for four years. Subsequently starred in "Male and Female," "Why Change Your Wife?" "Everywoman," "Senorita," "Swim, Girl, Swim," "Campus Flirt," "Rio Rita," "42nd Street," "Registered Nurse." Married popular star Ben Lyon and in 1937 they moved to London where they became active on radio and television in "Life with the Lyons." Surviving are her husband, a daughter, and son.

DARK, CHRISTOPHER, stage and screen actor for over 25 years, died Oct. 8, 1971 in Hollywood of a heart attack. His widow and daughter survive.

DARVI, BELLA, 44, Polish-born film actress, committed suicide Sept. 10, 1971 in Monte Carlo. She went to Hollywood from France in 1952 and appeared in "Hell and High Water," "The Egyptian," and "The Racers." She was divorced from Alban Cavalade, a French businessman.

DISNEY, ROY O., 78, Chairman of Walt Disney Enterprises, died of a cerebral hemorrhage Dec. 20, 1971 in Burbank, Calif. With his late brother Walt started cartoon studio in 1923 in Hollywood that became multi-million dollar business. His widow and son survive.

EAMES, VIRGINIA, 82, stage, silent and talking film actress, died of a heart attack in Hollywood on June 10, 1971. Began career in 1906, and for several years worked in films with her husband True Boardman who died in 1918. Played Shirley Temple's mother in a series of pictures. Surviving is her son, tv writer True Boardman, Jr.

EDWARDS, CLIFF, 76, singer, stage and film performer, died in Hollywood on July 17, 1971. From Hannibal, Mo., became widely known as "Ukulele Ike;" appeared in over 100 films, and sold more than 74 million records singing and playing his ukulele. Introduced such hits as "Ja Da," "Singin' in the Rain," and "When You Wish upon a Star." Pictures include "Hollywood Revue of 1929," "Marianne," "Good News," "Lord Byron of Broadway," "Saratoga," "The Women Men Marry," "Girl of the Golden West," "International Squadron," "The Falcon Strikes Back," "American Empire," "Fun and Fancy Free." He was twice married and divorced.

EPHRON, PHOEBE WOLKIND, 57, writer of stage and screen comedies, died Oct. 13, 1971 after a long illness in her NY home. With her husband Henry Ephron, collaborated on such screen comedies as "Desk Set," "Daddy Longlegs," "Captain Newman, M.D.," "Look for the Silver Lining," "No Business Like Show Business," and "Carousel." Her husband and four daughters survive.

EVANS, RENEE, 63, dancer and screen actress, died Dec. 22, 1971 of a heart attack in Hollywood. Appeared in many Busby Berkeley productions. Surviving are her husband, retired actor John Alban, and actress daughter Diane Evans.

FARRELL, GLENDA, 66, screen and stage actress, died May 1, 1971 in her NY home after a long illness. After Bdwy success, made film debut in 1931 in "Little Caesar," subsequently appeared in "Gold Diggers" and "Torchy Blane" series, "I Love Trouble," "Heading for Heaven," "Girls in the Night," "Secret of the Incas," "Susan Slept Here," "Girl in the Red Velvet Swing," "Lady for a Day," "Johnny Eager," "Middle of the Night," "Kissin' Cousins," "Talk of the Town," "Hi, Nellie," and "The Disorderly Orderly." In 1963, won TV Emmy for her performance in "A Cardinal Act of Mercy." She is survived by her second husband, Dr. Henry Ross, and actor son, Tommy Farrell. Burial was at West Point.

FEALY, MAUDE, 90, actress and drama coach, died Nov. 9, 1971 in Woodland Hills, Calif. After successful stage career, became actress in silent and talking films, appearing in many DeMille productions. No reported survivors.

FERNANDEL, 67, French film comedian, died Feb. 26, 1971 of cancer in his Paris home. Born Fernand Contandin, began career in music halls; made film debut in 1931, subsequently appeared in 150 pictures and gained international fame. Among his films are the "Don Camillo" series, "The Sheep Had Five Legs," "Around the World in 80 Days," "The Well-Digger's Daughter," "Paris Honeymoon," "Topaz," "French Touch," "The Dressmaker," and "My Wife's Husband." A son survives.

FLIPPEN, JAY C., 70, versatile stage and screen actor, died Feb. 3, 1971 in Los Angeles during an operation for internal hemorrhaging. Career began in vaudeville and minstrels in his native Little Rock, Ark. at 16. Became vaudeville, radio, and Bdwy star, and moved to Hollywood and films in the late 1940's. Appeared in over 50 pictures, including "Lemon Drop Kid," "Two Flags West," "Bend of the River," "Winchester 73," "The Wild One," "Carnival Story," "Far Country," "Six Bridges to Cross," "Man without a Star," "Strategic Air Command," "Kismet," "Oklahoma!," "Cat Ballou," and "Hellfighters." In 1963 his right leg was amputated but he continued to work in films and on tv. Served as president of AGVA. Survived by widow, screen and tv writer Ruth Brooks.

GHERARDI, PIERO, 61, Italian scenic and costumes designer, died June 7, 1971 in Rome. He received an "Oscar" for his costumes in "La Dolce Vita," and one for his scenery in "8½," both by Fellini. He also worked on other Fellini productions.

GILBERT, BILLY, 77, stage and screen comedian, died Sept. 23, 1971 in a Hollywood convalescent home. Born in Louisville, Ky., while his parents were on tour with the Met Opera. Film career began in 1930 and he appeared in over 300 movies. Is probably best remembered as the man with the funny sneezes. Among his films are "3 of a Kind," "Toast of New York," "Life of the Party," "Espionage," "The Great Dictator," "Tin Pan Alley," "His Girl Friday," "Safari," "Women in War," "Anchors Aweigh," "Trouble Chasers," "Fun and Fancy Free," and was the voice of Sneezy in "Snow White and the 7 Dwarfs." Surviving is his widow, former film actress Lolly McKenzie.

GLENN, ROY, 56, screen, stage and tv actor, died Mar. 11, 1971 in his Los Angeles home. He was national secretary of AFTRA. A native of Pittsburgh, Kan., he had appeared in "Golden Boy," "Guess Who's Coming to Dinner," "Great White Hope," many Tarzan films, and the "Amos and Andy" tv series. Two sons, and a daughter survive.

GOMEZ, THOMAS, 65, film, theatre, and tv character actor, died in a Santa Monica hospital after 3 weeks in a coma. Born in NYC, began his career on stage in 1923. His film credits include "Singapore," "Captain from Castille," "Key Largo," "Phantom Lady," "Kim," "Merry Widow," "Magnificent Matador," "The Looters," "The Conqueror," "Trapeze," "John Paul Jones," and "Summer and Smoke." No reported survivors.

GOODE, JACK, 63, musical comedy performer, died in NYC of acute infectious hepatitis on June 24, 1971. His films include "Flying Down to Rio," "Poor Little Rich Girl," "Top Hat," and "Swing Time." He also appeared on tv in Jackie Gleason's "The Honeymooners." Surviving are his widow, Australian actress Renalda Green, and a son.

GORDON, ROBERT, 76, a leading man in many silent films, died Oct. 26, 1971 in Victorville, Calif. Career began in 1917 and extended to 1929 during which time he appeared in such pictures as "Huck and Tom," "Missing," "Greatest Menace," "Night Ship," "Danger Signal," "On the Threshold," "Tom Sawyer," and "Hearts and Spangles." For past 25 years had been involved in real estate. His widow and two daughters survive.

HATTON, RAYMOND, 84, actor on stage, tv, and film, died of a heart attack in his Palmdale, Calif., home on Oct. 21, 1971. From Red Oak, Iowa, he appeared in 1912 in Hollywood's first feature, "The Squaw Man," and subsequently in almost 500 other pictures. His last was "In Cold Blood" in 1968. Other credits include "Hunchback of Notre Dame," "Bell of Penance," "Three Wise Fools," "Top of the World," "The Big Cage," "Polly of the Circus," "Honeymoon Lane," "Trent's Last Case," "Partners in Crime," "Treasure of Ruby Hills," "Twinkle in God's Eye," and many westerns. No reported survivors.

HAYTON, LEONARD GEORGE (LENNIE), 63, composer, conductor, and arranger, died of a heart ailment in Palm Springs on Apr. 24, 1971. He received Academy Awards for scoring "On the Town," and "Hello, Dolly!" He had been music director for MGM and 20th Century-Fox. Surviving is his wife of 23 years, singer-actress Lena Horne.

HEFLIN, VAN, 60, versatile stage, tv, and screen actor, died after a heart attack in his Hollywood home on July 23, 1971. In 1942 the native of Walters, Okla., received an "Oscar" for his performance as supporting actor in "Johnny Eager." Other film credits include "Outcasts of Poker Flat," "Flight from Glory," "Pulham, Esq.," "Santa Fe Trail," "Kid Glove Killer," "Shane," "Madame Bovary," "The Prowler," "Tomahawk," "Battle Cry," "Woman's World," "Under Ten Flags," "Greatest Story Ever Told," "Once a Thief," and "Airport." Twice divorced, surviving are two daughters and a son.

HELTON, PERCY, 77, screen and stage actor, died in Hollywood Presbyterian Hospital on Sept. 11, 1971. Began his career at 3 with his parents in vaudeville, followed by Broadway success. After 1937 he appeared in over 200 films, including "Call Me Madam," "20,000 Leagues under the Sea," "Butch Cassidy and the Sundance Kid," and "The Set-up." No reported survivors.

GLENDA FARRELL (1959)

VAN HEFLIN (1959)

HAROLD LLOYD (1934)

HOLMES, STUART, 87, leading man of silent films, died in Hollywood Presbyterian Hospital from a stomach ailment on Dec. 29, 1971. Chicago-born, began his career in vaudeville there, subsequently appeared in plays, and was star of first Fox feature, "Life's Shop Window." Other film credits include "Daughter of the Gods," "The Scarlet Letter," "New Moon," "Prisoner of Zenda," "Four Horsemen of the Apocalypse," and "Devil's Island." Several nieces and nephews survive.

HOLT, SETH, 47, director, died in London on Feb. 14, 1971. He was an actor before he turned to directing film "thrillers." His credits include "The Lavender Hill Mob," "Kind Hearts and Coronets," "The Lady Killers," "The Nanny," "Scream of Fear." No reported survivors.

JONES, T. C., 50, stage and screen actor, and female impersonator, died of cancer in Duarte, Calif., on Sept. 25, 1971. After appearing on Bdwy and in his internationally acclaimed one-man show "Mask and Gown," he appeared in such films as "Promises," "Three Nuts in Search of a Bolt," "Unlocked Window," "The Name of the Game Is Kill," and "The President's Analyst." Surviving is his widow.

KING, DENNIS, 73, English-born singer and actor of stage and screen, died of a heart ailment in a NYC hospital on May 21, 1971. Probably best known for his first film in 1930 with Jeanette MacDonald, "The Vagabond King," repeating the same role that made him Broadway's matinee idol. Other films include "Paramount on Parade," "Fra Diavolo," and "Between Two Worlds." Two sons survive.

KIRKLAND, MURIEL, 68, stage, tv, and film actress, died of emphysema and complications in a NYC hospital on Sept. 26, 1971. Among her screen appearances were "Fast Workers," "Little Man, What Now?" "The White Parade," "Hold Your Man," "Cocktail Hour," and "Nana." Surviving is her actor-husband Staats Cotsworth.

LENNART, ISOBEL, 55, Brooklyn-born stage and screen writer, was killed in a traffic accident Jan. 25, 1971 in Hemet, Calif. Three times nominated for an Academy Award; her screen credits include "Merry Andrew," "Anchors Aweigh," "Two for the Seesaw," "Please Don't Eat the Daisies," "Inn of the Sixth Happiness," "The Sundowners," and "Funny Girl." Survived by her husband, actor John Harding, a son, and daughter.

LEWIS, TED, 80, band leader and entertainer, died of a heart attack in his NYC home on Aug. 25, 1971. With his battered top hat and opening line "Is everybody happy?", became internationally famous jazzman. Appeared in two films, one based on his life entitled "Is Ev'rybody Happy?" and "Here Comes the Band." His widow, former dancer Adah Becker, survives.

LIGHTNER, WINNIE, 71, former film comedienne and musical comedy star, died of a heart attack Mar. 5, 1971 in her home in Sherman Oaks, Calif. Began career as popular vaudeville performer, before appearing in such films as "Gold Diggers of Broadway," "Show of Shows," "She Couldn't Say No," "Life of the Party," "Sit Tight," and "Dancing Lady" after which she retired to marry the late film director Roy Del Ruth. A son survives.

LLOYD, HAROLD, 77, one of the film's greatest comedians, died of cancer in his Beverly Hills home on Mar. 8, 1971. He was born in Nebraska, and after struggling as a comedian under the name of Lonesome Luke, a pair of horn-rimmed glasses without lenses and a shy, bumbling, accident-prone characterization made him the highest paid screen actor of the 1920's. Many of his escapes from disaster are film classics. Beginning in 1913, he made almost 500 pictures, from one reel to full length, among which are "Grandma's Boy," "Doctor Jack," "Safety Last," "Why Worry," "Girl Shy," "Hot Water," "The Freshman," "For Heaven's Sake," "The Kid Brother," "Speedy." After his first talkie, "Welcome Danger," in 1929 he made "Feet First," "Movie Crazy," "The Milky Way," "The Cat's Paw," "Professor Beware," and "The Sin of Harold Diddlebock" that eventually was released as "Mad Wednesday." In 1962 he issued a compilation of scenes from his old movies entitled "Harold Lloyd's World of Comedy." He was married to actress Mildred Davis, his leading lady in several films. She died in 1969. A son and two daughters survive.

LLOYD, HAROLD, JR., 39, died from undisclosed causes on June 8, 1971 in a North Hollywood sanitarium. He had been under care since suffering a brain hemorrhage in 1965. Had appeared in 14 films, but always worked in the shadow of his father's fame. Two sisters survive.

LOCKWOOD, KING, 73, film actor for over 50 years, died of a massive stroke in Hollywood on Feb. 23, 1971. Survived by his widow.

LOWE, EDMUND, 81, versatile stage and pioneer film actor, died after a long illness Apr. 21, 1971 in the Motion Picture Country Hospital after a long illness. His suavity, athletic build, and good looks made him a matinee idol. California-born, he began his career in stock, followed by Bdwy, and in 1923 his film career was launched, with eventually over 100 pictures to his credit. Appeared in "The Silent Command," "The Fool," "East Lynne," "What Price Glory," "This Thing Called Love," "Born Reckless," "Dinner at 8," "Gift of Gab," "Dillinger," "Good Sam," "The Cockeyed World," "Call Out the Marines," "The Misleading Lady," "I Love That Man," and "Wings of Eagles." Retired in 1960 after "Heller in Pink Tights" because of ill health. He was married and divorced 3 times.

LOWERY, ROBERT, 57, singer-actor, died in his Hollywood home on Dec. 26, 1971. Kansas City-born, began his career as singer with bands and orchestras. Appeared in "Wake Up and Live," "Young Mr. Lincoln," "Shooting High," "Star Dust," "Drums along the Mohawk," "Four Sons," "Private Nurse," "Dangerous Passage," "Prison Ship," "Dangerous Passage," "Heart of Virginia," "The Rise and Fall of Legs Diamond," "Charlie Chan in Reno," "Free Bond and 21," "The Navy Way," "Thunderbolt," "Combat Correspondent," "Cow Country," and "Lay that Rifle Down." He was divorced from actresses Jean Parker and Barbara Farrell. No survivors reported.

LUKAS, PAUL, 76, stage, radio, tv, and screen actor, died of heart failure in a Morocco hospital on Aug. 15, 1971. Budapest-born, after serving in Austro-Hungarian army, turned to the stage. Made film debut in "Samson and Delilah" and came to U.S. in 1927 to make debut with Pola Negri in "Loves of an Actress." Among his many films were "Address Unknown," "The Lady Vanishes," "Captured," "Secret of the Blue Room," "Little Women," "Strange Cargo," "Captain Fury," "Three Musketeers," "Dodsworth," "Confessions of a Nazi Spy," "Uncertain Glory," "Deadline at Dawn," "Berlin Express," "Kim," "20,000 Leagues under the Sea," "Four Horsemen of the Apocalypse," "Roots of Heaven," and "Fun in Acapulco." He received an "Oscar" for his performance in "Watch on the Rhine" in 1943. His second wife survives.

LYNN, DIANA, 45, pianist, stage and screen actress, died of a brain hemorrhage in Los Angeles on Dec. 17, 1971. Los Angeles-born, career began as pianist and made her film debut at 12 in "There's Magic in Music." Subsequent films included "The Major and the Minor," "Henry Aldrich Gets Glamour," "Miracle of Morgan's Creek," "And the Angels Sing," "Out of This World," "Our Hearts Were Young and Gay," "Our Hearts Were Growing Up," "Ruthless," "Texas, Brooklyn and Heaven," "My Friend Irma," "Friend Irma Goes West," "Bedtime for Bonzo," "Peggy," "Meet Me at the Fair," "Track of the Cat," "You're Never Too Young," "The Kentuckian," "Annapolis Story," "Henry Aldrich Plays Cupid," "The People against O'Hara," and "Plunder in the Sun." Surviving are her second husband, Mortimer Hall an executive of the NY Post, a son and 3 daughters.

MANN, HANK, 84, reputedly the last of the original Mack Sennet Keystone Kops, died in a South Pasadena Hospital on Nov. 25, 1971. Born David Lieberman, began his career in films in 1912, and appeared in comedies until 1943 when he became a makeup man, but made occasional appearances in pictures until 1960. Was starred in his own comedy series, and appeared in such films as "Modern Times," "The Last Dictator," "Smokey," "The Garden of Eden," "Hollywood Cavalcade," and "My Favorite Spy." His widow survives.

McGOWAN, OLIVER F., 64, stage and film actor, died in his sleep Aug. 23, 1971 in Hollywood. Had appeared in over 20 films, and on all tv channels. Retired in 1950 but returned to Hollywood in 1956. No reported survivors.

McGUINN, JOSEPH FORD, 67, veteran screen actor, died of a heart attack in Hollywood on Sept. 22, 1971. Born in Brooklyn, went to Hollywood in 1930 after brief career on stage. Appeared in many westerns for Republic and Columbia. Surviving is his widow.

McHUGH, MATHEW, 77, character actor in silent and talking films, died of a heart attack Feb. 22, 1971 in North Ridge, Calif. Career began in Mack Sennett comedies, and appeared in over 150 movies, including "Street Scene," "The Glass Key," "Barbary Coast," and "It Happened in Flatbush." His widow survives.

McMAHON, HORACE, 64, stage and film actor, died Aug. 17, 1971 from a heart ailment in his native Norwalk, Conn. Appeared in over 130 films, usually as a gangster. Credits include "Detective Story," "Double Wedding," "The Detectives," "Roger Touhy, Gangster," "Alexander's Ragtime Band," "Gangs of Chicago," "Gangs of New York," "Gangs of New Orleans," "The Gracie Allen Murder Case," "My Sister Eileen," "The Thin Man," "Rose of Washington Square," "Birth of the Blues," "Beau James," and the tv series "Naked City." Surviving are his widow, actress Louise Campbell, a son and two daughters.

MURPHY, AUDIE, 46, Texas-born screen actor, and most decorated soldier of World War II, died in a plane crash near Roanoke, Va., on May 28, 1971. Film career began in 1948 with "Beyond Glory," followed by "To Hell and Back" (his autobiography), "The Kid from Texas," "Red Badge of Courage," "Destry," "Night Passage," "No Name on the Bullet," "The Quiet American," "The Unforgiven," "Cimarron Kid," "World in My Corner," "Showdown," "Bullet for a Badman," "Apache Rifles," and the tv series "Whispering Smith." Survived by his second wife, and two sons. Burial was in Arlington National Cemetery.

O'CONNOR, HARRY M., 98, one of the screen's oldest actors, died of pneumonia on July 10, 1971 in the Motion Picture Country Hospital. Career began in 1910, after appearing in vaudeville, and many road companies. Had roles in D. W. Griffith's films, and those of many other pioneer directors. Had been in retirement for several years. No reported survivors.

PARKER, CECIL, 73, British-born film and stage actor, died Apr. 20, 1971 in his Brighton, Eng. home. Screen debut in 1928 in "Woman in White," followed by "Silver Spoon," "Dark Journey," "The Lady Vanishes," "Caesar and Cleopatra," "First Gentleman," "Quartet," "Under Capricorn," "Man in the White Suit," "Ladykillers," "Court Jester," "Admirable Crichton," "Tale of Two Cities," "Indiscreet," "Iron Maiden," and "Pure Hell of St. Trinians." No reported survivors.

RAFFERTY, CHIPS, 62, Australia's best-known film and tv actor, died of a heart attack in Sydney on May 27, 1971. Career began in 1938 and was known in U.S. from such films as "The Wackiest Ship in the Army," "Mutiny on the Bounty," "The Overlanders," "40,000 Horsemen," "Massacre Hill," "Kangaroo," and "Desert Rats." No reported survivors.

RAINE, NORMAN REILLY, 76, prolific screen writer, died July 19, 1971 in Motion Picture Country Hospital in Woodland Hills, Calif. Probably best known as the creator of the "Tugboat Annie" series, he won an "Oscar" in 1937 for his "Life of Emile Zola" screenplay. Other credits include "Adventures of Robin Hood," "A Bell for Adano," "Nob Hill," "Eagle Squadron," "Each Dawn I Die," "Private Lives of Elizabeth and Essex," "Fighting 69th," "Captain Kidd," and his last in 1953 "Sea of Lost Ships." Survived by his second wife.

REDWING, RODD, 66, veteran Indian screen actor, died of a heart attack in Los Angeles on May 30, 1971. Educated in London and NYU, appeared on Bdwy before beginning film career with DeMille. Coached countless actors in gunplay for screen and tv, in addition to playing in hundreds of films. His widow survives.

RENNIE, MICHAEL, 62, British-born screen, tv, and stage actor, died in Harrogate, Eng., June 10, 1971, while visiting his mother. Made film debut in 1940 in "Dangerous Moonlight," subsequently appeared in over 100 pictures, including, "Trio," "The Day the Earth Stood Still," "Black Rose," "Thirteenth Letter," "Phone Call from a Stranger," "Five Finger," "Les Miserables," "The Robe," "Demetrius and the Gladiators," "Desiree," "Island in the Sun," "Omar Khayam," "Mary, Mary," "Third Man on the Mountain," "Lost World," "Hotel," "Devil's Brigade," and "The Power." Became U.S. citizen in 1960. Was in popular tv series "The Third Man." Surviving are his mother and a son.

RIANO, RENIE, age unreported, stage and screen actress, died July 3, 1971 after a long illness in the Motion Picture Country Hospital, Woodland Hills, Calif. Celebrated her 60th year as an actress in 1969. After moving to Hollywood in 1937, appeared in over 150 features, including "Tovarich," "You're A Sweetheart," "Outside of Paradise," "Spring Madness," "Thanks for Everything," "Four's a Crowd," "Disputed Passage," "Kit Carson," "Whispering Ghosts," "Blondie for Victory," "None but the Lonely Heart," "3 Is a Family," "Take It or Leave It," "The Time of Your Life," "Maggie and Jiggs," series, "Barefoot Mailman," and "Clipped Wings." Was in tv series "The Partridge Family" and "Mayberry R.F.D." A daughter survives.

PAUL LUKAS (1963)

DIANA LYNN (1962)

AUDIE MURPHY (1966)

ROMANOFF, MICHAEL, 79, self-styled Russian prince and popular Hollywood restauranteur, died in a Los Angeles hospital after a heart attack on Sept. 1, 1971. Made initial appearance in Hollywood in 1927 as technical adviser on films about Russian life. After opening his restaurant, Romanoff's, became one of the first citizens of Hollywood. Retired in 1962. His widow survives.

ST. CLAIR, YVONNE, 57, vaudeville, night club, and film dancer, died Sept. 22, 1971 in a hospital in Seattle, Wash. Retired in 1938, enrolled at USC, and became an aeronautical engineer. Appeared in such films as "The Great Ziegfeld," "Anna Karenina," "A Night at the Opera," and "A Midsummer Night's Dream." Survived by her mother, costumes and stage designer Jessie Hall, and actor-son Mark Dempsey.

SANDE, WALTER, 63, character actor, died at Chicago's airport of a heart attack while waiting for a cab on Nov. 22, 1971. Film career began in 1943 as a result of his Japanese ship models. Among his many films were "I Love a Soldier," "Tucson," "Strange Bargain," "Joe Palooka," "Canadian Pacific," "Bad Boy," "Kid from Texas," "Dark City," "Tomorrow Is Another Day," "Fort Worth," "I Want You," "A Place in the Sun," "The Racket," "Payment on Demand," "Rawhide," "Red Planet Mars," "Blueprint for Murder," "Apache," "Wichita," "Texas Lady," "Bad Day at Black Rock," "Johnny Tremaine," "Sunrise at Campobello," "The Gallant Hours," and "I'll Take Sweden." No reported survivors.

SANTLEY, JOSEPH, 81, veteran of Broadway and Hollywood, and more recently tv director and producer, died in his West Los Angeles home on Aug. 8, 1971. Born in Salt Lake City, attained stage stardom at 9, graduating into musical comedies with his wife, Ivy Sawyer, as co-star. Went to Hollywood in 1929 to direct series of short subjects, before becoming feature director and writer. His over 50 pictures include "Smartest Girl in Town," "Swing Sister, Swing," "Spirit of Culver," "Sleepy Lagoon," "Earl Carroll Vanities," "Make Believe Ballroom," and "When You're Smiling." Became popular director and producer of tv musical and variety shows. His widow survives, as do a daughter and two sons.

SEDGWICK, EDIE, 28, "superstar" of Andy Warhol movies in the mid-1960's, died Nov. 16, 1971 in her Santa Barbara home. Coroner listed probable cause of death as acute barbitural intoxication. Had appeared in "Restaurant," "Kitchen," "Afternoon," "Beauty II," "Vinyl," "Face," "Prison," "Poor Little Rich Girl," and "Ciao Manhattan." Surviving is her husband, Michael B. Post.

SHEARER, DOUGLAS, 70, Canadian-born pioneer in sound recording, died Jan. 5, 1971 in a Culver City hospital. He had received 12 Academy Awards for sound recording and related inventions. He retired in 1968, and is survived by his widow, two sons, and his sister, actress Norma Shearer.

SKOURAS, SPYROS P., 78, Greek-born motion picture magnate, died of a heart attack in his Mamaroneck, NY home on Aug. 16, 1971. Retired as chairman of 20th Century-Fox in 1969 after 27 years with the company. Surviving are his widow, 2 sons and 2 daughters.

SPEWACK, SAMUEL, 72, Russian-born co-author with his wife Bella of stage and film comedies, died of cancer in a NYC hospital on Oct. 14, 1971. Pictures written by the Spewacks include "The Nuisance," "Three Loves Has Nancy," "The Gay Bride," "The Cat and the Fiddle," "Weekend at the Waldorf," "When Ladies Meet," "Move Over, Darling," and "Kiss Me, Kate." His widow survives.

SPIVY, 64, who operated and entertained in night clubs, died Jan. 7, 1971 in the Motion Picture Country Hospital in Woodland Hills, Calif. In private life, Spivy LeVoe, became an international favorite in clubs, and then turned to character roles in films. She appeared in "Requiem for a Heavyweight," "The Fugitive Kind," and "Auntie Mame." Three sisters survive.

STEINER, MAX R., 83, composer, died Dec. 28, 1971 in a Hollywood hospital. A perennial nominee for "Oscar," he received three Academy Awards for the scores of "The Informer," "Now Voyager," and "Since You Went Away." Other notable scores he composed were "Gone with the Wind," "Life with Father," "Johnny Belinda," "So Big," "Treasure of Sierra Madre," "King Kong," "Dark Victory," "Four Wives," and "The Old Maid." His widow survives.

JOSEPH SANTLEY (1952)

TERRY, PAUL H., 84, pioneer in animated cartoons, died of cancer in a NYC hospital on Oct. 25, 1971. Before Walt Disney's creations, he was producing hundreds of "Aesop's Film Fables" for silent pictures. In over 40 years he produced more than 1100 animated films and "Terrytoons" to amuse people of all ages around the world. Born in San Francisco, became news photographer and cartoonist before turning to animation. After selling his company to CBS in 1955, he retired. A daughter survives.

TISSOT, ALICE, 81, French actress of stage and screen, died of cancer in Paris on May 5, 1971. Her greatest U.S. success was "Women in Green Hats," but appeared in support of Fernandel in several films, and in "Ignace," "The Glory of Faith," "Last Desire," and "Mirages of Paris." No reported survivors.

TSIANG, H. T., 72, Chinese film actor and writer, died July 16, 1971 in Hollywood. Born in San Francisco, became editor of its Chinese newspaper before moving to Hollywood. Appeared in over 25 pictures, and 50 tv productions. His films include "Purple Heart," "Keys of the Kingdom," and "Oceans 11." Also noted for his poetry, and 5 novels. No survivors reported.

VICKERS, MARTHA, 46, former model and screen actress, died Nov. 2, 1971 after a long illness in a Hollywood hospital. Born in Michigan, her Hollywood career began in 1942 in "Wolf Man," followed by "The Falcon in Mexico," "The Big Sleep," "The Time, The Place, and the Girl," "That Way with Women," "Love and Learn," "Bad Boy," "Daughter of the West," "Alimony," and "The Big Bluff." She was divorced three times, and left a son and two daughters.

WESTERFIELD, JAMES, 58, screen actor, and stage director-actor, died Sept. 20, 1971 after a heart attack in Woodland Hills Motion Picture Country Hospital. After success as a Bdwy and summer theatre musical producer-director, appeared usually as a tough policeman in such films as "On the Waterfront," "That Funny Feeling," "Blue," "A Man Called Gannon," "Burn," and "True Grit." Surviving is his widow, actress Fay Tracey.

WILKERSON, GUY, 70, stage and screen actor, died of cancer on July 15, 1971 in Hollywood. From Bdwy, moved to Hollywood in 1920 and appeared in over 200 films, mostly westerns. His widow and daughter survive.

WOLFF, FRANK, 43, screen actor, took his own life in a Rome hotel Dec. 12, 1971. Born in San Francisco, he appeared in minor Hollywood parts before moving to Italy in 1959 and attaining stardom there. His film credits include "The Verona Trial," "Four Days of Naples," "There Was Once the West," "The Matriarch," "America, America," "Salvatore Giuliano," "The Lickerish Quartet," and "Death Walks on High Heels."

YOUNG, CARLETON, 64, screen, radio, and tv actor, died of cancer in Hollywood on July 11, 1971. Played title role in radio's "Ellery Queen," and "Count of Monte Cristo" series, and tv's "Wyatt Earp" and "Loretta Young Show" series. His film credits include "The Kissing Bandit," and "His Kind of Woman." His widow, two sons, and a daughter survive.

INDEX

251

253